# PUBLIC PARTICIPATION
# AND PLANNERS' BLIGHT

# PUBLIC PARTICIPATION

### AND

# PLANNERS' BLIGHT

*by*

*NORMAN DENNIS*

*with a foreword by*

*A. H. HALSEY*

FABER AND FABER
3 QUEEN SQUARE
LONDON

*First published in 1972*
*by Faber and Faber Limited*
*3 Queen Square London WC1*
*Printed in Great Britain by*
*Western Printing Services Ltd, Bristol*

*ISBN 0 571 09952 1*

© *1972 Norman Dennis*

# CONTENTS

# CONTENTS

# PLATES

# DIAGRAMS

# TABLES

# ACKNOWLEDGEMENTS

My thanks must go first to the Reverend W. J. Taylor, Vicar of St. Mark's, Sunderland, and the many active members of the local residents' association in both East and West Millfield. The best photographs in the book were taken by my neighbour, George Edwards.

The Research Grants Committee of the University of Newcastle upon Tyne generously made a contribution to the costs of preparing the manuscript for publication. Mrs. R. C. Rule's help was, as usual, invaluable.

None of these will mind, I know, if I take this opportunity to thank most of all my wife, Audrey, and my children, Julia and John. I will not list their virtues nor my debts to them, but their tranquillity and good humour provide me with working conditions which are ideal and which all researchers must envy.

N.D.

# FOREWORD

This book documents the second phase of Norman Dennis' exploration of the relation between government and people. His first book in this series, *People and Planning*, has been widely and loudly praised for its compelling analysis of planning under modern urban conditions — a critique of its scientific status and a challenge to its political legitimacy.

The story of Millfield as a slum-clearance area in Sunderland was begun in that book. Here, in this book, it occupies the centre of attention as the concrete example in an analysis of the power relations between a group of citizens and their city bureaucracy. The dichotomy of 'them' and 'us' has been a familiar feature of the description of urban working-class culture at least since Richard Hoggart wrote his account of Hunslet twenty years ago. For Hoggart and his period, relations of mistrust between working-class families and the representatives of larger-scale organizations were fractionalized individual exchanges. Norman Dennis carries this analysis of working-class life further into the post-war experience of deliberate civic intrusion into traditional neighbourhoods. The new element here is the incipient formal organization of traditionally unorganized communities — a new development of *Gemeinschaft* in the face of increasingly pervasive bureaucratic power. The reader will find here, I believe, an essentially new definition of the significance of local politics.

A. H. HALSEY

13

# TIMETABLE OF PLANNING AND PARTICIPATION IN MILLFIELD

1952 :
Statutory Development Plan approved by Minister. Millfield to be redeveloped by 1972.

1965 :
Council approves five-year clearance programme 1965–70. West Millfield to be cleared 1967–8. East Millfield to be cleared 1968–9.

MAY 1967 :
Conservatives take control of Sunderland after twenty-two years of Labour rule.

NOVEMBER 1967 :
Millfield Residents' Association formed. Chairman of the planning committee announces that the plans for Millfield will be re-examined and that public participation will be sought.

FEBRUARY–MARCH 1968 :
Corporation's survey of all pre-1914 dwellings started and completed in Millfield area.

14 NOVEMBER 1968 :
First participation meeting. Corporation representatives present new proposals for East Millfield to the committee of the Millfield Residents' Association.

13 DECEMBER 1968 :
Second participation meeting. Millfield Residents' Association presents twenty-one resolutions relating to the proposals of November 14th 1968.

| | |
|---|---|
| 7 FEBRUARY 1969: | Third participation meeting. Corporation representatives present revised proposals for East Millfield to the committee of the Millfield Residents' Association. |
| 14 FEBRUARY 1969: | Fourth participation meeting. Millfield Residents' Association presents nine additional resolutions relating to the proposals of February 7th 1969. |
| 31 MARCH 1969: | Corporation representatives present new proposals for West Millfield to public meeting. |
| 23–27 JUNE 1969: | Exhibition of West Millfield proposals of March 31st 1969. Also on display – East Millfield proposals of February 7th 1969, virtually unaltered. |
| JULY 1969: | Millfield Residents' Association begins to state its case publicly. First letter to Town Clerk, July 21st 1969. |
| 7 AUGUST 1969: | Sunderland planning committee considers the Millfield Residents' Association correspondence of July–August 1969, and the state of planning and participation in the area, as analysed in the planning department's document entitled *Millfield: Progress Report*. |
| 5 SEPTEMBER 1969: | Representatives of the Millfield Residents' Association called to the Town Hall to discuss the July–August correspondence with the planning (emergency) sub-committee. |

6 OCTOBER 1969:     Planning officers explain the survey of
                    February–March 1969 to the Millfield
                    Residents' Association committee.

9 OCTOBER 1969:     *Millfield: Progress Report* seen by Millfield
                    Residents' Association.

OCTOBER 1969 ONWARDS: Millfield Residents' Association reverts to
                    normal machinery of local councillor,
                    M.P., newspapers, etc.

PART ONE

# INTRODUCTION

# CHAPTER 1

# ADMINISTRATIVE DECISIONS
# AND THE REDRESS
# OF GRIEVANCE

Discussions of authority and the individual and schemes for administrative reform are as old as philosophy itself. But only with universal suffrage in the twentieth century has the millions-strong state developed centralized organizations in the interests of education, health, housing, income security, the planning of new and the replanning of old towns and the regulation of the economy. State intervention in education, public health, safety and welfare in factory and mine and to a lesser extent in housing had developed in the nineteenth century. It was not until the reforming Liberal government of 1906 that state services in their modern form made an extensive appearance. The First World War, the post-war depression, the general strike and long-term mass unemployment in coalmining, cotton and ship-building all strengthened attitudes which favoured govern-mental control.

## *The Donoughmore Report*

By 1929 liberal English collectivism as a subject of philosophical justification was on the wane. In 1925 J. H. Morgan disturbed English complacency (a legacy of Dicey's dicussions of the rule of law) by maintaining that his countrymen were now less well protected than their continental counterparts from despotic actions by officials. It was becoming increasingly necessary to recognize the need for a system of administrative law to match the growth of state intervention.[1] In 1931 C. K. Allen followed Morgan in calling for 'a wholesome body of administrative law' as the means by which public authorities would be made responsible for their actions.[2]

Morgan and Allen might have lain unnoticed if their publications had not been followed by a remarkable polemic by the then Lord Chief Justice, Lord Hewart. *The New Despotism*[3] gave the impression that 'when honest men were abed, civil servants were stalking the streets at dead of night, disguised in masks and cloaks, with daggers in hand, waiting to pounce on any undefended powers which they might be able to snatch for their fell purposes'.[4] Whatever its merits as history or political science, the book sparked an agitation which quickly led to the setting up of a government committee to investigate the problems to which it had drawn attention.

The committee reported in 1932.[5] It distinguished three types of government decision. A decision, first, was judicial if there was a dispute between parties, the disputants presented a case, facts were ascertained by the evidence adduced, legal arguments were submitted, and there was a finding on the facts and an application of the law of the land to the facts so found. Such decisions were properly within the province of the courts. 'No consideration of administrative convenience, or of executive efficiency, should be allowed to weaken the control of the courts and . . . no obstacle should be placed by Parliament in the way of the subject's unimpeded access to them.'[6] The presumption should always be in favour of safeguarding 'the rule of law and the liberty of the subject' and using the ordinary courts.[7] Where Parliament decided that certain judicial issues were not suitable for decision by the ordinary courts, then reference should be made to an independent assessor or assessors. Where such issues commonly arose from the work of a department then permanent specialized tribunals should be set up to deal with them.[8] In certain very exceptional cases, the decision would have to be left to the administration itself. Secondly, the Donoughmore committee identified what it called quasi-judicial decisions. These were judicial in so far as they involved a dispute, the presentation of their cases by the parties and the ascertainment of the facts. They were not fully judicial in that they concerned not the respective individual rights of the disputants, but the public interest. The Minister was the proper authority to reach the final decision on the public interest. Only in exceptional cases ought it to be entrusted to a tribunal. Thirdly, there were administrative decisions. In an administrative decision the grounds upon which the decision-taker acts and the information and other considerations he chooses to weigh before reaching his decision 'are left entirely to his discretion'.[9] There is no legal obligation upon the administrator charged with making such a decision to collate any evidence or to consider any submissions.

These distinctions failed to touch the problem of which decisions ought to be left to the unimpeded discretion of the administration, and which ought to be defined as judicial and quasi-judicial.

## The Franks Report

To Hewart and the pamphleteers of the 1930s state intervention seemed to be reaching unbearably large proportions. But during the Second World War another programme of reform was prepared, much more far-reaching than that of 1906. The Labour governments of 1945–51 were able to put it into effect. The indiginities of poor-law attitudes were to be abolished. Unemployment was to be reduced or its effects mitigated. Charity's grey-faced paternalism would be replaced by facilities and opportunities available to each citizen, and those facilities and opportunities would be rightfully his. Freedom would be enlarged through the income-maintenance and health services and by eliminating or controlling the sources of insecurity and fear. Through housing and town-planning legislation the exploitation of the weak by the strong would be prevented, and difficulties would be placed in the path of unscrupulous individuals who sought to reap profit from public developments or who placed personal gain above the common good. The reputation of the commentators of the previous decade sank, and their contributions seemed almost as remote as the rumblings of a Belloc or the medieval fantasizing of a Chesterton. Criticism atrophied.[10] 'The man in the back street', though he did not realize it at the time, was neglected by the lawyers, whose discussions tended to hang at the rarified heights of the British Constitution, and by those reformers who took it for granted that the only rights which would be violated would be those of the unduly selfish, rich and powerful. Donoughmore's emphasis on the primacy of the courts as the guarantee of redress was regarded as unrealistic, backward-looking and, so far as ordinary people were concerned, irrelevant. Little attention was being paid to the question of disputes and grievances in the Beveridge Report.[11] Its spirit was the 'readiness to sacrifice personal interest to the common cause' — the common cause of the prevention of want, and the diminution and relief of distress.[12]

In the late 1940s and early 1950s, however, there was a weakening in the tendency to see the Welfare State in the abstract, in terms of individual interests versus the public good. The question was raised once again: What happens when actual persons are confronted with the specific decisions of public authorities which they feel are damaging and unjust? The tone was no longer so strident and it was no longer so simple to dismiss complaints as solely the protests of the privileged. Lord Denning, not a Hewart, published his *Freedom Under the Law* in 1949.[13] W. A. Robson, scarcely an exponent of *laissez-faire*, published his *Justice and Administrative Law* in 1951.[14] Concern was shown at the still growing practice of allowing public authorities to determine matters within their jurisdiction without judicial control or scrutiny, i.e. to define more and more decisions as administrative decisions. Legislation was increasingly stating that where a Minister was satisfied that certain facts existed then he could exercise the powers specified in the enactment. The courts were strengthening the doctrine that local authorities were to be free from judicial interference to decide those matters which Parliament considered were best dealt with by them by virtue of their knowledge and experience. This doctrine was pushed furthest when applied to the decisions of planning authorities.[15]

Such was the climate of opinion into which the Crichel Down affair erupted. In 1937 725 acres of land at Crichel Down, Dorset, had been compulsorily purchased. Local farmers had been promised that when it was freed they would be afforded an opportunity to bid for it. The promise was not honoured. The resulting agitation led in 1954 to a public inquiry and the resignation of the Minister of Agriculture. But the inquiry roused rather than allayed public disquiet. For the report clearly disclosed that the maladministration from which the landowners had suffered revealed no grounds of illegality. There was no legal redress.[16] The inquiry itself had not been set up because the aggrieved parties had a statutory or common law right to be heard. They had no such right. The inquiry was purely the result of the volume of adverse public comment.

Immediately following the Crichel Down affair two pamphlets appeared. The Inns of Court Conservative and Unionist Society published its *Rule of Law*,[17] and R. H. S. Crossman published his Fabian pamphlet *Socialism and the New Despotism*[18] in which he felt it was necessary to argue that when they attacked the excesses of bureaucracy or defended the individual against its incipient despotism socialists need not feel that they were betraying their principles. The most important consequence of the Crichel Down affair, however, was the appointment of a new government committee. Its task was to investigate in the light of modern developments and experience the problems which Donoughmore had looked at thirty years previously, the balance between private right and public advantage, between administrative efficiency and fair play for the individual.

The Franks committee was set up in 1955 and reported in 1957.[19]

Like Donoughmore, Franks differentiated judicial and non-judicial decisions, but was only slightly more explicit about the basis upon which decisions should be allocated to one category or the other. Judicial decisions emerged from legislation which could be embodied in a system of detailed regulations. Non-judicial decisions emerged from legislation where it was desirable to preserve flexibility, where decisions should not be tied by precedent and rule. Flexibility of decision was somewhat vaguely linked with certain areas of public policy. In the pursuance of such public policy 'a wise expediency' was the proper basis for adjudication and the decision could rightly be left to the administration.[20] Again, the fundamental problem of the conflict between private interests and public interests was stated but not solved.[21]

Franks nevertheless vastly improved the existing state of affairs. It was no longer sensible, Franks argued, to talk as though the ordinary courts could act as the average Englishman's bulwark against the arbitrary powers of the state. Instead, the system of administrative tribunals ought to be extended and improved. Tribunals were favoured because, as compared with the courts, they were cheap, quick, informal, accessible, and knowledgeable. But Franks wanted them to be made more court-like than they were. They ought to be freed from their Ministries. They ought to be made more capable of deciding on the facts and applying the rules to them without any consideration of executive policy. In relation to both tribunals and public inquiries, Franks laid down a number of general principles which were intended to ensure that openness, fairness and impartiality should be obtained to the fullest possible extent. As Robson says, the intention of the reforms was 'to bring the decision-making process more into the light of day, instead of being shrouded in secrecy and mystery'. Ministerial policy was to be 'transferred from the realm of the unknowable to the sphere of the ascertainable'.[22] These and other measures proposed by Franks were embodied in the Tribunals and Inquiries Act of 1958.

Omissions from the Franks report have been touched upon. What tests could be applied in the determination of the degree to which decisions should be rule-bound? Who was to define, within the very broad limits of Parliament's stated intentions, the domain of wise expediency? What was public policy in a concrete case? A second defect of the Franks report was the large number of problematical citizen-authority relationships with which it was unable to deal. Franks was limited to investigating existing arrangements for public inquiry and for reference to tribunals. The vast area of decision-taking in which no formal procedure was prescribed by Parliament and where, therefore, determination was a matter of administrative discretion was outside its scope. Because it had been an *ad hoc* inquiry, not a procedure required by statute, the Franks committee's terms did not even permit it to examine the Crichel Down case which, as the Franks committee itself stated was widely regarded as the principal reason for its appointment.[23] It was called upon to examine, that is, only the decisions which were already relatively justiciable. It was unable to discuss those procedures of public decision-taking altogether outside the range of tribunals and public inquiries. The Franks committee recognized that in this excluded area of administrative decision-taking the individual was virtually unprotected against unfairness or error, but it was precluded from making any recommendations. By the second half of the 1960s in Millfield, Sunderland, where the case study reported in this volume was carried out, what constitutes 'public' policy as against private welfare, and what the aggrieved citizen may do in the face of such decisions had become questions of central importance.

*Planning in the Aftermath of Franks*

The Tribunals and Inquiries Act of 1958 was well received.

In town planning, however, satisfaction with the reforms in the procedures at public inquiries was more than counterbalanced by growing discontent with other aspects of the planning process. The number of appeals against planning decisions, where there was provision for such appeal, rose from 4,500 in 1953 to no fewer than 13,500 eight years later. This was partly a reflection of the great increase in the number of planning decisions which had to be made. Partly it was indicative of the ebbing public confidence in the acceptability of the unchallenged judgement of the local planner. Many of the planners' decisions were, furthermore, outside the scope of public inquiry, and the machinery of redress did not include reference to an independent tribunal.

The appeals system itself was basically unchanged, in spite of Franks and further minor improvements which followed the Saffron Walden chalkpit case. The final outcome of a public inquiry remained unquestionably a decision of policy and not a definition of law. Inspectors were not required to possess legal training; they sat alone; their report need not be restricted to evidence presented at the inquiry; the Minister was not bound to accept the inspectors' findings; and he could reach his final conclusion on facts or considerations of policy beyond the appellant's knowledge. The local authority whose decision was challenged at a public inquiry had legal and technical experts and public funds at its disposal while the private appellant was often too poor or diffident to secure legal representation. Even when he was able to afford a solicitor, he may have been at work when the public inquiry was held, and therefore unable to hear what was made of his case.

Among people who were not recipients of its results, planning continued to command a very high prestige. In 1967 a sample of students at Leeds University ranked eight professions on various criteria. Town planning received the highest scores on the following criteria: it was the most creative, exciting, proud, influential and socially useful; of the eight, planning required the most initiative and was the profession most concerned with formulating policy.[24] The post-Franks period showed no improvement, however, in satisfaction with the planning process either among planners or the professions in closest contact with them. In May 1962, for example, a committee was set up by the council of the Incorporated Association of Architects and Surveyors to investigate town planning procedures. It reported in 1963. 'In the professions dealing with town planning', the report said, 'there is a general belief that, however well founded a planning application may be, its approval or otherwise is as often as not a matter of whim and chance.' The failings of the existing procedures, the report continued, were so serious as to bring the administration of town and country planning into 'profound public distrust'.[25] The report, which was mainly concerned with planning permission and development control (a subject which the case study of Millfield does not touch) suggested that independent professionals should attend meetings of local planning committees. This would help to ensure that the applicant secured a fair hearing, and did not have to depend entirely upon the way in which the planning department chose to present his case. At the end of December 1969 the Royal Institute of British Architects submitted a formal statement to the Minister of Housing which spoke of the existence of 'massive waves of public protest' against current planning practices.[26]

While public confidence was crumbling, there was disillusionment in the planning profession with existing legislation and the planners' role.[27] The profession emerged, however, with an enlarged conception of its task. Town planning, it was argued, had become too closely identified with physical processes; the social end-product had been left by planners to other reformers. 'The rediscovery of social planning seeks to remedy this, because it elevates concern for the social environment to the same rank as that for the physical environment. In this way, "happiness" or "satisfaction", seen as the ultimate end of human conduct, becomes a planning objective.'[28] With happiness as their wider objective, the planners' tactics had to be reconsidered. In the past utopia had been a rigid concept which allowed for no evolution. Planning now needed to take fuller account of change and become more open-ended and less rigid. These ideas are embedded in an argument for freer choice in the community. The community's values must be allowed to develop rather than be imposed.[29] Whatever else might be said, by entering upon this road the planning profession was moving away from those types of decision for which Franks had developed improved methods of redress. Franks had concentrated on those decisions which were relatively rigid, in that they had to be taken in accordance with set rules, and the 'Franks' solution' was to reduce the discretionary powers of the administration.

In the 1960s, therefore, the planners were paying the price in growing public disesteem for the fact that they had been relatively untouched by the Franks' reforms.[30] But with this more ambitious definition of their role they began to adopt various schemes which would allow them to combine flexibility with public approval. The solution was to be greater public participation. Coventry local planning authority, for example, held meetings in connection with the 1965 review of its development plan at which elected representatives and officers were able to hold discussions with members of the public. In 1964 the Ministry of Housing and Local Government's Planning Advisory Group (PAG) started its study of the future of development plans. Its findings were published in 1965, in what is popularly known as the PAG report. The PAG report recommended that local authorities should be required to afford opportunities for detailed comments, representations and objections to be made on draft plans. They should be required also to take these views into account on deciding whether to amend the plans before finally adopting them.[31]

In May 1967 the Minister of Housing and Local Government announced that he intended to improve and modernize the system of town and country planning. The White Paper Cmd. 3333 of 1967 closely followed the recommendations and arguments of the PAG report. An effective and up-to-date system, the White Paper said, must ensure full public participation in the planning process. Participation would enable people to state their points of view at a time when they could influence decisions. This would be a means of 'safeguarding satisfactorily the interests of those affected by planning proposals'. That was one side of the coin, the wish to reduce opposition and raise the level of public consent. The other side of the coin was the wish for greater flexibility — the wish to expand the boundaries of discretion and 'wise expediency'. The need for formal Ministerial approval for every detail of the local planning authority's proposals under the 1947 system had given rise, as the White Paper put it, to meticulous procedures which were so time-consuming as to be real hindrances to the general progress of planning. They robbed planning of all flexibility. The new safeguards introduced by public participation must not be bought at the price of holding back important developments to such an extent that both private and public interests may be damaged. The White Paper accordingly distinguished two levels in the modernized planning process. The local planning authority would need to bring before the Minister for his approval only the broad recommendations of policy and principle. It would then be enabled to deal in its own right with the positive detail implied by these principles.

The details would be worked out in what were termed local plans. Opportunities for comment and consultation would be granted as a right to local interests; but the local authority would be the body which would decide whether to arrange a local inquiry or hearing. The local planning authority would be required to consider the representations; but it would be open to the local planning authority to modify the plan or not. The revised plan would be readvertized. Interested parties who had not had the opportunity to make representations on the previous version would be permitted a hearing on the new version. Again it would be for the local planning authority itself to decide whether to incorporate any further changes. The Minister would be informed of the fact that a certain local plan had been adopted. After a period of six weeks it could be confirmed by the local planning authority. It would then become part of the statutory development plan for the area. Only in exceptional cases (for example, when it was particularly controversial or when it related primarily to developments to be carried out by the authority responsible for drawing it up) would the Minister call in the plan for his own decision and hold a public inquiry under one of his own inspectors.

The recommendations were incorporated in the new Town and Country Planning Act of 1968. Local planning authorities had obtained the flexibility they desired.[32] Local planning authorities in preparing local plans had to take such steps as would 'in their opinion' give adequate publicity to any relevant matter arising out of the surveys carried out by them under the Act and to the matters the authorities proposed to include in the plans. Anyone the local planning authority expected might desire to make representations had to be made aware that they had the right to do so, and local planning authorities had to take such steps as would in their opinion provide adequate opportunities for such representations to be made. The planning authority had to inform the Minister of the steps it had taken in order to obtain consultation. It had to inform him also about the consideration it had given to the views expressed. For the purposes of considering objections the local planning authority 'shall cause a local inquiry or other hearing to be held by a person appointed by a Minister or, in such cases as may be prescribed by regulations under this part of the Act, by the authority themselves'. The Tribunals and Inquiries Act of 1958 would apply to such inquiries and hearings. The Act was passed on October 25th 1968, but the provisions for participation were not intended to be brought into operation until later. The experi-

ence of selected groups of local authorities, including Sunderland, was to be considered first.[33]

Participation in Millfield was initiated in November 1967. It
coincided with the introduction of the White Paper of 1967 and
the passage and first year of the Planning Act of 1968. The legal
obligation to operate the participation system of the Act was not,
however, placed upon the local planning authority during this
period.[34] The Millfield participation also took place contem-
poraneously with the sittings of the parliamentary committee
on public participation in planning, which had been appointed
in March 1968 to consider ways of involving the public more
closely in the work of local planning authorities. Its report was
published on July 28th 1969.[35] The Skeffington committee
not only formed part of the general background to the Millfield experience. The chairman of the Sunderland planning
committee was himself a member. Skeffington's developing
recommendations were, therefore, as far as the local planning
authority was concerned, the (somewhat ill-defined) rules of
the participation game.

### NOTES

1 J. H. Morgan, 'Remedies Against the Crown', in Gleeson Edward
Robinson, *Public Authorities and Legal Liability*, London: University of
London Press, 1925. See also A. V. Dicey's *The Law of the Constitution*.
This was first published in 1885. It ran through various editions in which
Dicey dealt with developments since 1885. The last edition was the
ninth (Macmillan, 1939).

2 Carleton Kemp Allen, *Bureaucracy Triumphant*, Oxford: Oxford University Press, 1931.

3 London: Stevens, 1929.

4 William A. Robson, 'Administrative Law', in Morris Ginsberg (Ed.),
*Law and Opinion in England in the Twentieth Century*, London: Stevens, 1959,
p. 198.

*Report of the Committee on Ministers' Powers* (the Donoughmore, or Scott
Report), Cmd. 4060, London: H.M.S.O., 1932. (Reprinted 1966.)

6 *Op. cit.*, p. 114.

7 *Ibid.*, p. 115.

8 *Ibid.*, p. 109.

9 *Ibid.*, p. 81.

10 Not quite. See C. K. (Sir Carleton) Allen, *Law and Orders*, London: Stevens, 1945.

11 *Social Insurance and Allied Services* (the Beveridge Report), Cmd. 6404, London: H.M.S.O., 1942. (Reprinted 1966.) Paras. 336(c), 394 and 395.

12 *Op. cit.*, p. 172.

13 London: Stevens, 1949.

14 London: Stevens, 1951.

15 Robson, *op. cit.*, p. 204.

16 *Report of the Public Inquiry Ordered by the Minister of Agriculture into the Disposal of Land at Crichel Down*, Cmd. 9176, London: H.M.S.O., 1954.

17 London: Conservative Political Centre, 1955.

18 Fabian Society Tract No. 298, London: Fabian Society, 1956.

19 *Report of the Committee on Administrative Tribunals and Enquiries* (the Franks Report), Cmd. 218, London: H.M.S.O., 1957.

20 *Ibid.*, para. 31.

21 For the inspiring language used to sidestep the issue, see paragraphs 26–32 of the Franks report.

22 Robson, *op. cit.*, p. 206.

23 *Op. cit.*, para. 15.

24 I am indebted to Dr. A. P. M. Coxon for access to his data. The Leeds' students, however, considered planning to be a relatively bureaucratic and manipulative profession (sixth out of the eight on the criterion of 'non-bureaucratic' and sixth on the criterion of 'non-manipulative').

25 *Architect and Surveyor*, July–August 1963.

26 *The Times*, December 31st 1969.

27 In the early and middle 1960s the planning profession reopened a question which the *Report of the Committee on Qualifications of Planners* (the Schuster Report), Cmd. 8059, London: H.M.S.O., 1950, had apparently settled. Was there such a thing as the specialized planner, or ought education for planning be rather a matter of a congeries of related specialisms? The 'specialized planners' were the victors in the 1960s' debate.

28 City and Council of Newcastle upon Tyne, *The Social Plan* (mimeographed), January 1968, p. 2. *The Social Plan* was the product of a department then under the direction of one of the principal architects of the measures which the planning profession undertook in the post-Franks' period. The views expressed therein are therefore of special significance. He was later to become chief technical officer—chief planner—at the Ministry of Housing and Local Government, as well as president of the Town Planning Institute.

29 *Ibid.*, p. 3.

30 In some instances later Franks' reforms did eventually apply to certain aspects of the planning process. In December 1968, for example, the Parliamentary Commissioner for Administration was, at the second attempt, successfully used to combat planning blight in Hockley, Essex. See *The Times*, December 30th 1968.

31 Ministry of Housing and Local Government, Planning Advisory Group, *The Future of Development Plans*, London: H.M.S.O., 1965. The local planning authority of Newcastle upon Tyne, whose department had been so influential in the Planning Advisory Group, actually approved the proposals of the PAG report on September 27th 1965, and went ahead with a PAG-type local plan for Jesmond. By 1968 the Development Control Working Group of the Newcastle planning committee officially included eighteen organizations in its procedure of consultation when considering planning applications.

32 Under the Act of 1968 all plans became highly flexible and could be changed as circumstances demanded. Millfield was planned under the statutory procedures of the Act of 1947.

33 In written answer No. 1248 the Minister of Housing and Local Government told the House of Commons on July 25th 1968 that certain groups of local authorities were being asked to prepare plans under the new Act. 'I have asked for assurances that proper attention will be paid to the views of the public and of objectors to plans.'

34 'The Sunderland County Borough Council have been invited to say whether they would be willing to prepare a development plan under Part I of the Town and Country Planning Act of 1968, *but they have not yet been authorised to do so*. I should stress that this request related solely to plans prepared under Part I of the 1968 Act *which has not yet been brought into operation*.' Ministry of Housing and Local Government letter reference UPD 2, dated August 22nd 1969. (Emphasis added.)

35 Ministry of Housing and Local Government, *People and Planning: Report of the Committee on Public Participation in Planning* (the Skeffington Report), London: H.M.S.O., 1969.

# CHAPTER 2

# PARTICIPATION IN MILLFIELD

Millfield lies down by the river. The men walk home from Sunderland Forge, from Doxford's shipyard and from Pyrex, have their dinner, and walk back to work when the buzzer goes. Their homes are single-storied terraced cottages built in the 1870s and 1880s, end-on to a busy shopping centre. All the more massive in contrast to the low cottages stringing away behind are the churches, the school, the Mountain Daisy, the Willow Pond, or the Buffs club. Scattered all round are little nonconformist chapels. Millfielders regard some of the streets as slums, but most seem to them to be solidly comfortable. (See Plates I–IV.) It is a small-family area. (See Diagram 1.) There are few immigrants from other parts of England. There are hardly any from other parts of Sunderland. It is artisan working class, mellowed by good wages, the mass media and Marks and Spencer's.

The homogeneity, solidarity and lack of social and geographical mobility of the inhabitants facilitates community action. (See Diagram 2.) If the action is militant, the strength of personal loyalties once formed means stable support. Within certain rather narrow limits, their customary dislike and indeed fear of militancy may be overcome by their very slowness to anger and tolerance, if the deviant is the accepted militant himself, to whom they feel committed even though they are unhappy about the dangers insubordination may bring.

Basically the Millfield situation is one of acceptance rather than protest and conflict. Both the men and the women with jobs are strongly organized at work, but in a variety of unions and only as rank-and-file members. Unionism at no point

touches local community affairs. People who are already politically active in the community are likely to owe favours for small

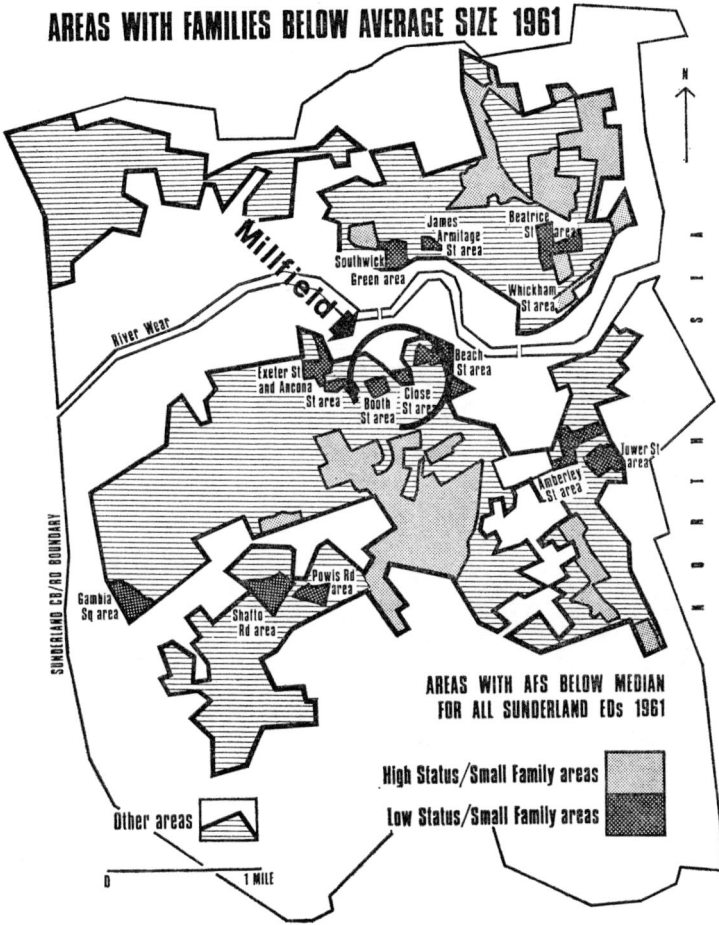

**AREAS WITH FAMILIES BELOW AVERAGE SIZE 1961**

Millfield

River Wear

James
Armitage
St area

Beatrice
St area

Southwick
Green area

Whickham
St area

Beach
St area

Exeter St
and Ancona
St area

Booth
St area

Close
St area

Tower St
area

Amberley
St area

SUNDERLAND CO/RO BOUNDARY

Powis Rd
area

Gambia
Sq area

Shallo
Rd area

**AREAS WITH AFS BELOW MEDIAN
FOR ALL SUNDERLAND EDs 1961**

High Status/Small Family areas

Low Status/Small Family areas

Other areas

0        1 MILE

*Diagram 1. A Small-Family Area*

grievances attended to by councillors, perhaps years ago—a new
bulb put in a street lamp, some tar laid to smooth out a depression in the front street. Political allegiance and personal friend-

ships coalesce and cut across each other. Conservatives have Labour attachments because their friends are Labour, and friends are friends through sharing contacts in the context of

## RESIDENTIAL MOBILITY 1961

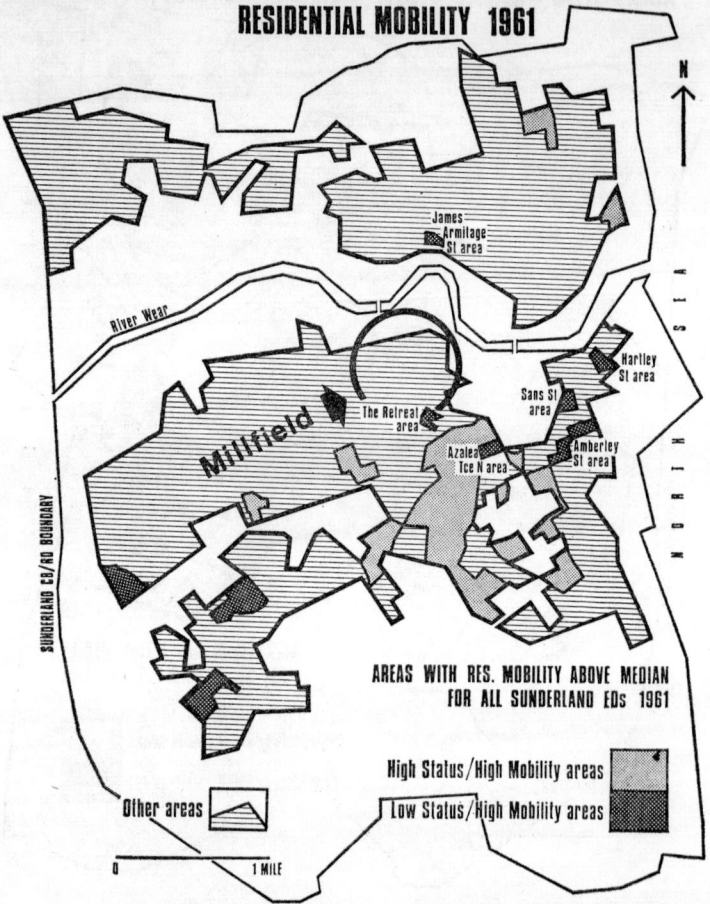

*Diagram 2. Lack of Geographical Mobility*

party-political affairs. In disputes with the ruling party of the Council, these complex patterns prevent the emergence of clear-cut and determined opposition.

The militant is likely, too, to have many ties of family and friendship in the locality. These friends and kinsfolk will have different levels of commitment to the particular point at issue. Those who are less committed, though they help the militant to go half the way, and on a personal, face-to-face basis are supportive if and when he runs into trouble, inhibit him from going all the way in militancy. What is more important, each of these friends and relatives will be integrated in a unique way into the life of the rest of the town, and have contacts of importance to themselves outside of Millfield. They may work side-by-side with the militant's opponents or his opponents' political supporters. They will almost certainly work or spend their leisure time with non-Millfielders whose good opinion they value and would dislike being tarred with the brush of their known friend's or relative's notoriety. The non-Millfielder, like the Millfielder himself (who tends to take it for granted that 'they' must know better than 'us' unless exceptionally provoked to take the opposite view), generally thinks of outspokenness as the work of 'the agitator' or at best 'the barrack-room lawyer', a useful figure, but one with whom it does not pay to be too closely identified.

In 1965 most of the area had been included in the Council's programme for clearance by 1967–9. Near the end of 1967, after several months of mounting anxiety in the area, the vicar of St. Mark's called a meeting. It was very poorly advertized—a note in his parish magazine and a post-card in a newsagent's window—but the meeting was full and people were excited. A residents' association was formed. Passion was fuelled principally by two groups. First, the Millfielders who resented both the clearance proposals and the indefiniteness surrounding them. In the second place there were those Millfielders who wanted to be rehoused but who were equally upset by the uncertainty.

The mass meeting and the activities of the residents' association received a good deal of publicity in the local press.[1] The

Council soon held a meeting in Millfield at which it announced the intention to revise the plans, make them concrete and involve the public in the whole process.[2]

The residents' association accepted that the local planning authority must be allowed time to prepare the plans; continued public agitation would be both inappropriate and impolite. The residents settled down to wait for participation. The association studied the new White Paper on housing.[3] It made a structural survey of members' property (virtually the whole of the area) through one of the town's main estate agents and surveyors. The street representatives casually collected opinions on members' preferences in the matter of compensation, slum clearance, rehousing, improvement, and so forth. The question of a housing association was explored. Public meetings were held, and the committee evolved its own policies for the area.

Increasingly these policies were taking the form of contingency plans: 'If the Corporation this, then the association that'. For the association found that months were passing with no word of the plans being sent (though through the local newspaper it was known that a survey of all pre-1914 houses in the town had been undertaken by the planning and health departments). Nor was there any word about participation, except for a news item in March 1968 that the chairman of Sunderland planning committee had been appointed to the Skeffington committee; he himself publicly gave credit for his appointment to the success of public participation in Millfield.[4] However, in 1968 the committee of the Millfield Residents' Association corresponded very well to Engels' celebrated description of the hand-loom weaver: quiet men with their little houses, godly and honourable, ready always to doff their caps to the rich and to the officials of the state. Participation would come, and the plans would come, but in the meantime—patience.

*The Proposals of November 14th 1968*

Exactly one year after the promise of participation, the Council phoned the chairman of the residents' association (the vicar of St. Mark's), and a meeting was arranged at very short notice, three or four days, for November 14th 1968.

The proposals centred round 688 dwellings in East Millfield which had been programmed in the statutory plan for redevelopment by 1972.[5] In 1965 they were included in the programme for demolition in 1968–9. The technical report on which the 1965 decision rested had estimated that 626 of the dwellings were at that time unfit for human habitation, i.e. were already legally slums in 1965.

The proposals of November 14th scheduled none of these houses for demolition as early as 1968–9. It was planned to clear by 1971–2 only 69 of the 688. Between 1972 and 1975 133 would be demolished; 110 between 1975 and 1978; and 134 between 1978 and 1983. The total clearance programme, stretching to 1983, was only two-thirds of the total of 688 which had been scheduled for clearance in 1968–9. In the proposals of November 1968 203 of the 688 dwellings were now in improvement areas. The plans for 39 of the 688 dwellings were not indicated.

Two main objections were raised to this programme. First, the quality of the research. The association was not convinced that the plan of November 1968 had been based on accurate and relevant data. It advocated, not only in the resolution specifically dealing with the surveys, but also in the wording of particular substantive resolutions, that decisions should be arrived at on the basis of ascertainable knowledge of the area.

A second objection was to the legal basis of the planners' proposals—rather, not so much objection, as the wish to be informed clearly about what the legal basis was.

On the question of the internal facilities of dwellings, Mr. Bews said that in these cottages an outside toilet was more hygienic than one inside.

Many people thought so. All this about 'inside toilets' was a gimmick. The planning department replied that 'for a house to be fit by Act of Parliament it has to have an inside toilet'. The secretary of the residents' association asked the Town Clerk's department whether the planning department's statement was accurate. Was it true to say that any Act of Parliament laid it down that the possession of an outside rather than an inside toilet was a specific item to be considered in the matter of 'fitness for human habitation'? The planning department denied that it had made that statement, but the secretary pointed out that the exact words had been noted as they had been uttered. The Town Clerk's department said that in its experience no dwelling would be condemned on those grounds alone. The secretary asked whether in law it was possible to condemn a dwelling on these grounds at all. The Town Clerk's department said that the relevant legislation did not include such a specific reference, but slum-clearance decisions were influenced by precedent in public inquiries, etc. The secretary asked whether either by Act, precedent or usage it would be true to say that the possession or not of an inside toilet was an allowable consideration in law in compulsory slum-clearance cases. The Town Clerk's department then said that it thought not.[6]

The third main objection raised to the proposals of November 1968 in public meetings, street representatives' reports and committee discussions was that short 'lives' to cottages of under fifteen years were punitive to the families affected. Spreading the clearance programme over fifteen years until 1983 would mean living in an area in which fifty cottages were being demolished this year and fifty next, with the constant unpleasantness of dust, vermin, vandalism and the accelerated decay of both the area and the dwellings for the remaining families. The association therefore proposed that the Corporation should discover which areas 'in fact and in law' could be properly represented for clearance in the next five-year programme and clear them. For the remaining areas it should adopt policies which would maintain them for at least fifteen years. The slums should be ascertained and cleared with all possible haste. Planning blight should be lifted from the rest of Millfield. The degree to which the general and detailed proposals of the association were individually or collectively desirable or feasible is open to debate. Such debate was elided by the Corporation's new plans, presented at the participation meeting of February 7th 1969.

## The Proposals of February 7th 1969

The first area to be cleared under the new proposals of February 7th 1969, 114 dwellings, were programmed for demolition by 1971. Three months before, in the November 1968 plans, these same dwellings had been proposed for clearance by 1975. Included among the 114 dwellings to be demolished by 1971 were twenty-seven dwellings which three months before had been in the programme for clearance in the period 1978–83. Half-a-dozen houses included in the February 1969 plan for clearance by 1971 had been given a life into the twenty-first century in the plans of November 1968.

The sixty-nine dwellings which in the November 1968 proposals had been earmarked for the first phase of clearance (on the grounds that they were structurally the worst in Millfield) were now to be cleared two years later; again, in accordance not only with survey findings but also with what the planning department said were the resolutions of the Millfield Residents' Association.

In the Corporation's previous proposals of November 1968 a group of 101 cottages had been scheduled for clearance in the period 1975–9 (the sort of short life against which the association spoke most strongly), accompanied by a recommendation that grants should be allowed if a 'crash programme' was undertaken. The new February 1969 plans retained the proposal to clear these cottages about the year 1978, but removed the recommendation to provide grants.

The Corporation's proposals of February 7th 1969 were discussed by the residents' association, and nine additional recommendations were prepared. In the main they spelled out still more clearly and in greater detail the association's basic policies:

to remove uncertainty; to establish the plans on the basis of reliable and relevant information; to develop sound plans for rehousing and redevelopment; to facilitate revitalization; to speed necessary slum clearance; and to put an end to planning blight. These resolutions were discussed with the planning department and the Council at a participation meeting on February 14th 1969.

Although at its inception it had been militant, in the sense that it had spoken publicly, the Millfield Residents' Association had accepted the rightness of quiescence as soon as participation was offered. In February 1969 there was still scarcely any support for, or indeed much thought given to publicity. Most members of the committee clearly regarded it as sometimes necessary, but always in bad taste. The new resolutions therefore merely became more exact and unambiguous versions of those which had been put earlier, the meaning of which appeared to have been mistaken by the planning department and the Council. In spite of some shaking which the association's confidence in the Corporation had received in these encounters, when the meeting of February 14th 1969 ended there remained a strong faith in the power of the facts and the weight of rationality in carrying participation to a correct conclusion.

## NOTES

1 e.g. *Sunderland Echo*, November 8th 1967.
2 This is an analysis of institutional, not personal factors. In spite of the occasional clumsiness of the designation, therefore, contributors on the political, elected side are mainly referred to as the Council. Contributors from the appointed side are referred to throughout as the planning department, the health department etc. My own contributions, as secretary of the residents' association, are attributed to 'the secretary'.
3 Ministry of Housing and Local Government, *Old Houses into New Homes*, London: H.M.S.O., 1967.
4 *Sunderland Echo*, March 20th 1968.
5 East Millfield covers census enumeration districts A34, 35, 36, 37 (north),

38 and 39 (north). This is the 'Deptford Road area' of the author's *People and Planning*, London: Faber and Faber, 1970. It corresponds to Robson's 'Deptford' in his text, but not on his maps. Brian Robson, *Urban Analysis*, Cambridge: Cambridge University Press, 1969.

6 Millfield Residents' Association minutes of participation meeting, November 14th 1968. The question of an outside toilet was irrelevant to clearance decisions.

# CHAPTER 3

# PARTICIPATION?

Millfield is divided roughly in half by the old Sunderland to Durham railway. The residents' association covered the whole of the area. When the word participation was first used about Millfield by the Council in November 1967 it was widely understood—no other thought was raised—that Millfield would be dealt with as a whole. The Corporation proposals of November 1968, however, dealt only with East Millfield.

The Corporation's proposals for West Millfield were not submitted for another five months, at a public meeting held on March 31st 1969.[1] A further three months were to elapse before residents were able to inspect the proposals at close quarters and see how they affected their own homes, at a public display of the maps on June 23rd–27th. Participation in West Millfield along the lines of the November 1968–February 1969 meetings had been frequently and firmly promised by both the Council and the planning department. June 1969 passed without any such meeting being held. Meanwhile, what on earth had happened to public participation in East Millfield?

The area was deteriorating due to Council neglect. Under the shadow of these uncertain plans (including road proposals in both East and West Millfield, but particularly in West Millfield) the morale and the will to maintain, much less improve, their cottages was now clearly collapsing. The association's membership and committee remained uniformly loyal. But even in so stable an area as Millfield it was unreasonable to expect a voluntary body to remain viable in the face of such difficulties. In July 1969 the patience of the association broke. The chairman of the association announced that unless Millfield's problems were quickly and effectively tackled, the residents would run candidates in the municipal elections in the Millfield wards.[2] At the same time, the secretary was instructed by the association to conduct all future business through the Town Clerk's department.

*Preparation for the Planning Committee Meeting of August 27th 1969*

On July 21st 1969 the Town Clerk's department was asked to obtain the answers to two questions. First, what was the status of the plans for West Millfield? Second, when would the promised participation meetings be started in West Millfield?

The Town Clerk's department replied that these questions would be put to the planning committee on August 27th 1969. This meant another delay of over a month. There was a considerable exchange of correspondence with both the Town Clerk's department and the planning department. Copies of a mimeographed letter were sent by the association to the leaders of the Conservative and Labour groups for distribution to members of the planning committee, explaining its requests for information on the status of the plans and the date of the promised participation meeting. All the members of the planning committee were sent a second letter informing them that the association had formed small deputations. These deputations would be available to discuss Millfield and especially to answer any questions members of the planning committee might like to put about Millfield's particular problems of the lifing of cottages, slum clearance, road proposals and other planning matters. The association's committee, the letter continued, would fall in entirely with the wishes of the planning committee members as to time and place of meeting. Several councillors replied, and two received deputations. Two days before the meeting a third mimeographed letter explaining the issues was sent to each member of the planning committee.

The local Member of Parliament had a special interest in

planning. (He had been the first Minister of Land and Natural Resources.) Unknown to the residents' association he also had a special sympathy for public participation in planning. The fact that he had not yet been approached by the residents' association, and that he himself (a conscientious constituency M.P.) knew little or nothing of the work of the association between November 1967 and August 1969 is an indication of the extent to which the association had confined itself to internal communication with the planning authority only. At the end of July 1969, however, the association instructed the secretary to contact him. Presumably as the direct result of his meeting with the secretary, the M.P. almost immediately made a statement to the press favourable to the association.[3]

The press was also used directly for the first time in a systematic way to draw attention to Millfield's problems.[4] In Sunderland's new central shopping and flat complex the planning department had erected display cases containing maps for the guidance of visitors. All the maps were wrongly oriented. The association drew a lesson from them, which was reported under a three column headline 'Sunderland upside-down maps pointer to Millfield misery'.[5] An opportunity was seized a few days later, after reports of serious vandalism in the new town-centre flats, to publicize the lack of information for Millfielders on the question of rehousing after clearance had taken place, as well as the question of compulsion when the superiority of the new accommodation could legitimately be doubted.[6]

Two days before the meeting of the planning committee *The Times* (London) carried a fourteen column-inch report on Millfield. 'This week Sunderland planning committee comes to grips again', the report said, 'with the urgent need to do what it can about Millfield, with the request for a date and arrangements for more participation.' *The Times* dealt with the pointlessness of Millfield's blight, and the lackadaisical pace of local planning. 'The 1957 non-plan; the 1965 non-plan; the 1969 non-plan: Tweedledee, Tweedledum and Tweedletwaddle.'[7]

The meeting of the planning committee was held on August 27th. Its decision in relation to the letters from the Millfield Residents' Association? To postpone a decision. The matter was referred to a sub-committee. The sub-committee was to discuss the letters with a deputation from the association composed of the secretary, the joint chairmen and two other committee members. The secretary of the association was informed of this decision. He replied that the committee would consider the invitation, no doubt favourably. The association's committee would decide the composition of the deputation. It would probably include the secretary and the two chairmen. If it did not, the Corporation could be sure that the association's representatives would have been chosen for their competence to express the association's view. The Town Clerk's department replied that, although it was appreciated that the composition of the representation was a matter for the association to decide, 'the Corporation feel that the attendance of the two chairmen to be of the utmost importance'. The purpose of the meeting, the Town Clerk's department said, would be to discuss the whole of the correspondence since July 21st. In preparation for September 15th, therefore, the deputation appointed by the association studied the accumulated letters.[8]

*The Meeting with the Planning (Emergency) Sub-Committee on September 15th 1969*

The Corporation representatives at the meeting comprised the members of the planning sub-committee, three senior officers from the planning department, the Borough Engineer and a senior officer of his department, the housing manager, two public health inspectors, a Corporation solicitor and some other officers. The proceedings opened at 7.50 p.m.:

*Council:* The meeting will be terminated at 8.30 p.m. I think the best way to begin is to ask the Millfield residents to say what they wish to say.
*Chairman of the association:* Well, as the secretary is the one who has been

47

principally concerned with the correspondence we are going to discuss, perhaps . . .

*Secretary:* I think that anyone who has looked at this correspondence will see that the contributions to it from the Millfield Residents' Association are considerably more bulky and voluminous than those from the Corporation. I am therefore somewhat surprised at the request. What the Millfield Residents' Association has to say on the subject we were asked here tonight to discuss has been said, after due consideration and careful thought, in those letters. . . . A very senior councillor said to me a fortnight ago, 'Nobody reads long letters'. Well, we are here at your request to discuss these long letters. All the Millfield Residents' Association representatives here have read them, I assure you. I assume you have too. What we have to say has been said as clearly as we could say it in our letters, and it does not seem possible to make it any clearer with an impromptu summary now. What we have to say is in the correspondence, and I cannot say it again without simply reading it out aloud to the meeting. I should of course be glad to clarify any particular points at the request of any members of this committee, who have no doubt studied the letters, and may have questions to ask about them.

The planning sub-committee did not discuss the correspondence. There was no further mention of it. No answers were received to any of the queries contained in the association's letters. Positively, however, further promises were made about participation in the future and these were felt to be a sufficiently satisfactory outcome.[9] The deputation left feeling (mistakenly) that the Corporation had at last given undertakings of such a nature and in such a context that beneficial results could not but flow from them for Millfield.

But no answers had been given by the planning committee or sub-committee to the question of the status of the plans; no information was given about the date of a participation meeting. The association, though happy with the promises, was puzzled. On August 27th the decision of the planning committee had been to put the questions, together with matters raised in subsequent correspondence, to the planning sub-committee of September 15th, to which the Millfield Residents' Association would be invited. Now the planning sub-committee had shied

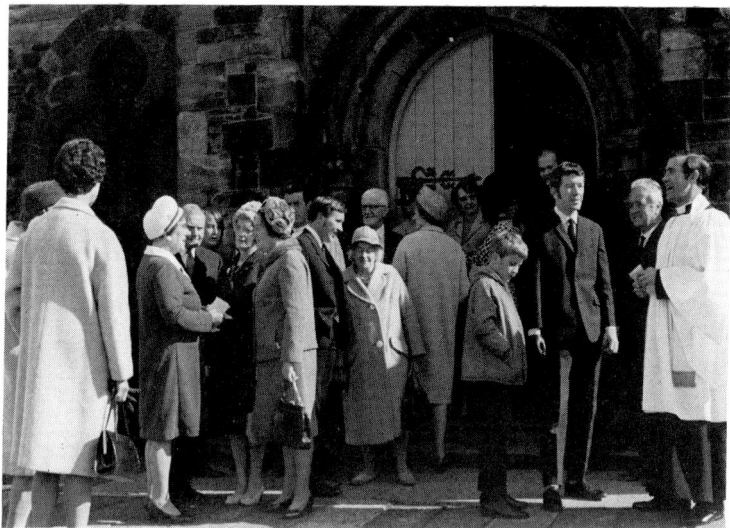

Plate Ia. St. Mark's Church, East Millfield

Plate Ib. St. Mary Magdalene's Church, West Millfield

Plate II. The Mountain Daisy

Plate III. Franklin Street Pentecostal

Plate IVa, b. 'Seem to them to be solidly comfortable'

Plate Va. 'Redevelopment . . .

Vb. . . . by 1972'

Plate VIa. Self expression—self-made front

Plate VIb. Self expression—self-made back

Plate VIIa, b. Potts Street in 1967

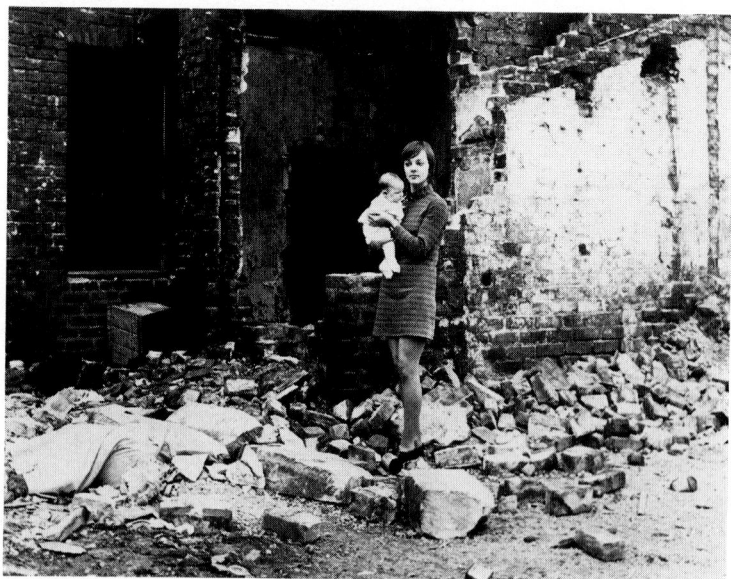

Plate VIIc, d. Potts Street in 1970

away from the correspondence. All this was strange. The insistence on the presence of the joint chairmen of the association was strange, especially in the light of the fact that, when the association asked for the minute requesting this, the secretary was told that it was the planning department's wish, not the expressed wish of the planning committee itself. Strangest of all was the obvious bewilderment of the planning sub-committee when the representatives of the Millfield Residents' Association had arrived on September 15th quite obviously prepared to discuss the correspondence and as a body happy to do so.

On October 9th, however, a document entitled *Millfield: Progress Report* was inadvertently shown to the vicar.[10] It had been presented to the planning committee on August 27th. The report characterized the relationship between the Corporation and the Millfield Residents' Association as 'reasonable' up to and including the letter of July 25th to the Town Clerk. The report continues:

> But between then and August 9th, nine further letters were received from the Millfield Residents' Association, six of them dated August 1st. ... The tenor of the letters dated July 29 ($2\frac{1}{2}$ pages long), July 30th (four pages long) and August 9th (three pages long) with all the innuendo and wilful misunderstanding inherent in this type of correspondence is best gained by reading them (they are of course available). . . . Subsequent to the drafting of this report two further letters have been received, as at August 22nd, comprising a total of ten pages, plus enclosures.

An appendix to *Millfield: Progress Report* dealt with the six letters from the association to the Town Clerk all dated August 1st, full versions of which were (the committee was told once more) 'of course' available. The planning department's 'answers' thoroughly vindicated the planners in the eyes of the planning committee on August 27th 1969 and as thoroughly discredited participation. The planners' report effectively terminated public participation in planning, with the blame for failure lying unmistakably with the association.

# INTRODUCTION

## NOTES

1 West Millfield covers census enumeration districts A45 (east), 46, 47 (east), 48 (east), 49 (east), 50, 51 and 52 (north), plus the south-east corner of A44. E.D.'s A49, 50 and the western edge of A51 are the 'Booth Street' area of the author's *People and Planning*.

2 *Sunderland Echo*, July 21st 1969.

3 *Sunderland Echo*, August 5th 1969.

4 There had been occasional letters on special subjects over the previous two years—the outbursts in the *Sunderland Echo* to which the planners' report referred.

5 The secretary was reported as saying this about the maps. 'They only make sense to that small band of strangers who happen to stand on their heads when they have any reading to do. Some people might think this is a niggling complaint. I sincerely wish it was. Unfortunately for everyone in this town—and I speak with particularly strong feeling about Millfield—it is only too glaringly symptomatic. When in small, simple things, a matter of a moment's thought, there is evident this attitude of carelessness about the task in hand, is it surprising that in large and complicated projects, involving the lives of hundreds of families over months and years, requiring complex information and sympathetic understanding, local citizens find nothing but frustration, dissatisfaction and misery with the quality of what is "planned" for them?' *Sunderland Echo*, August 5th 1969.

6 'The issue is a straightforward one. Is the Council satisfied that what it will give the people of Millfield is on balance superior to what will be taken away? In some of the slum streets there is no problem: anything is better than the disgraceful, broken-down hovels in which families have been left to rot for so long—and as often as not cottages that have rotted because of the proposals for slum clearance, still not implemented. But is Mill Hill, in the balance of advantages and disadvantages, superior to Booth Street? Is Lumley Tower on the whole better than St. Luke's Road? Is Gilley Law to be preferred to Oswald Street?' *Sunderland Echo*, August 26th 1969.

7 'Prophet of Blight in the North', *The Times*, August 25th 1969.

8 Appendix I (*The Correspondence of July–August 1969*).

9 Appendix II (*Meeting Between Millfield Residents' Association Representatives and Corporation Representatives, Town Hall, Monday September 15th 1969*).

10 Appendix III (*Millfield: Progress Report*).

PART TWO

# THE STATUS OF THE PLANS

CHAPTER 4

# LIFING

In the 1952 statutory development plan for Sunderland, in common with virtually all pre-1914 working-class housing in the town, Millfield had been given what is now termed a 'life' lasting only to 1972. The proposals presented to the Millfield Residents' Association at the participation meeting on November 14th 1968, and the proposals as further amended and presented on February 7th 1969, gave different groups of these houses new lives of different lengths – to 1975, to 1978, to 1983, to the end of the century, and beyond the end of the century.

Twenty years of blight and four years of great uncertainty had brought distress both to families which had been looking forward to being rehoused by the Council and to those who objected to the loss of their home and residence in the Millfield community.

> 'It's not so much the life of the property that's the matter. It's all these short lives, one after the other.'
>
> 'They keep saying "another five years". But then it goes on for twenty.'
>
> 'New rumours! Why won't they set our minds at rest for the few remaining years we have? We are entitled to know what's in store. We can't live in peace, not knowing what is going to happen.'
>
> 'The Corporation is very crafty. They let it go down. They let it deteriorate. A little bit worse! A little bit worse! Then they can get them cheap.'

## The Planning Department's Case

National legislation (the latest measure being the Housing Act of 1969) made subsidies available for houses which, after improvement, had a further life of fifteen years. More substantial grants were available for dwellings which after improvement had a life of thirty years or more. The simplest case for the planning department to put (and one which in the frame of participation between local government and residents would be conclusive) was that this national legislation compels the local authority to life all properties for the sake of those families who might wish to take advantage of the improvement-grant system. Surprisingly, this argument was not used until very late in the participation meetings, after several alternative answers to the residents' objections had been given.

The main argument, sustained by the planning department throughout the meeting at which the lifing proposals were principally discussed (December 13th 1968), was that lifing was not a policy at all. It was merely a statement of what was going to happen anyway. The following are four statements by the planning department, taken from different parts of the tape-transcript of the meeting:

> 'It isn't a policy, you see. We haven't tried to give them five, ten or fifteen years.'
> 'We put lives on to the best of our ability. What the life actually is. Nothing to do with what we want, or what the Corporation plans.'
> 'If someone gets a mortgage, there will be a surveyor's report. The assumption is that their assessment is the same as ours.'
> 'Another thing. Supposing the Corporation was willing to give mortgages on these properties. We would be bound to send a competent surveyor. And we would have to tailor the repayments to the life of the property.'

On page nine of the tape-transcript the argument appears for the first time that the authority is obliged to give lives because of grants. 'We can't give a standard grant unless the property has a life of fifteen years or more. We can't give a discretionary grant unless it has a life of at least thirty years.' The main reason given up to that point was the necessity to give this information to prospective purchasers, landlords, and owner-occupiers in assisting them to reach reasonable judgements about their investments in property.

'If you placed yourself in the position of the prospective purchaser, would you still say, "No lives"?'

'If you came to our department and asked about buying property, you'd expect to be told about lives.'

'But people write to us and ask, "What is the life?" We get queries from the Land Search. The development plan says 1972. Rightly or wrongly we in law have to say that. But informally we say, "So-and-so many years". We have to advise people when our advice is sought.'

'I must make one point about this life business. If a solicitor comes to us, we must give him the life of the property. You must advise people like this, otherwise they'll play hell with us.'

'If there was no plan, if there was no year by year clearance programme, how could anybody know what he was buying? He would have nothing to base his investment on. Things can happen nationally that throw the predictions and the plans out, but what protection has such a person got unless there is a plan of some kind?'

### The Effects of Lifing As Such

There were several grounds for objection to the planning department's lifing policy, especially to the short-life proposals.

1. Some residents took the view that the great body of Millfielders, who by and large were neither buyers nor sellers of property, but were settled in what they would wish to be their life-time homes, were being sacrificed to the interests of the relatively small number of buyers of property—that is, even if the predictions were accurate and dependable.

2. Some residents wanted to move from Millfield, but were unable to sell their cottages because of the short lives:

'We want to be out of Ravensworth Street to improve ourselves. A ten-year life is no good to me.'

'We are in the older houses in Ravensworth Street. We can't sell them. Now we are landed with them until 1978. We've tried to move for years, now we still can't move.'

'We want to get another mortgage before we get too old for one.'

3. Some wanted to stay, but were unable to raise the loans for modernization and maintenance because they could not mortgage their houses. The vicar told the planning department's representatives that such people 'have no hope of getting a mortgage on their home, especially the older folk'. Some people, he told them, had been in tears at a public meeting held on November 19th 1968. 'They feel trapped. They can't face another seven years, yet they can't raise the money to improve the property to make it habitable for themselves, because they can't get a mortgage anywhere on a short-life house.'

4. The vicar also described for the Council and planning department the blight which Millfield had suffered for many years due to planning proposals. 'The fact that you say that property has five, or ten or however-many years of life has effects that wouldn't operate if you did not say that', he said. 'Take the people in Ravensworth Street, they can't decorate, they can't spend money repairing or modernizing. In other houses people weep, they have cried to me because their houses are in such a condition because of blight.' The vicar put the problem in concrete terms—comparing Thornhill Terrace, where the town's planning officer lived, with a street of two-storied, substantial Victorian houses in Millfield, in the development plan for redevelopment by 1972, but not in the area subject to the November 1968/February 1969 planning proposals. 'If Thornhill Terrace was programmed for 1982, would the property retain its present standard? Even in, for example, Broxbourne Terrace, a house has stood there for months and can't be sold simply because all these streets are in the development plan for redevelopment by 1972.' Both in committee and at public meetings all the residents who commented on this aspect of the proposals expressed some version of these sentiments: 'Giving a life of five or seven years is just asking for five or seven years of quick deterioration.'

Residents objected to the planning department's judgement that in a few—or even in many years' time, their own house or street would have fallen below the standard they set themselves in their own housing. Into the indefinite future, they saw maintenance and improvement proceeding, if it was not artificially retarded or stopped by planning proposals. The secretary of the association put the point to the participation meeting in these words:

> 'I believe (and this is my personal opinion, there has been no decision on this in committee), I believe that if it wasn't for the life that had to be given for those people who were going to be given or not given improvement grants—it is because of improvement-grant policy that you give lives—if it wasn't for the life that you give in order to "help" people, and there was no life on the property, Mrs. Brown and Mrs. Russell and people like them wouldn't bother too much about improvement grants. They'd be pleased enough to put their own money in. . . . If people thought it was their home, and were assisted, by the way, by the Corporation controlling the people who weren't pulling their weight, who were pulling the area down . . . In other words in Millfield if people weren't offered these improvement grants which require lifing, then they'd be improving out of their own money continually and very happily.'

(Clearly, that argument depended upon empirical data. Was Millfield, or was Millfield not the kind of area to which that argument applied?)

5. Residents, finally, were suspicious of the quality of the council houses which they would be offered when their own were demolished. In their view, their present accommodation was superior to what they would be likely to be offered by the Corporation when they were rehoused, and would remain superior if not blighted. 'There'll be some right mugs going into them', a committee member said about the new town-centre flats. 'I'd rather have our cottages any day and at any price.' 'Rising damp!' he said. 'What about your own Council estates? There is disgraceful verdigris up at Downhill. I know. I've seen it. What are you going to do, start demolishing your own houses?' A councillor agreed that the conditions of some of the Corporation's newest houses meant that they were inferior places 'to actually live in' than Millfield cottages. He himself

was taking part at that time in an inquiry into the quality of houses at Doxford Park (Silksworth New Township).

## The Unreliability of the Lifing Predictions

The above points were, so to speak, arguments against progress as such, arguments for never saying in advance that any property would be demolished, against planning ahead. If the lifing predictions were accurate forecasts of the fate of the property a number of years ahead then it would be simply obscurantist of Millfielders to object to them; they would be refusing to face up to the facts.

It was the association which put the point that there were two sorts of predictions, one much more difficult than the other (and that it was the more difficult of the two that the planning department had insisted was its sort of prediction).

The first sort depended, the association said, upon the power of the predictor to bring about a certain state of affairs. Thus in housing it was possible to say that various relevant facts were known in the here-and-now. The condition of the property in the here-and-now could be known. So could legislation. So could the resources of the residents. On the basis of this information plans could be devised. These plans would take the form of undertakings on the part of the planning authority to take certain actions to bring about a certain result at some time in the future, by operating on the known current circumstances in 'appropriate' ways. The secretary of the association said that the following line of reasoning was entirely possible:

'Now, we cannot guarantee, by any means, that our plans cast so far into the future, will eventuate, will come to fruition. But at any rate it is logically possible to say, "Well, I want to preserve this property, if I can, for fifteen (or thirty) years, and I'm going to start now to try to do it". That is in fact what Mrs. Brown does in her cottage, Mrs. Russell in hers, Mr. Tingle in his, Mr. Watson in his. That is what everybody does. It is a thing that is possible, though it may fail in practice.'

He continued: 'But if you say in the void, "Well, I believe this will happen in twenty years' time, thirty years' time", and then base current policies on it, I think that is a logical impossibility.' What the secretary called 'a logical impossibility' is the second type of prediction. This was the type of prediction the planning department was claiming to make.

The programme of redevelopment by 1972 shown in the statutory development plan approved in 1952 had included four areas which contained most of Sunderland's pre-1914 dwellings. (See Diagram 3.) One of these areas, roughly a mile square, included Millfield. (See Diagram 4.)[1] The type of dwelling included in the 'by 1972' programme in this area is shown in Plate V. Both West and East Millfield were programmed for clearance and rebuilding (or redevelopment for some other use, e.g. industrial expansion) within the first twenty years of the 1952 plan. Diagram 5 shows at a larger scale the area of East Millfield, so programmed.

Blight took several forms. The relatively small number of families wanting to sell their houses were put at a disadvantage in relation to buyers. Overall, of course, what the sellers lost financially, the buyers gained. What was blight for the vendor was benefit for the purchaser, and the depressed prices of blighted property enabled families to become owner-occupiers who would have otherwise been compelled to remain tenants of private landlords and perhaps, eventually, become council tenants. From that point of view, while blight in the long run makes the redevelopment proposals (if persisted in) a self-authenticating statement—they are their own voucher—in the short run the spread of owner-occupation means that they build up their own opposition, because the attitude of owner-occupiers to demolition and council rehousing tends to be significantly less favourable than that of renters, not least because their homes become an important vehicle for self-expression. (Plate VI.)

The redistribution of wealth from sellers of property to buyers of property due to blight is both considerable and completely arbitrary. The sellers naturally suffer from a sense of injustice. The buyers, perhaps illogically, once they are themselves by the fact of purchase in the position of potential sellers, begin to share the blighted area's resentment against the system from which they have been so recently the gainers. As the plan

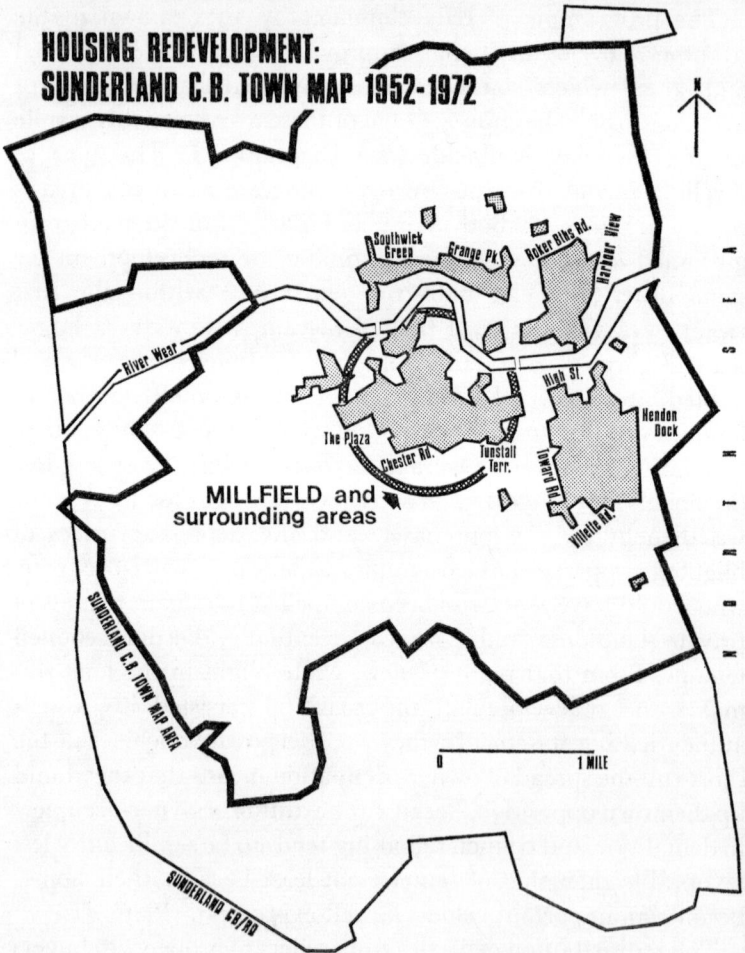

HOUSING REDEVELOPMENT:
SUNDERLAND C.B. TOWN MAP 1952-1972

N

Southwick Green
Grange Pk
Roker Blhs Rd.
Harbour View

River Wear

High St.

Hendon Dock

The Plaza
Chester Rd.
Tunstall Terr.
Tavern Rd.
Villette Rd.

MILLFIELD and surrounding areas

NORTH SEA

SUNDERLAND C.B. TOWN MAP AREA

SUNDERLAND CB/RD

0          1 MILE

*Diagram 3. Redevelopment by 1972—Sunderland C.B.*

approaches the date of its completion, cottages in an area such as East Millfield can be sold only at a price which is so low that it is experienced by the owners as unsaleability.

Blight also took the form which Millfielders most resented (see p. 56 above), the deterioration of property due to lack of maintenance and the failure to keep it up-to-date in its amenities.

## 'By 1972' – Development Plan 1952 and Reviews

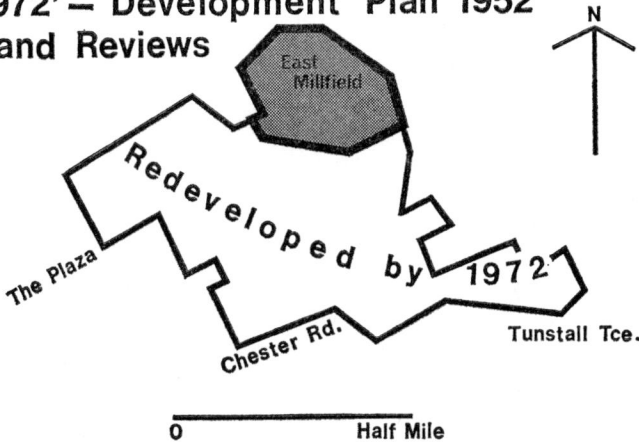

*Diagram 4. Redevelopment by 1972—Millfield Area*

Decisions on whether and to what extent to repair or refurbish were taken in the knowledge that redevelopment was expected to be completed by 1972. Lack of environmental maintenance and improvement by the Council contributed heavily to this deterioration. Again, this can be most clearly seen when the blight was lifted. Westbury Street was a street Millfielders were by no means convinced ought to have been retained in any of the plans presented in participation meetings. It was given a fifteen-year life in November 1968 and February 1969. As soon as fifteen-year grants began to be given, one resident completely rebuilt the front wall of his cottage. In the better streets of Millfield post-blight improvements were correspondingly more widespread and intensive.

The mile-square area circled in Diagram 3 and shown again in Diagram 4 was blighted in 1952 in the interests of redevelop-

# 'By 1972'—Development Plan 1952 and Reviews

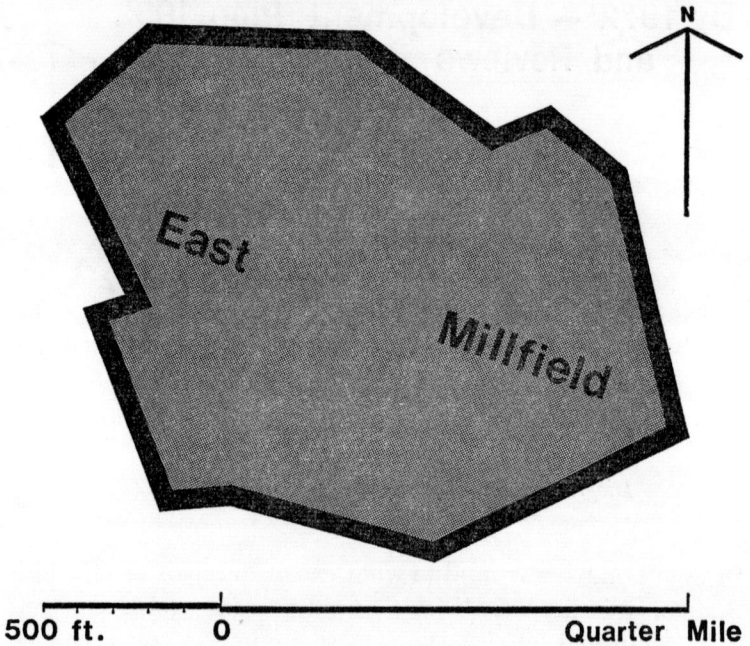

500 ft.          0                              Quarter Mile

*Diagram 5. Redevelopment by 1972—East Millfield*

ment, clearance and rebuilding which would take place by 1972. This included the whole of East Millfield. In May 1965 the Council approved the clearance of most of East Millfield by 1968–9, but excluded certain areas from the clearance proposals. (See Diagram 6.) It announced no plans for rebuilding. The new proposals of November 1968 phased only a corner of the area for clearance by 1972. (See Diagram 7.) The amended proposals of February 1969 substituted a different area for clearance by 1972. (See Diagram 8.)

Late in 1970 the *actual* redevelopment which was to take

# 'By 1972'—Council Decision 1965

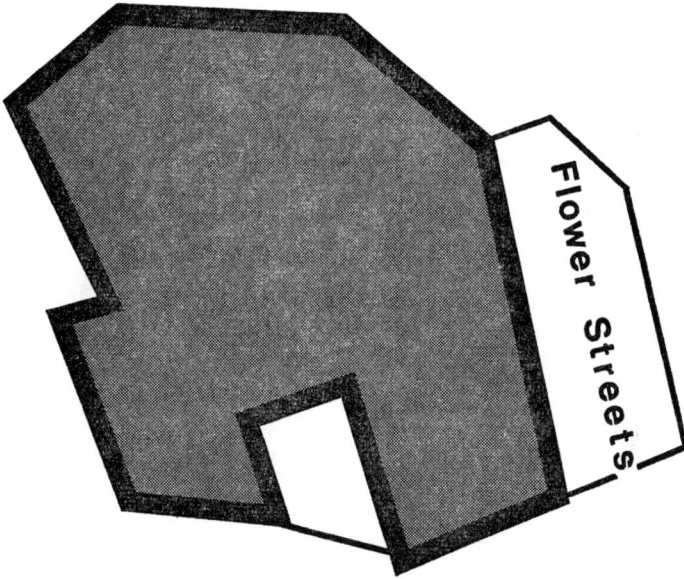

*Diagram 6. Clearance in East Millfield—Plan of 1965*

place in East Millfield by 1972 was announced. Ten houses were to be built by a private developer on a site less than forty-five yards square, which had been 'cleared' by a bomb during the Second World War. (See Diagram 9.) This already-cleared forty-five yard square site was the total redevelopment in the mile-square area shown in Diagrams 3 and 4 and apart from the Peacock Street area and the Beach Street area this constituted the total redevelopment carried out or actually planned for completion 'by 1972'. The fruit of twenty years of blight for Millfielders was the housing committee's recommendation that 'the developer be requested, as far as possible, to give priority to the residents of the Millfield area when offering the houses

# 'By 1972' — November 14th 1968

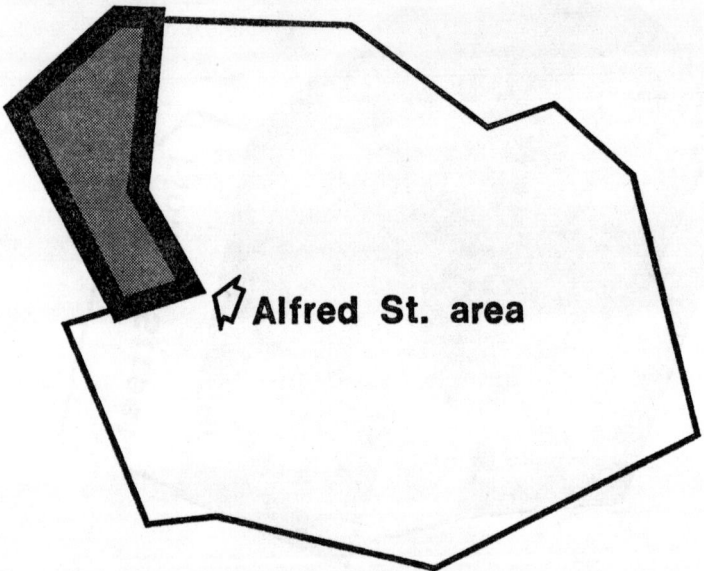

*Diagram 7. Clearance in East Millfield—Plan of 1968*

for sale'.[2] 'Strict conditions' were attached to the planning permission for eleven more. There was to be a landscaping scheme, and samples of the external materials to be used had to be submitted to the planning department for approval. This was to make certain that any new dwelling fitted in with the 'proposed new image of Millfield'.[3] Diagram 10 gives the sequence of lifing predictions in three typical districts in East Millfield. In order to give graphic representation to the magnitude of the successive changes in the predictions, their lack of dependability, the scale runs from 1911 to 2011, that is, for a full century.

# 'By 1972' – February 7th 1969

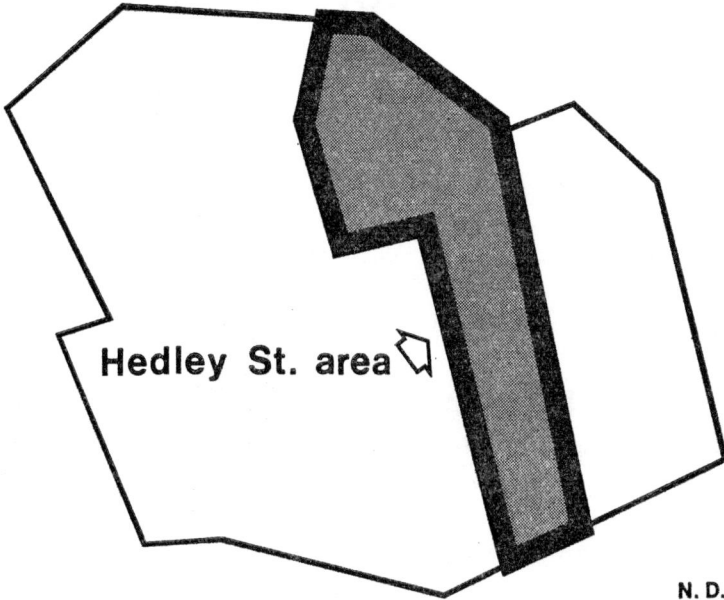

*Diagram 8. Clearance in East Millfield—Plan of 1969*

The Granville Street area, as Diagram 10 shows, was blighted from 1952 by the programme for demolition by 1972. This was confirmed in the quinquennial review of 1961. It was blighted especially by the firm slum-clearance programme based on the technical report of the planning and health departments in 1965. When the date for slum clearance came, 1968–9, a further period of blight was imposed by a new life terminating in the late 1970s or early 1980s. In practice, grants were being allo-

65

cated by 1970 on the basis of demolition at some time between 1985 and the year 2000.

Close Street, Hadrian Street and Westbury Street were also

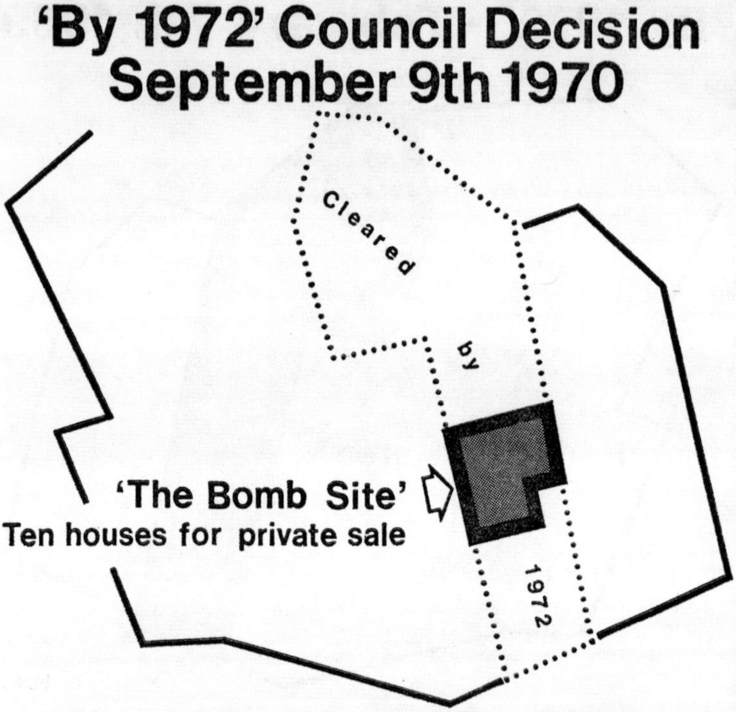

**'By 1972' Council Decision September 9th 1970**

'The Bomb Site'
Ten houses for private sale

*Diagram 9. Redevelopment of East Millfield—Plan of 1970*

programmed for redevelopment by 1972, and then included in the 1965 programme for clearance by 1968–9. In 1968 they were given a further life until at least 1990. In practice grants were being given by 1970 on the basis of demolition at some time between 1985 and the year 2000. In June 1970 the Corporation decided to undertake a study to determine whether it was feasible to extend the lives of these streets beyond the year 2000.

The Flower Streets (of which Fern Street is one) were blighted for nearly twenty years by the programme of redevelopment by 1972. When the terminal date of the redevelopment programme approached, the Flower Streets were given lives to an undetermined time somewhere in the twenty-first century.

# Changes in Lifing (Demolition) Dates

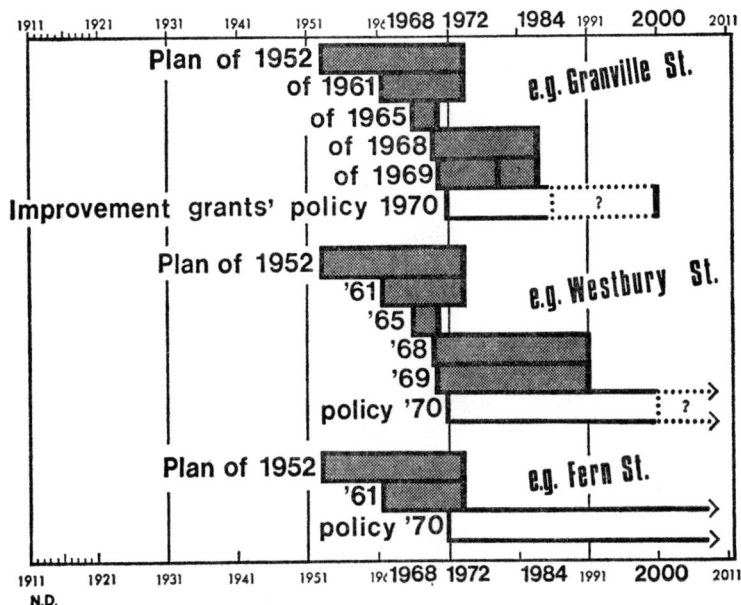

*Diagram 10. Changes in Lifing Dates*

Because so many policies had been offered and then either reviewed or quietly forgotten as 'unrealistic', different institutions and persons took different views about what current or likely policies would be.

*Mrs. McDermott:* We live in Cromwell Street. We were told that Standard Grants would be allowed. A neighbour [Mr. McDermott's brother] has just bought his cottage outright. The Corporation told him he could have a Standard Grant . . . But when he went to the Building Society to raise some money for his half of the improvement grant the Building Society said, 'It could easily be down in five years'. How could it be down in five years unless the Corporation pulled it down? How did they get this idea? Because the Building Society is still going off the old plan for Millfield! The old Corporation plan! The old Corporation life!

*Planning department:* We can't give a Standard Grant unless the property has a life of fifteen years or more. We can't give a Discretionary Grant unless it has a life of at least thirty years. But we try to be helpful.

The same problem of uncertainty and indefiniteness affected Mrs. Connolly in a different way. 'We wanted to get a mortgage ten years ago. We couldn't sell the house then. Yet if it had been known then that Ravensworth Street in these plans is going to be up until 1975 now, we could have sold it!'

Here is a typical letter from the planning department to an enquiry from Millfield about the life of a particular cottage:

> Although it was expected, when the development plan review was submitted in 1959, that the property would be redeveloped before 1972, it is now clear that this is unrealistic. The Council is now prepared to consider applications in this area for Standard Grants on the qualifying basis of a life expectancy of at least 15 years . . . The information contained in this letter is believed to be accurate and is based on the present decisions and policies of the Council. Nevertheless, it is given without prejudice to changes in those policies and also without accepting any legal responsibility for supplying such information.

The enquirer had lived in Millfield for many years. She had suffered for many years both mental anxiety and physical blight because of the '1972' programming. In 1959, looking forward only a dozen years, the planning department still judged that the street would be redeveloped by 1972. In 1970 the planning department were forecasting a life of a further fifteen years. Would she have been worse off trusting her own judgement on whether the area was declining into slumdom or being maintained by the inhabitants than she was trusting the judgement of the outside expert, whose judgements consistently proved to be unsound?

## *The Planners' Response*

What was the status of the new lives, the lives of November 14th 1968, as drastically altered three months later in the plans of February 7th 1969? That was the question put in the letter to the Town Clerk's department on July 21st 1969. It did not raise the very difficult issues of lifing as a policy. It did not raise the question of lifing as it applied to Millfield. It did not even ask for the justification for particular lives attached to particular streets in the proposals. It merely asked for an indication of the status of the plans as at mid-July: what *degree of reliability* could now be placed upon them? The point was raised again in the association's letter of July 30th to the planning department:

> It is essential for the people of Millfield to know soon whether their house *does* have a life of thirty-plus years, and so on, and that these facts be publicly announced with great firmness so that families can start again to repair and improve their homes with some confidence in the future. Of course, definiteness of long life is a *sine qua non* for financial institutions which families need to approach for the necessary resources for major improvements. Because of the continued indefiniteness of the plans, Building Societies and so forth 'will not touch Millfield'.

In making their report to the planning committee meeting of August 27th, which was to have discussed the two original issues in the letter to the Town Clerk's department of July 21st (the status of the plans and the date of the first participation meeting for West Millfield), the planning department selected twenty-six points from the association's letters of July 29th, July 30th and August 9th. The quotations from the letters and the planning department's comments covered four sides of foolscap. The essential point of the association's correspondence, as it had been of its resolutions, was 'uncertainty'. In the report of August 27th by far the briefest item quoted and commented on by the planning department was this. *Date of letter*: July 30th. *Point raised by the association*: It is necessary to know definitely whether houses have a long life. *Planning department's comments*:

Agreed. That was the planning department's whole answer to this crucial and complex problem.

What was said at the August 27th meeting of the planning committee by the planning department (as distinct from what was written into the report) is not known. It may be that verbally the planning department placed before the planning committee a clear and fair picture of how the problem of the status of the proposals presented itself to Millfielders, and satisfied the planning committee on the question of the status of the proposals. No such clarification, if it was made, was ever transmitted to the residents' association or to Millfielders through any other source or agency.

Confusing and contradictory, as distinct from definite and clear public statements continued to appear in a desultory fashion. The one change made to the proposals of February 7th was the deletion of 'by 1978' from the phasing key of the map, as this phasing related to the Millburn Street area. A letter to the *Sunderland Echo* dated June 25th 1970 read: 'I wonder if you could give me any information as to when Millburn Street is due for demolition.' The answer? 'Millburn Street is included in the third phase of the Millfield redevelopment proposals, *with clearance scheduled by 1978.*'

The planning department might have stated that experience had proved that its own views and proposals were only one element in a complex pattern of influences, including central government policy, party-political ideologies and manoeuvres and the state of public opinion. Not only did it not do so: these arguments appeared to form no part of the planning department's conception of the world in which it had to operate. Allowing for some disingenuousness on its part, the record suggests compellingly that the department's attitude was that to the extent that political parties, local councillors, residents' associations or the rate of economic growth distorted its proposals and falsified its predictions, so much the worse for economic fluctuations and the democratic system of local government.

These were not constraints of which account had to be taken in elaborating its blighting proposals of what would happen 'by 1972' given only its own presuppositions and wishes. There was no recognition in the department's statements that for twenty years its plans had caused deep and wideranging distress, all to no purpose. (Rather, exactly, to what turned out to be ten private houses on a bombed site.)

Millfield had become more and more dubious about the desirability as well as the likelihood of the benefits for which planning blight was supposedly the unavoidable and worthwhile price. In the participation meetings, therefore, Millfielders were anxious to know at least what degree of reliance could be placed upon the new proposals. At the time of the participation meetings they did not know the end of the story, which is shown in Diagram 9, but they knew the story up to that point. Diagram 9 seems to be a convincing confirmation of the reasonableness of their desire to be informed about the status of the new plans, as the status of the old had been so unsatisfactory to them. Participation, however, yielded them no answer.

### NOTES

1 As compared with Diagram 3, Diagram 4 excludes areas to the north and east which had been cleared for industrial use (Beach Street) and a small area to the west which had been redeveloped for housing (Peacock Street West).

2 Approved by the Council September 9th 1970. The builder was to be granted an option also, at a price to be agreed, on adjacent sites for a further fourteen houses, as and when the sites became available. The recommendation of the finance committee that the Council's mortgage scheme should be extended to cover the purchase of these ten houses was also approved, but no mention was made of preference for Millfielders.

3 *Sunderland Echo*, February 2nd 1971.

# CHAPTER 5

# DEMOLITION

---

## Doubt and Certainty

Ever since its foundation in November 1967 the status of the plans had been a key issue for the residents' association. At the first participation meeting with the Corporation this issue was raised again and again. In the notes on the meeting sent by the association to the local planning authority the point was made that the proposals in the booklet presented to the meeting were not only tentative proposals. If consultation were to take place they must of course be tentative. But they were *tentative* tentative proposals. Even if the Millfield Residents' Association immediately agreed to every word of them they were not proposals which would come into operation as stated. Whatever the Millfield Residents' Association did or did not agree to, they left the Corporation free to do what it liked. 'Until the overall clearance programme is prepared, and clearance rates established for the whole of the borough', the Corporation's proposals read, 'it is possible to indicate only the order of priorities of clearance for Millfield. The following clearance dates, which are based on the maximum life of the properties, must be confirmed in the light of this revised programme.'[1] 'Confirmed' was a euphemism. It clearly could only mean confirmed, altered, or abandoned. In the same notes a query was put to the planning authority about their recommendations in the proposals booklet. The planning authority recommended that the views of the association should be sought and its support solicited in improving the better houses. 'Subsequently', the planning authority recommended, 'the general aims for the area, and the suggested priorities for clearance, should be publicised to inform the local residents and eliminate uncertainty.' The Millfield Residents' Association asked, 'Subsequent to what?' As the proposals also stated that 'in carrying out ... environmental improvements it may be necessary to clear some long-life houses, for instance, in order to make proper garaging facilities available', it was obvious (and the association pointed this out) that no one in the areas even of the long-life properties could feel free of anxiety until plans were made final.

The association's resolutions gave 'an end to uncertainty' pride of place. Halfway through the meeting of December 13th 1968 the vicar despairingly cried, 'We needn't go any further! The whole thing is blown open by what we've heard tonight. The proposals are *not* phased as the booklet described. It will just drag out and drag out. Like the people in Beach Street!'

The secretary took up the same point.

'The prospect of this dragging on and on from what has transpired at this meeting is looming very large indeed. We must find some way quickly of reaching conclusions on these matters. Within some definite time span we've got to be able to say that this or that proposal has been accepted, or that either on policy grounds you reject it or on the grounds of practicality they cannot be fulfilled.'

When a new set of demolition proposals were put to East Millfield at the participation meeting of February 7th 1969 one of the Millfield Residents' Association's principal concerns was still the confidence that could be placed in them. On February 14th, however, the planning department answered this question far more firmly than the Millfield Residents' Association— before the answer was given—had thought possible, as the following extract from the meeting shows.

'Now', the secretary said, referring to the proposed clearance area, 'resolution 22 takes up the question, What is to happen to the areas which are not found to be unfit ...?'

'Well, if I could just comment on that', the planning department

73

replied. 'Properties in the areas marked Phase 1 (that's the area we've just been talking about) . . . Those are likely to be represented for clearance in 1971. That's two years—two years plus—from now. There's very little we can do in that short period.'

'But of course we don't know which areas will be unfit there. Those areas which are *not* unfit . . .'

'I don't know whether we're both on the same wavelength here', the planning department said. 'As the whole area is going to be cleared . . .'

'Well, we don't know that . . .'

'. . . in 1971—that is two years plus from now—what do we do in the meantime . . .?'

'We are wondering what is going to happen (in this resolution) to the fit properties and those properties which cannot be included in the clearance areas, when these decisions on unfitness have been made. If the whole of Phase 1 *is* cleared, then this resolution doesn't apply to anything in that area.'

'That's the implication, that . . . these areas will be cleared *en masse* . . .'

'So as not to leave, as it were, odd pieces here and there?' the vicar asked.

The health department interposed an answer, 'That's it exactly.'

On February 14th, that is, the planners dismissed Millfielders' fears about continued uncertainty not merely with confidence, but with scorn. What happened then?

1. *In East Millfield:* The slum-clearance plan of 1965 had scheduled 688 dwellings for demolition in 1968–9. Thirty-one of these had been cleared by 1968. The clearance plans of 1965 had then been replaced by the proposals of November 1968. These in turn had been radically altered by the proposals of February 1969. The proposals of February 1969 were apparently to be considered by the Corporation in the light of the association's resolutions of February 14th 1969. As it turned out, on March 19th the health committee approved the planning department's February clearance plan, quite unaltered. The Council passed the plan on April 9th. It therefore had the same status as the 1965 plan, which had been abandoned. This clearance plan was displayed at the exhibition at the end of

June. Most members of the committee of the Millfield Residents' Association were now reasonably confident that the February 7th/March 19th/April 9th plan could be depended upon, though the secretary was not as confident as the planning department had been on February 14th when it had regarded as incomprehensible his proposition that parts of the clearance area might prove not to be unfit.

2. *In West Millfield:* The position in West Millfield was extremely peculiar. The 1965 plan had phased 361 dwellings for clearance in 1967–8, as we have seen. Later, another twenty-three dwellings were added. None of the 384 had been touched. On March 19th the health committee approved the clearance of most of the 384. They were to be demolished under two distinct compulsory purchase orders, one area in 1970, the other in 1972. The twenty-three added dwellings were included. But — an unfathomable quirk — about forty at the south end of Washington Street and six in Bell Street which had been in the 1965 programme were now excluded from the 1969 programme. They stuck out like a sore thumb in the midst of the demolition proposed for 1970 and 1972.

These proposals were approved at the same meeting of the health committee as had approved the East Millfield clearance plan, and both sets of plans had exactly the same status. Yet the first public meeting called by the planners in West Millfield did not take place until March 31st, and at the meeting it was emphasized by both the Council and the planning department that the plans were conditional upon local opinion expressed through participation. There would be a public exhibition to give everyone the chance to see the plans, and then participation of the East Millfield type would take place. The exhibition was mounted at the end of June. Yet six weeks before, on April 9th, the Council had included the displayed proposals in the official programme of slum clearance up to the end of 1972.

What, then, was the status of the slum-clearance plans? The clearance plans for East Millfield now seemed fairly firm. But what of West Millfield? Would West Millfielders be participating on a matter which had already been decided, and which their representatives could not alter? If slum clearance was not now alterable by the Millfield Residents' Association or other local representations what degree of reliance could Millfielders place upon them being carried out within the planned period?

By October 6th 1969 the clearance proposals were formally very much firmer than they had been at the time of the planning department's remarks in February. Since February the clearance proposals for 1971 had been approved by the health committee and passed by the Council. The meeting of October 6th was preoccupied, as usual, with the problem of indefiniteness in the lifing, but not in East Millfield the clearance, areas. On the basis of the exchange between the planning department and the secretary on February 14th about the Hedley Street area (Diagram 8) the vicar, before going on to discuss the areas where uncertainty did still exist, indicated this area where the planners had been so adamant there was now no such problem.

*Chairman of the association:* Right. Let's get things clear. Get this straight. The brown area here will be cleared by 1971 . . .
*Planning department:* We can't say that. Take the Washington Street area. When the Public Health lads went there they found properties reasonably fit, in a block. Now there is a controversy in the Council over this. Until the Health lads go in, about eighteen months before clearance is done, when they assess which is fit and which is unfit, if there is a pocket like Washington Street the Corporation has to decide whether it ought to stay . . .
*Chairman of the association:* So there may be blocks that may *not* be taken. . . !
*Planning department:* We are as certain as we can be. That is what we think at present. That is all we can say.

Millfielders had to cope not only with the fact of uncertainty. They had to cope with uncertainty which took the form of a series of plans which were presented as certain until the last minute. They had to live simultaneously in the real world and in the world of the planners' fictions. Certainly as late as August 1967, and perhaps later still, the planning department was issuing letters to enquirers from West Millfield to the effect that 'this area could be cleared during 1968'.[2] Such letters included the standard disavowal of all responsibility for the statements they contained.

The best account of why there was chronic uncertainty presented as certainty about Millfield's future was given by the planning department at the meeting of October 6th 1969. The chairman of the association had once more brought up the question of Millfield's now permanent state of anxious suspense. 'This uncertainty', he said. 'A young couple in Close Street built a bathroom onto their cottage. But at that time it was programmed to be demolished by 1969, so they built it only one brick thick. Now they want to put the other course in. They went to the Building Society and asked for £125. Close Street now has fifteen-years-plus. But the Building Society said, "No. The property is too dicey. The Corporation can't make up its mind." '

The planning department's reply was that the difficulties were appreciated. 'We know it's difficult,' the planning department said. 'Even the Flower Streets, that now have thirty-plus years. [Aside.] Wasn't it down for redevelopment by 1972?' A colleague was consulted. The fact was confirmed. Redevelopment by 1972 remained the statutory status of the area.

'It was down for redevelopment by 1972 on the development plan', the planning department continued. 'That plan was prepared about 1950, the time when it was thought, "Brave New World". Unfortunately, when the time came to review the development plan (we weren't there then) the opportunity wasn't taken. Town Maps ought to be reviewed every five years. But there are big shifts in thought', the planning department went on. 'In 1948 we had to plan for twice the 1939 volumes of traffic. That looks silly today. So now we are having to do complicated "O and D" surveys; and the Government have said, "No review of the development plan until you get the traffic sorted out."'

The planning department gave other reasons why quinquennium by quinquennium the unrealistic redevelopment programming remained unchanged in the official plan. 'Then there is a new shift', the department said. 'This participation (this is a part of it) means that all sorts have to be done. Can't review the development plan until *these* are seen to!' There was yet another obstacle: 'Now we have to co-operate with other authorities, with seven other local authorities in the Tyneside area. That is why it has not been reviewed.'

The planning department concluded, 'We know it is unsatisfactory for you. That is why we have this survey of all pre-1914 houses. Eventually we will get a Corporation housing policy. But until there is a Corporation housing policy, there can be no review.' The planning department's final words on this particular topic were, 'There can be no review until about 1972 at the earliest, daft though it is.'[3]

*Delay*

A particular street which lies in an area where uncertainty had ended — which was at last at the end of the planning/clearance trail — Potts Street, will be taken as an illustration of this process of planned demolition. On the basis of the technical report of the planning department and the health department it had been included in the official Council resolution of May 1965 for clearance in 1967–8. It was the subject of the official Council resolution in the spring of 1969 for clearance in 1970. The 'by 1972' plan caused some physical deterioration; the 1967–8 plan caused more. The 'in 1970' decision, which at last resulted in an application by the local authority for a compulsory purchase order, completed it.

As some families spontaneously left the area, their former homes remained empty.[4] On May 12th 1970, a year after the announcement that the estimated year of clearance was 1970, but several months before the public inquiry and the airing of objections to the compulsory purchase order, the first report appeared in the local press about the slum-like conditions of Potts Street. The headline read, 'Derelict Property Peril to Children' and the photograph's caption read, 'The back yard of a house in Potts Street, Millfield, where rubbish is being dumped after dark'. A spokesman for the health department was quoted as saying that it was normal practice to seal off the entrances to derelict property. He promised to investigate the case. 'But he pointed out that the street is scheduled for demolition under the Millfield Plan.' The report contrasted the derelict houses with 'the brightly painted cottages in the rest of the street'. (In fact the area had deteriorated badly in the previous three or four years, especially in the back lanes.)

By September 1970 newspaper reports showed the spread and acceleration of dereliction. 'Guarding Her Home Against Vandals: Soldier's Wife Tells of Lone Fight.' Vacated houses had become the playground of teenagers. 'Every night of the week, says Mrs. Snaith, boys and girls invade the houses. They throw stones at the shattered panes of glass. When the stone throwing is over they adjourn to the houses, drinking beer and singing and shouting.'[5] (Plate VII.) What were readers to think? Potts Street is a slum and the decision to clear it is self-evidently correct. These sensational reports (which are accurate) are the first most people outside of Millfield would have noticed about Potts Street. 'I didn't know Potts Street was that kind of area!' It was not that kind of area throughout its existence— until 1965 and especially 1970. The compulsory purchase order was not confirmed by the Minister until the end of December 1970.[6] By the time the bulldozers arrive in such an area, perhaps a year later still, it is certain that there will be almost complete agreement in the street that clearance cannot be quick enough. The press will carry reports of protests from its residents that it is inexcusable that they should live for a moment longer in such appalling slums. Eventually the archives of Sunderland museum will receive a set of photographs of Potts Street which will record for posterity the cottages as they were before they were cleared. They will leave no doubt that clearance was the only possible course of action.

A superficial glance at Millfield's problems would suggest, perhaps, that the residents were chasing a phantom of complete assurance about their future. This interpretation would be erroneous. The people of Millfield, as working-class people, live all their lives with uncertainty, not simply victims of time and chance, as we all are, but with uncertainty in the texture of their employment, their income, their education and their health. What they objected to was not uncertainty as such, but further gratuitous and meaningless uncertainty. They objected to uncertainty that was not explained to them in any rational way, because it was, indeed, irrational, and which led to no results which could be indicated by those who had created it as in any way beneficial to anyone.

### NOTES

1 Sunderland Planning Authority, *Millfield: Clearance and Improvement*, November 1968, mimeographed, paragraph 27.
2 For example, letter L2B DC, dated August 8th 1967.
3 Millfield Residents' Association minutes of meeting of October 6th 1969.
4 After a certain date families coming to live in a clearance area in Sunderland are 'ineligible' for rehousing by the Corporation. In practice this means that they are rehoused under onerous conditions. The 'expiry date' for the Washington Street area was March 13th 1970, i.e. almost ten months before the C.P.O. was confirmed, and twelve months before clearance actually commenced.
5 *Sunderland Echo*, September 21st 1970.
6 *Sunderland Echo*, December 31st 1970. (Official Notice.)

PART THREE

# THE PLANNERS' EVIDENCE

# CHAPTER 6

# THE ISSUE

In studying the records presented below the reader may be assisted by a knowledge of how the Millfield Residents' Association came to have them. They did not begin as research data. This research started as community action, pure and simple. In November 1967 I had completed a research project on Sunderland's housing. It had been undertaken along the lines I favoured at that time to the exclusion of all other research styles, particularly in the striving for independence from all parties to the social situations being examined. This preference involved me in frequent disputes with Jon Davies, my colleague at the University of Newcastle upon Tyne. He believed that such data were uselessly pallid and that to find out what was really at stake, for whom, it was necessary for the researcher to commit himself fully to a situation and study the consequences.[1]

At this very time, November 1967, the vicar and the Council were calling their separate meetings to discuss the planning proposals for Millfield. I was living in Millfield (I was born there, and returned in 1963). I attended these meetings, feeling free to do so now that my housing and planning research had been completed. As a result of a contribution or two I made from the audience I was invited to join the committee of the Millfield Residents' Association. I became secretary in mid-1968. The joint chairmen (the vicars of St. Mark's and St. Mary Magdalene's) and I were professional elements in an organization composed of wage-earners or retired wage-earners and their wives, with a small admixture of 'corner shop' owners (three).

The records which this book analyses were maintained for several months exclusively in connection with the work of the residents' association, in order to make certain that any communications from the association to its members were accurate and entirely reliable. This felt need for full records was the product of the indefiniteness and changeability of the planners' statements about Millfield, together with the secretary's (I return to describing my own part as that of 'the secretary') growing conviction that in an area such as Millfield history was always being rewritten against the residents. *Scripta manent*, what is written, remains.

Almost all subsequent meetings with the Corporation were tape-recorded and the full tape transcript sent to the Council (as were records of all public meetings). They were sent to all members of the committee of the Millfield Residents' Association for their own use and for circulation among members. (The three most important meetings which were not tape-recorded were those of November 14th 1968, September 15th 1969 and October 6th 1969; full notes were taken at these meetings, so far as possible verbatim.)

Why did the Corporation allow meetings to be tape-recorded? First, for the purely organizational reason that formally the Corporation representatives were attending meetings of the association. The Corporation had no 'constitutional' basis from which to object. More important is the second reason: the Corporation representatives almost certainly had no conception that what they were saying was anything but completely creditable to them. They therefore did not think there was any reason to object to having their words preserved. Thirdly, their indifference to being recorded was probably a reflection of their unconscious depreciation of a body like the residents' association. Any notion that anything it could record could be analysed, and even more, that what was recorded and analysed could reach an effective audience would not readily enter their minds. Fourthly, a related point, the combination of promises and procrastination at later stages suggests that at any rate some appointed or elected officials believed that it did not matter too much what was said; like all these committees of busybodies in slum areas they would soon fall to squabbling amongst themselves or, in the face of delay and lack of information, lose their morale and vanish. Why worry about what there might be to answer for, if one can be quite certain that there will be no one to answer to?

A year elapsed between the promise of participation given by the Council at the public meeting in November 1967 and the presentation of the East Millfield plans to the residents' association. During that year the Council did not contact the association. The association, however, had been developing certain views on what residents' participation might mean. Rightly or wrongly, the Millfield Residents' Association had come to the conclusion that its role ought to be a modest and limited one. It took the view that it had neither the resources nor the expertise to direct the Corporation on what Millfield required.[2] After the planning department had presented its proposals of November 14th 1968 the association's resolutions consistently embodied this view. The resolutions made no statements about which specific areas ought to be condemned or given lives of various lengths. In all cases the resolutions said to the Corporation 'find out the relevant facts and come to a conclusion based on those facts which carries conviction for the people of Millfield'.

For the association, that is, participation did not mean usurping the functions of the planning department, still less claiming authority which lay with the Council. Whenever the planning department or the Council appeared to press the association into too ambitious a role, the association reaffirmed its own limitations—again rightly or wrongly. When it was suggested, for example, that the association could and should authoritatively decide which of several possible routes a trans-Millfield road should take, derision is not too strong a word to describe the attitude of the committee, an attitude shared by many of the people in the streets.

Participation for the association meant something modest. It meant simply that the residents should be persuaded by the Corporation that the proposals were such as would result in the betterment of their condition. Alternatively, if Millfielders were being asked to bear some degree of suffering in the interests of posterity or for the benefit of their fellow-townspeople (or their fellow-citizens in the region or the country at large) then the justification of placing theses burdens on Millfielders should be put to them in terms of (i) equity and (ii) the facts of the situation.

Insuperable problems may or may not have arisen in participation of this sort. Irreconcilable clashes of interest on a large scale might have appeared among Millfielders themselves. Irremovable conflicts between Millfield and the rest of the town might have emerged. Intransigent interest groups might have fought it out among themselves in the area; or the area might have united to fight uncompromisingly and obstructively against the legitimate wishes of other districts in Sunderland. Millfield might have succumbed to even the most threadbare argumentation; or it might have stubbornly held out against the most conclusive findings. Great problems might have arisen; or, on the contrary, harmony might have reigned in an atmosphere of sweetness and light.

Which groups, over which issues would have revealed what degree of openness to conviction by what kind of appeal to fact, emotion or ethics are questions which have now gone unanswered into history. The questions remain unanswered because participation never reached the point at which they were realistically raised. Discussions were less over positive projects than over the initial issue of the accuracy and relevance of the facts upon which the Corporation purported to erect the whole edifice of its proposals.

The problem of the quality of the planning department's surveys was raised at the earliest participation meeting (at which the plans and the basis for the plans were made known for the first time). The proposals booklet, *Millfield: Clearance and*

*Improvement*, was given to each committee member. It referred to both interviews in connection with the state of Millfield's housing and inspections of the houses. The booklet said that every family had been interviewed or been asked to complete a questionnaire, and that *each house* had been inspected.

> The inspection of each house was carried out in order to determine: (a) its condition — taking into consideration its repair, stability, evidence of rising and penetrating dampness and its overall appearance; (b) the facilities it contained—i.e. which, if any, of the standard amenities of bath, hot and cold water, wash-hand basin, sink and internal w.c., it contained; (c) the family structure—the number of families in the dwelling, the number of adults and children, the rooms occupied by each family and whether owner-occupied. Further information was obtained regarding the age of each building, number of floors, the rateable value, and whether improvement grants had been applied for.

The minutes of the meeting, mimeographed copies of which were in the hands of the committee members for several days before they were approved, and a copy of which was sent at the same time to the Council say this about the planning department's verbal statement on this question:

> The planning department described seven studies which had been carried out on the condition of dwellings in the area under discussion . . . (iii) Dampness: The planning department asserted that a survey had been carried out by the health department which showed the distribution, prevalence and severity of rising and penetrating damp in dwellings in the area. Surveys had been carried out on 'repair', 'stability' and 'general maintenance' with regard to the area's dwellings.

Many of the other points made by the planning department were debated, and in due course the meeting came to consider the survey. Mr. Somers owns a general store in Cornwall Street and is accordingly at the hub of many information networks in the area.

> Mr. Somers queried the claim, made by the planning department verbally and written into the proposals booklet, that every family had either been interviewed personally or had completed a questionnaire. 'No-one came to 17 Cornwall Street.' The planning department consulted the computer print-outs and said that in May this year [1968]

evidence had been collected in respect of Nos. 1–16 Cornwall Street. Mr. Somers said there was no survey of the property of any of the members in Cornwall Street by the Corporation.

Throughout the year the committee of the Millfield Residents' Association had been meeting and rank-and-file members had been avid for any news of what the Corporation was doing in the area.

> Mrs. Drummond said that the survey described had not been carried out in Ravensworth Street among the members she represented. Mrs. Connolly supported this.
> Mr. Tingle said that no-one from the Corporation had inspected the properties in Westbury Street in the manner claimed.

The chairman of the committee used the word 'accusation' to describe this scepticism about the internal inspections. 'There is an accusation that no-one went *inside* the houses to examine the property—that it was a matter of a few minutes question and answer at the door.'

The planning department therefore asked the health department to comment. The health department said that inspections had been carried out in Alfred Street and Cornwall Street. The minute reads, 'The information the planning department had was taken from the Count Book, and related to an actual inspection prior to representing it to the Ministry as a slum clearance area'. The health department checked and was able to say that the survey was carried out in March 1967.

> *Planning department:* So you did inspect the properties internally?
> *Health department:* Yes.
> *Planning department:* There you are, then.

The question was about the claim that all pre-1914 dwellings in the borough had been internally surveyed in preparation for the Millfield proposals; certainly, that all the Millfield houses had been internally surveyed in preparation for the Millfield proposals. The planning department's references were clearly to the survey which had been announced in the *Sunderland Echo* in February 1968. ('The planning department consulted the computer print-outs and said that in May this year [1968] evidence had been collected in respect of Nos. 1–16 Cornwall Street.') Now the health department was saying that 69 of approximately 700 houses in the East Millfield planning area had been internally inspected—and the inspections had taken place not in May 1968, but in March 1967. 'There you are, then.'

The secretary was uncertain at the meeting what the planning department had stated in detail when it had announced the survey in the *Sunderland Echo*. Of one thing he had no doubt, however: that it had been explicit that it would be an interview survey only. On checking back in the *Sunderland Echo* files he found the press release in the issue of February 10th 1968. The survey, it said, would take the form of personal interviews. *It would not involve the inspection of the properties.*

Whatever else, the matter was confused. The secretary did not at that time know what the position in fact was with regard to the surveys. Some of the committee members, by contrast, thought that the planning department had successfully demonstrated that all the internal inspections had been completed. However, at a packed public meeting in the church hall on November 19th 1968, called by the Millfield Residents' Association to transmit the Corporation's proposals to the residents (they were also widely circulated in the news-sheet of the Millfield Residents' Association, *Fair Play*), there were many other objections that the claimed surveys had not been carried out.

One of the resolutions of the Millfield Residents' Association, resolution No. 5, therefore proposed that the Corporation 'ensure that future surveys in connection with its proposals for Millfield be carried out in such a way as to yield information of due accuracy, detail and relevance'.

As the next chapter shows, resolution No. 5 was the cause of still further confusion on the question of whether or not Millfield's cottages had been inspected. It also throws, however, a flood of light on the attitudes and behaviour of the planning department when faced with the necessity to explain itself to the consumers of its services.

NOTES

1 See his study, *The Evangelistic Bureaucrat*, London: Tavistock Publications, 1972.
2 Report of the policy sub-committee of the Millfield Residents' Association dated April 29th 1968.

CHAPTER 7

# 'VERY, VERY FEW HOUSES
# WERE INSPECTED'

The second participation meeting was on December 13th 1968.
Its purpose was to present the residents' counter-proposals for
the area. Following their study of the Corporation's proposals of
November 14th, the Millfield Residents' Association had prepared its resolutions Nos. 1–22. The meeting of December 13th
lasted from 6.30 p.m. until after 11 p.m. The transcript covers
forty A4 pages of single-spaced typing. A quarter of the way
through the meeting the planning department is recorded as
terminating another discussion to say: 'Now just a sec.! The
other thing I'd like to comment on is item 5. I don't quite know
what this means, but the implication seems to be that the
survey that has been carried out is a load of rubbish.' From that
point onwards, for over three hours, nearly all the discussion
turns on the association's resolution No. 5.

*Resolution No. 5:* That the Millfield Residents' Association, on the basis
of its own professional survey and on the basis of widespread local knowledge, request the Corporation to ensure that future surveys in connection with its proposals for Millfield be carried out in such a way as to
yield information of due accuracy, detail and relevance.

The planning department were being asked to show that
their planning proposals for Millfield were rational—that they
were based upon knowledge of the researched facts.

What was meant by 'the' survey had been swaddled in doubt
by the proceedings of the meeting of November 14th. In several
statements on December 13th the planning department now
made its meaning quite unequivocal.

'You see, this survey has largely been done by the medical staff.'

'My information is that they have *all* been done.'

'Can I just interpolate a very quick point there? The card survey he is mentioning is this overall survey of all the pre-1914 houses. Not just Millfield. The whole lot of them.'

The Council at one point said that in order to devise lifing policies for houses it was not actually necessary to carry out internal inspections. 'When you're dealing with a survey on buildings', he said, 'it is the structure that you are interested in, which determines the life of the property, not how well the person's got it fitted out inside. So on that basis you don't necessarily have to go into each house individually to find out what the life of the house is.' The planning department responded to that statement in order to reinforce the fact that all the properties had been internally inspected. 'They have in fact been in anyway.'

At another point the planning department confidently addressed a housing inspector. 'Would you like to say whether or not the houses were inspected—*inside*? I think that is what people seem to be doubting.'

The Council followed the planning department in stressing that the department was claiming that Millfield had been internally inspected as part of a particular survey, that of all of Sunderland's pre-1914 property. 'We have the complete picture of all of the pre-1914 houses in the whole of the town, so that we know precisely what it looks like roughly.'

The association did not deny—it asserted—that any sensible planning would start with sketchy surveys and proceed to more detailed and definitive surveys. Problem areas ought to be picked out, the Millfield Residents' Association said, by rapid and economical studies; and then such further detailed investigations as might prove necessary for proposals of statutory force should be undertaken. The association's objection was that the planning department appeared to have produced proposals—

once again—which were based upon inadequate surveys. The planning department's claim that the surveys were of the necessary detail, relevance and accuracy was disputed.

In trying to justify its pre-1914 survey, the representatives of the planning department (and to a lesser extent the health department representatives) tied themselves into such knots in the course of the discussion of December 13th that the secretary of the association attempted to have the subject dropped. The planning department, however, insisted that the discussion should continue.

'I am concerned with this statement No. 5, which suggests that the survey is inadequate and should be done again.'

'Could I have a seconder . . . ?'

'Wait a minute, now!'

'Could I have a seconder . . . ?', the secretary repeated.

'Just let's get to the bottom of this question', the planning officer replied. '*You've* raised it under item 5.'

What was the association's case against the planning department at the meeting of December 13th? In general it was put by the chairman. 'May I say this', the vicar said at one point, 'what came out of the public meeting[1] was the fact that very, very few houses were examined internally as to structure and so forth.'

At another point he remarked: 'Actually, it was the opinion from the meeting that the only area where the houses were individually examined externally and internally are the houses in the Alfred Street and Cornwall Street area. And in Cornwall Street a number of those houses had not been examined *internally*.'

Again: 'Well, this is what, this is the unanimous opinion of the committee, that it is *not* sufficient, because the Alfred Street area has been condemned, Cornwall Street, and yet these houses over here [the Hedley Street area] are considered to be, by the people, considered to be in much worse condition.' (See Plate VIII.)

Here is another quotation in which the vicar makes the same point: 'Well, you must appreciate this. We are simply representatives of quite a number of people—about 450 people [families]. Now, we can only go on what has been stated in the public meeting. But this came up time and time again. You get that, "They didn't come to my house!", something like that.'

Individual members of the committee said that the planners had not carried out the claimed internal inspection of their own particular homes. In some cases individual members of the committee claimed that even the door-to-door survey, not involving internal inspections, had not been carried out. The manner in which the planning department handled these complaints at the meeting of December 13th can be illustrated from the cases of Mrs. Drummond, Mrs. Connolly and Mr. Watson. (These are additional to the complaints of Mr. Somers and Mr. Tingle at the meeting of November 14th.)

### The Internal Inspection of Mrs. Drummond's Cottage

The vicar had just said that the problem arose 'from the fact that so many people at the public meeting of November 19th did say that their houses had not at all been surveyed in the way they considered it should have been surveyed in order to produce proposals of this sort'. The planning department had replied that if only they had the addresses of the complainants, then from the figures they had brought to the participation meeting they could, they said, tell the story 'which we think would prove that we must have been inside'. This was interrupted by Mrs. Drummond who gave her address. The planning department then read from the computer print-out:

'Owner-occupied, fair repair, fair rising damp, fair stability, fair penetrating damp, fair general maintenance. It's a fair building. It has a bathroom with a bath, a hot and cold water supply, a hand-wash basin with a hot and cold water supply. It has an outside w.c. It has no kitchen sink—it uses the hand-wash basin. I've got the age and rateable value.

94

There are four rooms, occupied by one adult male, four female adults, making a total of five persons.'

It is, of course, impossible to say that 'fair' repair, 'fair' dampness, etc. are untrue descriptions of almost any building in the country. The planning department had said specifically, however, that Mrs. Drummond had no kitchen sink.

Mrs. Drummond objected. 'Well, we have got a kitchen unit in! We haven't got a hand-wash basin. We've got a kitchen unit.'

'That's what he said', was the planning department's rejoinder. (That is *not* what the planning department had said.)

The planning department then enumerated the heads of information contained in the computer print-out—repair, stability, etc. The fact that the information was on the computer tape was presented as self-evident proof that internal inspections must have been carried out. 'Now, we can only get this information by going inside.'

At the public meeting and at the participation meetings of November 14th and now again on December 13th Millfielders protested that the planning department's computerized information had not been obtained by internal inspections of their homes. The planning department's reply was that the evidence that internal inspections had been carried out lay in the very fact that information was contained on a computer tape.

Mrs. Drummond does not take up the planning department on the logic of this point. She answers instead with a surprising piece of concrete information. She knows how the information was obtained. 'You didn't get this information from *me*', she says. 'You got it off the woman at the other side of the road. You've never been to my house!'

Had the planning department carried out the claimed internal inspection? Mrs. Drummond now claims that far from having been inside her cottage, even the door-to-door questionnaire, which was undoubtedly filled in, was completed by the Corporation surveyors, when they obtained no answer at Mrs.

Drummond's door, by asking a lady at the other side of the road.

The planning department asks, 'Is it *correct*?'

'No, of course it isn't!', exclaims another committee member, a local newsagent.

The owner-occupier herself, Mrs. Drummond, and now Mrs. Callum have made it quite clear that the information is incorrect in certain particulars. The planning department, however, continues its own line of reasoning. 'Well, is it correct? Let's know if it is correct, please!'

Mrs. Drummond, flustered by now, changes the subject and turns to defending her home from the accusation that it is only 'fair'. 'It's in *good* maintenance order.' She is therefore denying that the planning department's description 'fair' is a correct description.

But the planning department says again, 'Is everything said correct?'

This repeated question, 'Is everything he said correct?', whenever Mrs. Drummond or another member of the committee point out items which are incorrect, apparently confuses Mrs. Drummond still further. She in a sense accepts the notion that what the planning department says is correct. She now excuses the description of her house as 'fair dampness' by pointing out, 'There's dampness in the whole street, because there's no damp course.'

'What we've said, what we've said in effect, is that this is a "fair" house.'

'Oh yes' (by now Mrs. Drummond has given up the struggle on the question of correctness), 'but when you want information you come to the *person*.'

'True, yes.'

'Well you didn't come to *me*! You took the words off another person. It mightn't have been true!'

The planning department then spoke. The tone of voice cannot be reproduced. It was patient, restrained, reasonable and condescending. 'The planning department is trying to make the point, and I can't personally prove his error, that we couldn't have this information, which is apparently correct, without somebody having been inside.'

Mrs. Drummond expostulates: 'But there's never been . . .!'

She is interrupted by the Corporation solicitor, who appeals to the good sense of the vicar, who must have been able to see that everything was in order, as the planning department had stated. 'This seems to be right, vicar. There doesn't seem to be anything wrong about this.'

### The Internal Inspection of Mrs. Connolly's Cottage

Mrs. Connolly gave her house as an example of one which had not been internally inspected in the survey of all pre-1914 property. 'In fact, I was out at the time, and somebody knocked on the front door, and your mother just happened to be coming up, and they said to this passer-by, "Has this lady got a bathroom?" She said "Yes". Your mother didn't even know who she was!'

Mrs. Connolly thus knew what had happened in the survey. Exactly as in Mrs. Drummond's case, the surveyors had asked a passer-by about the amenities of her cottage. The whole incident had been reported to Mrs. Connolly by the mother of a friend of hers. The surveyors had knocked, received no reply, and asked an unknown passer-by.

Later in the meeting the discussion returned to the subject of Mrs. Connolly's cottage.

'Do you mind me asking what's down about my . . . ?'

'Give us the number.'

'I know I'm right. There's been nobody to my house.'

'Has anybody got a line yet?' the planning department joked.

'Number 4. Right. The information that we've got for No. 4 Ravensworth Street is that it is a single storey property. It is owner-occupied. Repair is good. Stability is good. Rising damp, a bit. Penetrating damp, a bit. General maintenance, good. A Class 1A property. It has a bathroom which has a bath with hot and cold water, no wash-hand basin and an indoor toilet in the bathroom. You have a sink with hot and cold water. So it is a fully modernized cottage.'

'Where you've got it from . . .!'

Mrs. Connolly, who lives a few doors away from Mrs. Drummond ('There's dampness in the whole street, because there's no damp course') is obviously delighted with this description of her house as 'Good' and 'Fully modernized'. A voice from the planning department ends the buzz. 'Attention, please!'

The planning department continues: 'Male adult, with two female adults . . .'

'Yes, a child.'

'Yes, well, over ten, you see.'

The chief planning officer addresses the planner reading from the print-out: 'Anything else?'

Mrs. Connolly says, 'Well, honestly, I don't know how you've . . .'

'I don't know what the colour of your eyes are, but . . .'

The planning department again asks the question, asked so frequently of Mrs. Drummond. 'Is this correct?'

Mrs. Connolly says in amazement, 'It's true! But I don't know how! My husband's away at sea! My girl is at school!'

The planning department says, 'Well, I can't help you with that one. But at least we've got the information.'

This was the closest the planning department got at the meeting to a correct description of checkable details. There was the error of calling a child an adult. Whether or not No. 4 Ravensworth Street was 'good' as compared with No. 10 (Mrs. Drummond's house) which was only 'fair' is another matter.

Whether the above exchange constitutes evidence that Mrs. Connolly's house was indeed internally inspected by the surveyors—who asked the lady across the road when they could get no answer at Mrs. Connolly's door—or internally inspected by someone else, is something for the reader to judge for himself.

### The Internal Inspection of Mr. Watson's House

Mr. Watson is a retired cobbler who still does occasional shoe-repairing in the shop attached to his home. The kitchen-living room seems always to smell strongly of freshly-baked spicey scone.

He was yet another of the sixteen-strong committee at the meeting of December 13th who objected that the claimed internal inspections had not been carried out. The sixteen included the vicar and the secretary, plus five members from West Millfield, where the question of inspections had not arisen. In effect, therefore, the strong objections of Mr. Somers, Mr. Tingle, Mrs. Drummond, Mrs. Connolly, and now Mr. Watson came from five of the nine members of the committee from the area under discussion. Mr. Watson challenges the planning department to produce the description of his home. The planning department reads from the computer print-out:

> 'There are two families at No. 24. Is that right? Now, in the first one there is an owner and a tenant, there is an owner-occupier and a tenant. The information that we've got on repair is—not very good, in fact. Now, the stability is fair. The rising damp is, you know, just a little bit. General maintenance—pretty good. In other words, a fair property generally.'

The planning department then proceeds from the 'little bits' and 'pretty goods' to the description of the amenities of Mr. Watson's home. (Mr. Watson was not disputing that he had been asked questions on the amenities at the door. He was disputing the claim that internal inspections had been carried out.)

'It has no bath or bathroom at all. It has no hand-wash basin. You share an outside toilet. You have a sink with hot and cold water, and your tenant has a sink with hot and cold water.

Now, to be quite honest, how on earth can we get this information?'

' "How on earth can you get the information about hot and cold water?" Is that down?'

'Yes.'

'Well we haven't got any!' (*Laughter for several seconds.*)

The chief planning officer asks hurriedly, 'What does this say about this sink? Just a second now!'

'Yes, I'm afraid you're down here that you've got a heater, with . . . so you've no heater at all?'

'We use a kettle—the fire or the gas stove.' (*Renewed laughter.*)

'We've dealt with about twenty-five—about twenty-odd thousand properties, so . . . Nevertheless, I agree that's an error to your advantage.'

### NOTE

1 The public meeting held on November 19th 1968.

# CHAPTER 8

# 'POSSIBLY SOME CONFUSION'

As might be imagined, the members of the committee were puzzled and confused by these proceedings. Although occasionally excited or upset it would be wrong to think that they were angry. The transcript and the tape recording of the meeting of December 13th show that they were still trying to untangle what was being said. They were probably blaming themselves for their own slowness of wit.

The issue was, however, one of considerable salience for Millfielders. They were, in the psalmist's phrase, an afflicted people. Much of the damage resulted from the unreliability of the planning department's plans for Millfield; and that unreliability was the direct consequence of the vagueness and vacillation of the planning department's data. To the residents the planning department's newest evidence was dubious because it appeared to be inaccurate about their own homes and streets. To the secretary, at least, it was dubious not only for that reason, but also because the planning department's account of the survey (as it had been put at the meeting of November 14th) seemed to fall short of full consistency and credibility.

So long as their plans were not backed by adequate survey — by facts about the dwellings, about at least their physical structure in relation to existing and/or proposed legislation — the totally unreliable predictions of 'lives' and the delays and uncertainties in slum clearance dates would continue.

Blight which is the more-or-less unavoidable cost of ultimate benefits is one thing. Blight which is not followed by improvement in some respect for someone is another. Millfielders had suffered from lives of fifteen years and less; when those fifteen years were up they were being asked to suffer another number of years of blight. Legislation had been altered, but when requests came from the residents that this legislation should be used for the benefit of Millfield, the requests were stubbornly blocked by the planning department—on the basis of 'the facts', the planning department's 'maximum lives' of the property. What were these facts? Were the facts sound enough to bear the weight of policy they were being asked to carry?

The planning department might have appeared on November 14th and announced that their proposals were predicated upon scant data. They might have argued that this was inevitable because of shortage of staff. They might have even argued, after all these years of plans, that it was still desirable at this late stage to get a broad general picture before concentrating on the detail of Millfield. (Such a sequence is obviously required at some time; it would have been disgraceful for the planning department to admit that in 1968 they were still at the stage of the broad picture.)

Millfielders might have objected, perhaps strenuously, but at least what the planning department said would have made sense. Millfielders would have had to realize that they were objecting to something which could not now be altered, the inefficiency of the Corporation; they would have been wise to forget it, and turn their faces away from the past.

On November 14th the planning department had said that the most thorough and far-reaching surveys had now indeed been completed. That would have been excellent news. But people said they had not been surveyed in the manner claimed. People said they had not been surveyed at all by the Corporation. That was why the association produced their resolution No. 5. It was critical of the Corporation, but essentially it asked about the future—that future surveys should show the necessary degree of relevance, detail and accuracy. The association showed no inclination to rake over the embers of November 14th.

When it was in progress the secretary attempted to terminate what seemed to him an arid debate. The planning department insisted, however, in taking the matter further, and participation found iself jammed at the stage of what could be termed 'extreme preliminaries'. It was not even a matter of how accurate the survey was, overall or in certain particulars. It was a matter of the planning department establishing that all the houses had been internally inspected.

### The Housing Inspector's Version

The planning department had initiated the discussion of resolution No. 5 and had pursued it with determination and confidence. The health department was present, and it soon became obvious that the planning department had arranged to call upon the health department to elucidate and confirm the planning department's descriptions of the surveys it had carried out in Millfield.

What was the health department's story on December 13th 1968? For most of the time it was an account of the processes of slum clearance, and clarified a point that the association had never regarded as unclear: that 'the' survey of Millfield had not been the formal slum-clearance inspections carried out by the health department prior to representing an area to the Minister for clearance under the Housing Act of 1957. The department was at pains to differentiate what it called 'the card-survey inspections' from 'the actual clearance inspections':

> 'I do think there is possibly some misunderstanding here, and some confusion of this card-survey inspection with the actual clearance inspections, and I'd just like to say what were the methods adopted and the purpose behind each inspection.'

The association was not puzzled by what happened in actual clearance inspections. The committee did want to hear, however, about the other inspection (the card-survey inspection, as

103

the health department called it), i.e. the survey carried out in connection with the plans of November 14th by the planning department and health department.

The association heard a lucid, detailed and sympathetic account of the processes of slum clearance, seen from the stand-point of the health department. All that was said about the card-survey inspection, however, was that it was not the actual clearance inspection, and that it gave only a general guide to the health department:

> 'The purpose of the card survey inspection was to inform us where future clearance areas in the borough are most likely to be found: in other words, to eliminate much of the time wasted by hit-and-miss methods previously used. We admit that. So don't for one moment con-fuse these inspections with the actual inspections that are used for the representation of clearance areas.'

At different places in his extended discourse the housing inspector made this point in various forms, but never described what items the disputed card-survey inspection covered, how the information had been obtained for the computer, nor who had carried it out.

The members of the committee were appreciative of the insight and information they had obtained on slum-clearance inspections, public inquiries etc. For the health department to use an economically obtained overview of the priority in the whole of the town and derive some idea of priorities for inspec-tion from it was eminently sensible. 'When we come to actual clearance inspections for representation, we've got a different picture altogether.' No reasonable person, presumably, would want to quarrel with anything in the several-page long tran-script of the health department's contribution.

When he had finished, however, the committee was no nearer to finding out about the card-survey inspection. The secretary therefore asked him about it.

'Can I interpolate a question of my own? You say it was a card survey, door-to-door, that went through the computer, implying, I think, that the internal survey was not put through the computer?'

At this stage the secretary, basing his view on what he had just heard and on the report in the *Sunderland Echo* of February 10th 1968, believed now that there must have been two surveys; the door-to-door card-survey inspection, which had not involved the internal inspection of the properties, and the internal survey which the planning department were still insisting had been carried out. When? By whom?

The secretary continued: 'Can I have a straight answer to this, please? Was it the card survey *only* that was put through the computer?'

'Yes.'

'It was the card survey only!', the secretary cried. 'So it was the door-to-door survey that has been read from these sheets.'

The card survey, also referred to as the door-to-door survey by the health department, had not involved the inspection of properties. If the card survey only had been used for the computer print-outs, therefore, they could not have included evidence of internal dampness, etc. It was not the health department which spoke next, but the planning department:

*Planning department:* No, the one's we did inside as well.
*Health department:* I think our man ought to be allowed to finish.
*Planning department:* Yes, so do I. Let him finish, for God's sake.

The health department then said, in a rather bemused way, 'There appears to be another survey that we know nothing at all about. So, the card-survey inspections serve *this* purpose, and nothing more . . .' There were then further elaborations on the process of slum-clearance inspections, public inquiries, and so forth.

Later, the secretary spoke for a second time to discover from the health department the relationship between the internal inspection of all the Millfield properties and the door-to-door surveys carried out in February and March 1968.

'Well, as this thing's gone on so long, Mr. Chairman', he said, 'I think I would just like to make quite sure what's being said. You are now saying that all the houses in the area covered by the map in the book [the proposals booklet of November 14th 1968] have been visited and internal inspections have taken place by public health personnel?'

'On the card survey, you mean?'

'No, not the card survey, the . . .'

'No, we haven't.'

'You *haven't*!', the secretary exclaimed.

'Now, Mr. Chairman', the chairman of the planning committee interposed, 'the secretary is trying to split hairs here. This is the first town in the country to go so deeply into a survey of pre-1914 houses, so that we can get a picture, as the health department said, without wasting time, and deeming an area unfit when it necessarily isn't. So we have started something in this country which is unique.'

'Deeming an area unfit when it wasn't necessarily unfit' was exactly what the secretary at this point was concerned about. The health department had been at great pains to differentiate between (1) the process of indicating where clearance inspections should be carried out (the card-survey inspections), and (2) the clearance inspections themselves, undertaken by the staff of the health department prior to representation. The Medical Officer of Health identified areas for representation after clearance inspections, and represented them when he thought he had a case which could survive a public inquiry. As the health department said, at a public inquiry the department had to put its head 'on the chopping block' and it would not do that unless it felt sure it would 'win'. But the November 14th proposals had defined clearance areas. What was the factual basis of the proposals? By now the secretary definitely wanted to know. For a third time, therefore, he asked the health department for clarification:

'Could I ask which parts you have done? It's not clear.

Which parts have you done?', he asked. 'Could I ask that question directly?'

'We have done all of Alfred Street and all of Cornwall Street.'

'And nothing else?'

'And nothing else in this area, in this area [East Millfield].'

It is somewhat ironic to note that this dialogue comes after the secretary's attempt to abandon the discussion, an attempt which had been thwarted by the planning department. The dialogue continued with a question from the planning department to the health department.

'Could I ask you, because there might be a genuine misunderstanding between our two departments. When did you become in charge of this section of the department?'

'Of this section of the department?', the health department said.

'Of your department.'

'In April.'

'Of this year? [1968].'

'Of this year.'

The planning department then began internal consultations in whispers and eventually it said, 'Now I am told that there was an inspection carried out into the former Millfield clearance area in 1967, and that this was carried out as an internal inspection by your department, and this is the information that is represented on these sheets. Now we want to get at the bottom of this, because—Now, is this fact? Were these properties inspected internally by someone from your department? You yourself had nothing to do with it. Were these properties inspected in 1967, because this is where all the apparent mistrust centres? Now, we must get this thing absolutely clear.'

This was the first time that the date 1967 had been mentioned at the meeting of December 13th 1968. It will be recalled that 'March 1967' had been mentioned at the meeting a month previously, November 14th, by the health department as the date when the sixty-nine houses of Alfred Street and Cornwall Street had been inspected. The above dialogue continues with an interpolation by the planning department: 'The health inspectors—a survey inside the old Millfield clearance area. You are now doing a very detailed thorough one for representation of the Alfred Street area.'

That remark is found on page 29 of the transcript. On page 35 of the transcript the health department quotes its report to the health committee of November 10th 1968. The planning department's plans included the clearance by 1972 of Alfred Street which was described in the planning department's proposals booklet of November 14th as 'probably the worst houses in the Millfield area and the majority are unfit'. Yet the report to the health committee of November 10th, as read out from the original by the health department at the participation meeting of December 13th, stated that: 'Preliminary inspections were *commenced* with a view to the representation of Alfred Street as a clearance area. The inspectors encountered *a high degree of general good maintenance*, and in view of this, *inspections were stopped* in this area, and attention is now being given to inspection in areas of greater priority in other parts of the town.' (Emphasis added.)

Quite apart from the detail that the health department was *not*, on December 13th, 'carrying out a very detailed' inspection in Alfred Street (which was what the planning department had affirmed only a few minutes before) this extract shows that four days before the planning department's plans were presented to the association, the health department had decided *not* to proceed further with 'the worst houses in Millfield'.

The dialogue between the planning department and health department then continues:

. . . 'You are now doing a very detailed thorough one for representation of the Alfred Street area.'

'We've started.'

'You've started. That's right.'

'*We've finished that.*'

'They were started in October [1968]', added another representative of the health department.

'Those are the one's we've done; and the Cornwall Street ones. There are only six houses not done in Alfred Street, they [the six houses] have not been done recently. *And Cornwall Street was done in March 1967.*' (Emphasis added.)

Once again the insisted-upon *internal* inspections of *all* the houses, 'not just Millfield but the whole of the town's pre-1914 dwellings' in February and March 1968 had been reduced to the internal inspection of the *sixty-nine houses* of the Alfred Street area *in March 1967*, with the additional information now that thirty-nine of the forty-five houses of Alfred Street itself had been internally inspected at some time since October 1968.

'Yes, but let's go back to this', the planning department said. 'There's someone called [name], I understand. Now this survey, that we've been told about, that [name] and [another name] carried out in 1967 by your department; and that information has been given to us here—on these cards. Now, was this internal survey carried out, or wasn't it, in 1967, because we must . . .'

'Yes, in 1967.'

'Now, this one that you've done since and subsequently for Alfred Street is a follow-up to that, again internal?'

'Yes.'

'And the fact is, then, the properties for which we have information on this print-out was the result of surveys carried out internally, by your department, in 1967.'

'That's right, in March 1967.'

Written down in the knowledge of what transpired at future meetings, that reads like an exposé of departmental and inter-departmental bungling, with the hapless families of Millfield as victims. Sociologically speaking, however, the anticlimax is at least as interesting in terms of bureaucratic rationality as the climax to the substantive issue, namely, whether, by whom, when, and in which properties internal inspections had been carried out. For the planning department interpreted it all as a vindication of the planning department's case. The next words, spoken with a sincerity which cannot for a moment be doubted, are:

> 'Now, you know, I don't know whether you have to take us on face value now. As a result of you saying this, we've asked the department who carried it out. You can either believe us or you won't believe us. But I can assure you that we, as people, have nothing to gain by telling lies.'

At least one of the members of the committee was still uncertain. She asked, 'It's only Alfred Street and Cornwall Street?' The readiness of the residents' association to accept any reasonable case is shown by the fact that it was the vicar who reassured her, 'No, the whole of Millfield'.

This interpretation was immediately pressed home by the planning department. 'Let us define the area. The health department will now help us on this.'

'I can't here. I only came into this in August [1968]', was the reply. The health department went on to say: 'The information that you have on there, on the card survey side, for Alfred Street and Cornwall Street, were taken from the inspections we did in March 1967.'

The health department was once more, that is, strongly suggesting that the March 1967 internal inspections were of Alfred Street and Cornwall Street only.

> *Health department:* The remainder of the houses in the Millfield area—
> *Planning department:* The area we are talking about here.
> *Health department:* The remainder were inspected, inside, by the cards that were returned—
> *Planning department:* By the public health inspectors inside the houses.

This was different again. What was *now* 'established' was that only Alfred Street and Cornwall Street had been internally inspected in 1967, and the rest of Millfield had been *internally* inspected *in 1968*. This was the version of the facts which re-appeared when the planning department, in summing up, clinched their case that *all* of Millfield's houses had been surveyed, and all had been inspected *internally*.

> *Planning department:* I pressed it, you see, because I believe you are entitled to know everything we can tell you. Now, there seemed to be some divergence as between the two departments, and I've been pressing and pressing because I want to [inaudible] this too. The difficulty seems to have been that your staff [the health department's staff] have changed since they did this inquiry.
> *Health department:* Yes, I had nothing to do with the card survey. All I did was to collect the cards in, when I took over from [name].

In so far as the health department is saying anything here, it is saying that the card survey, the survey of February–March 1968, did include the internal inspection by staff of the health department. That was consistent with the press release of February 10th 1968, in respect of the involvement of the health department, but inconsistent with it in that the press release had said internal inspections would *not* be undertaken.

'Yes', the planning department concluded. 'The planning department doesn't do all this detail all the time. That is why . . .' That is why the planning department knows less? Not at all.

> '. . . that is why it is more knowledgeable in a way what the other departments are doing than the department itself. So I hope I've done as much as we can to establish to you that this is a genuine survey, because I was particularly concerned, you see, with what was said under point 5, that the survey wasn't adequate. I think it is.'

### The Meeting of February 14th 1969

At the participation meeting of February 14th 1969 the Millfield Residents' Association presented its additional resolutions. The tape-transcript shows that the secretary made occasional references to the quality of the surveys. There was no suggestion at all, however, that he any longer doubted that internal surveys had been carried out in all the houses. The confused discussions of December 13th had left him with the impression that the Corporation's case had been satisfactorily established on that point. When particular problems arose, his contribution was simply, 'In this or this particular area, granted that internal surveys had been carried out in March 1967 and the door-to-door surveys in February–March 1968, if fuller surveys were to alter the picture, what then?' It had been the health department's reiterated point on December 13th that the actual clearance inspections often threw up additional or different data which altered the original intentions of the Corporation.

Half-way through the meeting of February 14th 1969, however, the planning department attempted to elucidate the position with regard to improvement grants and lifing. This revived in the committee a discussion of the inspections, with interesting results. The planning department began a detailed description of the improvement grants system. The lecture was informative, without touching on any problems that had been worrying the committee. 'The point about the improvement grants which seems to be a little bit, not quite grasped, is that a standard improvement grant, given a life expectancy of fifteen years, is really to install various amenities, like water supply (a heck of a lot of houses in this area don't in fact have inside water), it is to provide these sort of things: a toilet, a hand-basin, a bath. It doesn't really help you to re-do the roof, to stop rising and penetrating damp, to attend to all your bulging walls', the planning department said.

All this was well-known to the committee. The planning department went on to explain the rationale of the refusal of grants. If the property could not last fifteen years, then it would be a waste of public money to subsidize improvement. Again, so far as the committee members were concerned this was uncontroversial, at least as a general statement. The question the residents were interested in was this: How did the Corporation

Plate VIIIa. 'Alfred Street has been condemned . . . '

VIIIb, c. '. . . and yet the houses in Hedley Street are . . .

'. . . considered by the people to be in much worse condition'

Plate IXa, b. 'We can't see any *sense* . . .' Westbury Street

Westbury Street

Plate IXc. 'We can't see any *sense* . . .' Granville Street

Plate IXd. Granville Street

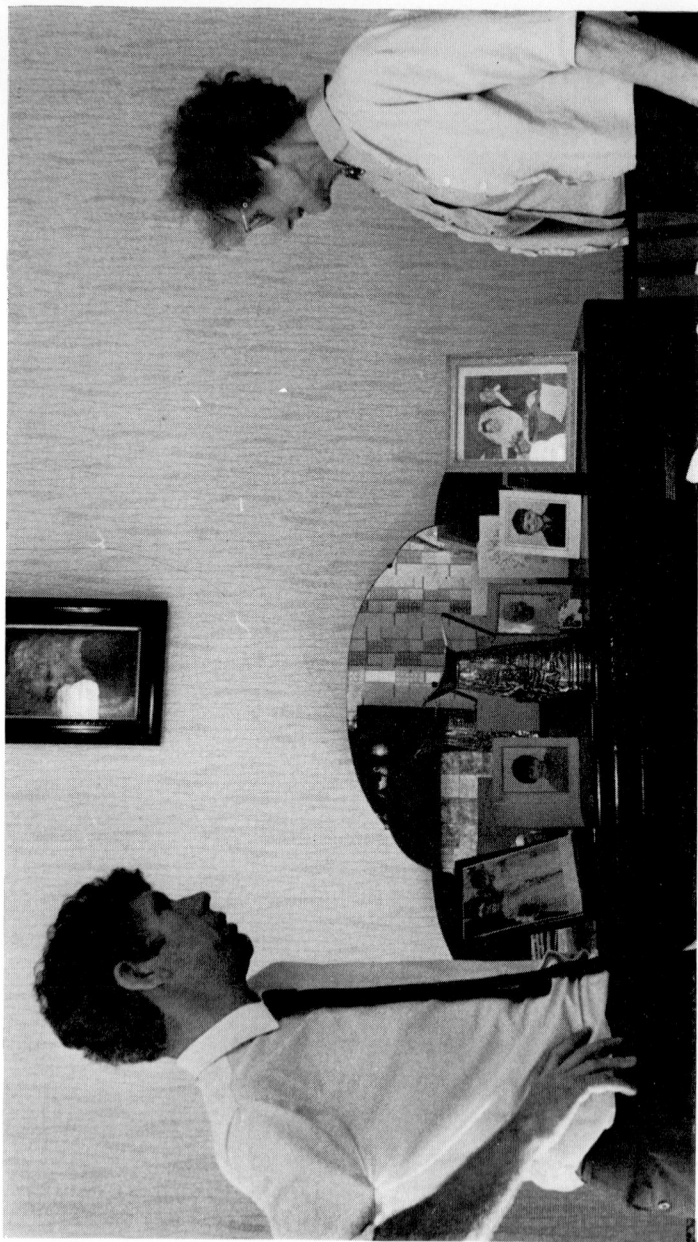

Plate X. Who benefits? A Pickard Street tenant

reach its decisions about lifing? The planning department, without being asked, went on to explain this point:

'So this is the way we look at the property when we inspect its potential for an improvement grant. And this isn't just done by the planning department. An architect goes out from the borough architect's department, and the Medical Officer of Health goes out. So that the consensus of opinion, as it were, of three different professions to decide whether a particular property is fit enough, or could be made fit enough, to rank for an improvement grant.'

This description of how decisions on lifing were made was analogous to the health department's description of the detailed clearance inspections prior to representation. It described what happened when an individual applicant approached the Corporation for an improvement subsidy. No one had at any time suggested that the improvement-grant inspectors from the architect's department did not do a thorough and competent survey when individual grant applications were before them. (In the field work for *People and Planning* I had accompanied the officer in the architect's department who carried out these inspections on several of his normal working days.)

The secretary made no comment. The planning department's point was taken up first by the chairman, and then by the two representatives from Granville Street. The point was, what was *the factual basis for lifing the different areas* in their proposals of November 14th 1968 and the much-revised proposals of February 7th 1969?

'If I can just come in here', the chairman of the Millfield Residents' Association said. 'This is the point. There is one street in this particular area under debate where the door stanchions are not in alignment, the windows and spoutings are not in alignment, and quite a number of the walls are bulging at the front and at the back. And yet this is included with the 15-year-plus area. The houses are derelict, if you like! And when we, as amateurs, look at the map, at the proposals here, and look at Westbury Street, which is next to and runs parallel with Granville Street, and we know Granville Street so well, we can't see any *sense*.' [Confused sounds of members of the planning department consulting each other, and of committee members expressing agreement with the chairman.] 'When you compare Westbury Street and Granville Street, you know, there *is* no comparison.' (Plate IX, and Table 1.)

TABLE I

### THE PROPOSALS FOR THE WESTBURY STREET AND GRANVILLE STREET AREAS COMPARED

| PROPOSAL DATE | WESTBURY STREET | GRANVILLE STREET |
|---|---|---|
| 1. *Development Plan of 1952 and Statutory Quinquennial Reviews* | 1. Cleared and redeveloped by 1972. | 1. The same. |
| 2. *Slum Clearance Programme Approved by Council in 1965* | 2. Cleared in 1968–9. | 2. The same. |
| 3. *Proposals of November 14th 1968* | 3. Standard grants until at least 1975. (That is, a life until at least 1990.) | 3. Clearance within fifteen years. (That is, 'by 1983'.) 'Within this period all these dwellings will have reached the end of their economic life even after improvement.' |
| 4. *Proposals of February 7th 1969* | 4. Unchanged from proposals of November 14th 1968, except that description *short term* improvement area dropped. | 4. Clearance in late 1970s or early 1980s. 'If a concerted effort is made in the near future by the owners to improve dwellings in this area, it is thought that they will not be affected by clearance proposals until the early 1980s. If, on the other hand, little im- |

| PROPOSAL DATE | WESTBURY STREET | GRANVILLE STREET |
|---|---|---|
| | | provement is effected, then they would fall for demolition in the late 1970s.' Reference was made to the proposals of the residents' association, giving the impression that the proposals had been *favourably* considered. In fact, in most of the area the availability of standard grants was cut from 'until 1973' to the end of 1971. |
| 5. *Public Announcements* | 5. Householders notified *en bloc* in June 1970 that the area had a further life of between fifteen and thirty years (1985–2000), and that an investigation was to be undertaken to see if it could be given a life of more than thirty years, that is, beyond the year 2000. Headlined in local press, July 1st 1970. Later announced that life of fifteen to thirty years would not be extended. | 5. None. But on applying individually for grants in the course of 1970, householders receive notification that the area is expected to have a further life of from fifteen to thirty years, that is, 1985–2000. |

There was a short incidental exchange between the planning department and the health department. The vicar had again mentioned the Granville Street area, and the planning department casually remarked, 'What we call the Short-term Improvement Area'. As casually, the health department said, 'We haven't been there yet'. Probably other members of the committee had taken little notice of that remark. But the street representative for Granville Street politely took it up.

'You say you've never been in Granville Street, yet the planning department says it's got to come down in a few years' time. You say it will be down before Westbury Street, yet the health department says, and we know this, that they've never been in the street.'

The second representative for Granville Street asked, 'If you've never been in the cottages, how can you say they're coming down?'

CHAPTER 9

# THE PLANNERS EXPLAIN TO
# THE PLANNING COMMITTEE

For several months the association's view about the surveys
remained that which had emerged from the discussions of
December 13th 1968, slightly clouded once more by the senior
housing inspector's gratuitous remark about Granville Street
at the meeting of February 14th 1969.

In June 1969, however, when the proposals for West Millfield
were put on public exhibition, the written information and the
maps on display included an explanation of the survey and the
way in which the results had been analysed and used, as well as
detailed descriptions of every cottage in the area. The reactions
of Millfielders were a combination of incredulity, incomprehen-
sion and indignation.

The quality of the planning department's data had not been
mentioned in the association's first letter to the Town Clerk's
department, that of July 21st 1969. Continued participation was
not at this time thought to be at risk, but the association's
committee was timid. It was anxious not to give any offence.
Certainly it was unwilling to give the Corporation a premature
and easy excuse for terminating participation on the grounds of
the association's belligerency. The secretary went even further
than the body of the committee in caution. Instead of writing
immediately to the Town Clerk's department, he once again
wrote to the chairman of the planning committee to say that if
he heard in a reasonably short time from the planning authority,
then he would 'willingly disobey' his committee's instruction.
No word was received, however, from the planning authority,

and the secretary accordingly wrote to the Town Clerk. The Town Clerk passed the association's letter to the planning department. The contentious issue of the quality of the surveys appeared in the reply to the planning department's letter of July 28th. The association's letter of July 29th said that the quality of the surveys was absolutely crucial. At public meetings many residents had complained that surveys had not been carried out by the Corporation. Many said that the condition and facilities of their own homes were grotesquely misdescribed by the planners. It was a similar story when the maps had been displayed in the June exhibition in West Millfield. In participation meetings and at ordinary meetings of the committee there were vehement denials of the planning department's claims to have inspected every house, and to have inspected every house internally. This was scarcely surprising, the association's letter of July 29th went on to say,

> when it is borne in mind that the planning department/health department's survey, which was not commenced until some time after February 10th 1968, was claimed to have been completed for the whole of the south side of the river (*8,000* pre-1914 dwellings!) by March 18th 1968. Anyone with any knowledge of survey technique would know that such a claim was extravagant in the extreme with the resources and personnel devoted to the task by the planning and health departments (with the assistance of some workers from other departments). Objections at public meetings and among Millfield Residents' Association committee members themselves that they have not been surveyed *at all* have always been denied by the planning department. But again, anyone with knowledge of door-to-door surveys can only look with amazement at the planning department's claim that in a single month, when *8,000* households were miraculously surveyed, in only 'a few cases' were people not in when the surveyor called. This is contrary to all known experience of surveys. These comments refer only to press releases from the planning department. In participation meetings with the association (of which tape transcripts are available) the story is, if anything, more sombre and less satisfactory still.

It was this letter which the planning department, in its report to the planning committee's meeting of August 27th, characterized as the turning point from previously reasonable relations with the Millfield Residents' Association. The letter referred to the fact that the association had recorded from the plans displayed at the exhibition a very large discrepancy between the facts of the situation and the scores allocated to different houses and streets by the planners.

How impartial and exact was the planning department in dealing with the question of the surveys as raised by the association in the letter of June 29th (i.e. assuming for the moment that the surveys had been carried out, and the association was in error, a fact which would have been neither improbable nor shameful)?

*Millfield: Progress Report*
*Item No. 7*
*Point raised by the association:* Regarding the survey of pre-1914 houses, 'There is a very large discrepancy between the facts of the situation and the "scores".'
*Planning department's comments:* Yet at the exhibition there were only six queries as to the accuracy of the survey.

The association's point, that is, was refuted by reference to the contents of the suggestion box from the June exhibition. Only six complaints about the quality of the surveys were received from West Millfield, that is, six complaints from 1,074 families.

But was this the strong point it appears to be in the planning department's comment on item No. 7? Not 1,074 but a total of forty-three slips were placed in the suggestion box. Three of the forty-three suggestions came from the same family in West Millfield. A further five came from East Millfield. One came from a housing estate at the other side of town. One came from a post-war street outside the area of the plan. Of all the items, therefore, 'only six' represented 14 per cent of the families submitting comments. Of the relevant population, families from West Millfield submitting slips, it represented 17 per cent.

If the planning department wished to argue any case from the suggestion box, then it might also have pointed out that on those grounds its proposal to retain the south end of Washington Street (see p. 75) amid a sea of demolition, a proposal very few people in the area could fathom, was complete nonsense. The only comment in the box from the south end of Washington Street read: 'Demolish as soon as possible— people cannot afford continual repairs; houses are damp; Villa Factory is noisy.' The comment from the post-war street outside the planned area also dealt with south Washington Street: 'Agrees generally with the clearance area but fails to see why south Washington Street has been left.' What becomes of the planning department's item No. 7, then, when it is open to counter-comment?

Item No. 8 was the second of the two in *Millfield: Progress Report* which dealt with the quality of the planning department's surveys upon which its plans were claimed to be based.

> *Item No. 8*
>
> *Point raised by the association:* 'The planning/health departments' survey which was not commenced until some time after February 10th 1968, was claimed to have been completed for the whole of the south side of the river (8,000 dwellings) by March 18th 1968. Anyone with any knowledge of door-to-door surveys can only look with amazement at the planning department's claim that, in a single month, 8,000 houses were miraculously surveyed . . .'
>
> *Planning department's comments:* As a matter of fact, it is quite within the capabilities of the planning department to survey 8,000 houses in a month, but it was never claimed that the whole of the south side of the river had been completed in that time.

This is probably the most interesting item of the twenty-six when rationality is the issue. The first thing to notice is that a section put in quotation marks by the planning department is significantly different in its sense from what was actually written. The planning department's extract from the association's letter consists of two sentences. One of them is an introduction to the association's case against the claim that 8,000 dwellings had been not simply surveyed, but internally surveyed in a month. This is a much more difficult and time-consuming job than gathering door-to-door information by questionnaire. The association had never doubted that door-to-door interviews had been conducted. The controversy was principally over the claim to have conducted *internal inspections* of all pre-1914 houses in the borough in preparation for the Millfield proposals. The sentences dealing with that case are completely missed out in the above 'quotation', without any indication of ellipsis. The planning department proceeds immediately to a second sentence about the much less controversial door-to-door interviews.

This second sentence from the association's letter simply has a word removed, again without ellipsis, and again altering the sense significantly. The point in the letter was not about the door-to-door surveys as such, but the claim that very few respondents were out when the surveyor called; not 'in a single month, 8,000 houses were miraculously surveyed', but 'in a single month, *when* 8,000 houses were miraculously surveyed, in only a few cases were people out when the surveyor called'. This, the letter from the Millfield Residents' Association had said, was contrary to all known experience of surveys. To have completed 8,000 door-to-door interviews in a single month with the resources available to the existing staff of the Corporation was, on the face of it, at any rate not completely impossible. But that was not the point the association had raised. It had said that to complete 8,000 internal inspections was or would have been a remarkable achievement for a month's work; but to maintain that *very few recalls were necessary*, i.e., that the planning department had successfully covered all houses in the way it claimed, was completely unbelievable. No one who has ever canvassed, interviewed, called at doors for any other reason or tried to obtain a high percentage response from material put out through the letter-box could possibly accept that. The association's points were not, however, allowed to appear before the planning committee; they were replaced by something masquerading as the association's points. Against the substituted points the planning department could at least put up a colourable case.

In the letter of July 29th to the Town Clerk's department the association had been in error in one particular matter. A *Sunderland Echo* report of March 18th 1969 was quoted by the secretary. In its press release, he said, the planning department had claimed to have completed the survey of 8,000 dwellings and that these constituted all the pre-1914 dwellings on the south side of the River Wear. The *Sunderland Echo* had not reported that. It had said that 8,000 dwellings had been surveyed; but from the districts named, some of these were clearly south and some north of the river. So far as the point the association was making is concerned, to have concentrated on the south of the river in the first instance and completed the survey of the dwellings there, before moving to deal with the area north of the river as a block, would, if anything, have marginally strengthened the planners' case that they had managed to complete their formidable task.

> As a matter of fact, it is quite within the capabilities of the planning department to survey 8,000 houses in a month, but it has never claimed that the whole of the south side of the river has been completed in that time.

The total survey covered about 17,000 or 18,000 dwellings (the planning department quoted different figures at different times, occasionally going as high as 20,000). Approximately half of these lay south and half north of the river. The association's criticisms were refuted only by a combination of a misquotation from the association's correspondence and an ambiguous and highly misleading answer from the planning department. The association, however, was not meant to see the report of August 27th, and was most certainly not expected to comment on it.

The question of the quality of the planning department's data is in a special category. Their claim to expertise and the legitimacy of their intervention in the housing decisions of the citizen are grounded upon their superior knowledge, the objectivity, the 'scientificality', of their facts. It is therefore unavoidable that not only the treatment of the association's correspondence should be examined; it is necessary also to attempt to reach some conclusion on whether or not, or in which way and how efficiently, Millfield was surveyed in preparation for the planning proposals. When the association was again able to meet Corporation representatives (at the meeting of September 15th 1969 at the Town Hall) the vicar strongly expressed the wish to be satisfied that the planning department had 'done its homework', i.e. that it had carried out reasonably adequate surveys of the area before elaborating its proposals for Millfield. The secretary-observer's record of the dialogue at the meeting of September 15th covers 13½ A4 pages of single-space typing. On the question of the surveys, the secretary made only one comment. Following the vicar's requests for evidence that the planning department had done its homework and the assurances offered on that score by members of the planning sub-committee he said only, 'You are saying that all the information will be forthcoming, and the Millfield Residents' Association will see it?'

> *Councillor:* We are all saying one thing with one voice.
> *Second Councillor:* We are prepared to supply it. Yes, we are.
> *Secretary:* Is this an authoritative statement, or is it only your own view?
> *Second Councillor:* I am not in the habit of making statements that are not authoritative. The association will be supplied with the reasons for the proposals . . .

He also made, however, a general remark about the knowledge of the members of the planning committee which, again, might have adversely affected the subsequent experiences of Millfield as a whole. Two senior members of the sub-committee (chairmen of important Council committees in their own right, including the chairman of the housing committee) had mildly said that they were at a disadvantage. They did not know, they said, what the issues were in Millfield. The chairman of the housing committee said, 'We are here as new boys. We want concrete proposals put as quickly as possible. Take it back, find out what people think'.[1] The secretary's retort was probably sharp and may not have been entirely devoid of emotion:

> 'Councillor, if I may address the councillor through the Chair, I do not believe that you are entitled to plead ignorance of the affairs of Millfield. Another councillor has just made a similar statement, that he is a new boy and has come fresh to Millfield's problems. We are here to discuss Millfield with members of the planning committee. The planning committee has undertaken to affect, and drastically affect, the lives of many hundreds of families. Millfield has been an issue since at least 1965, when the Council first approved definite plans for substantial slum clearance in the area. It has been a burning issue since 1967, when the new plans were promised. It is simply not good enough for members of the planning committee to turn round now and say, "I am a new boy, the problem is new to me". You are not entitled not to know about Millfield.'

As a result of the meeting of September 15th the Millfield Residents' Association met the planners—for the last time—on October 6th. It was not a participation meeting such as had been held previously. In November and December 1968 and in February 1969 chief officers, the chairman of the planning committee, as well as councillors and junior officers had been present. On October 6th only three planning officers attended the meeting. One of the officers made notes—the first record the Corporation had ever kept of any public meeting in Millfield or meeting with the association. The meeting had a single purpose —to show clearly and definitely that the planners had carried out the surveys as originally claimed.

### NOTE

1 They had been chairmen of their respective committees and *ex offici* members of the planning committee since mid-1967—i.e. for eighteen months before the November 14th 1968 proposals were presented to the Millfield Residents' Association.

# CHAPTER 10

# THE PLANNERS EXPLAIN TO
# THE MILLFIELD RESIDENTS'
# ASSOCIATION

At the meeting of October 6th the contentious survey was described very fully. The planning department handed out copies of the card which had been used in the door-to-door survey. Excluding the section 'for office use', the card showed the following headings:

Name
Street name
Dwelling number
Type of property (number of storeys)
Owner-occupied or tenanted
Repair
Stability
Rising damp
Penetrating damp
General
Facilities
  In separate bathroom
    Bath: hot/cold
    Bath: none/shared/sole use
    Wash-hand basin: hot/cold
    Wash-hand basin: none/shared/sole use
  Individual facilities
    Bath: hot/cold
    Bath: none/shared/sole use
    Wash-hand basin: hot/cold
    Wash-hand basin: none/shared/sole use
    W.C.: in/out
    W.C.: none/shared/sole use

> Sink: hot/cold
> Sink: none/shared/sole use
> External tap: none/shared/sole use
> Occupants
>> Number in family
>> Adults: male/female
>> Children: male/female
>> Total
>> Permitted number
>> O/C [meaning not known]
> Weekly rent
> Rooms

The planning department's address on the subject then followed. With very minor interruptions, it covers seven A4 pages of single-space typing of the association's minutes.

The three queries in October 1969 were: First, how could the planning department reconcile the shortness of the time taken over the survey with the richness of the results? Secondly, had the internal surveys been accurate enough? Thirdly, *when* were the internal inspections carried out?

1. *Were 8,000 houses surveyed in a month?* The planning department answered the first query without being asked: 'We went round the doors saying, "Good morning! Is this 26 Westbury Street?" Started like that. Then asked the questions. We got so expert on this that we could do it in a minute—two minutes—three at the most.'

The survey of as many as 8,000 houses in a month was therefore explained satisfactorily (so long as it could be assumed that there was nearly always someone to answer the door, that no surveyor was ever kept talking, and so long as he could be transported instantaneously from one interview to another).

2. *Which houses were inspected internally?* But what about the *internal* inspections of *all* the houses. No, not *all* the houses. 'On the top left of the card you can see the basic questions on structure. We did not ask those questions. There was no point in asking those questions in, say, the "ABC" streets.[1] It was only in

the worst areas that we asked the health department to ask those questions.' The planning department has asked itself, ' "Who is the most expert person?" The health department. Gave them all those areas which had been in the old clearance area [the 1965–70 programme].'

So, the health department had been responsible for the internal inspections of all the houses in the old clearance areas, including Millfield. Furthermore, the internal inspections were not, after all, those of March 1967. (See page 109.) The planning department was back to its claim that the internal inspections had been carried out as part of the survey of February–March 1968 ('which would not involve the inspection of properties').

The association was at last presented with at least a plausible version of what had happened. It was not impossible that the health department had internally surveyed all the houses of the old 1965–70 programme (about 2,000 properties) at some time between February 10th 1968 and the date on which the proposals for the Millfield area, presented at the participation meeting of November 14th 1968, were approved by some *ad hoc* Corporation committee. If that had been the first and consistent explanation then the only difficulty — but of course a very serious one — would have been to account for the fact that dozens of Millfield families (at least) were adamant that their own houses had not enjoyed such an internal inspection.

There was more to the explanation given on October 6th than this. The Millfield Residents' Association was concerned not only about whether the surveys had been carried out, but also whether they were sufficiently detailed to justify the policies which were based upon them. The planning department on October 6th were prepared to say that they were sufficiently detailed. Because, after the computer results were known (the door-to-door surveys and the internal surveys by the health department of the 1965–70 clearance areas), 'We said to the health department, "By this computer print-out, these streets seem to be rather poor, go and look at them". There are two of them, one who has 23 years' experience, and the other with 21 years' experience. That is 44 years' experience altogether. That is a lot of experience. "You go and tell us if the computer print-out is a lot of rubbish". '

This full and detailed history of the surveys put an entirely different complexion on the proposals of November 14th and February 7th—and on the previous discussions of 'the adequacy of the surveys'. By a mammoth effort 'nineteen-odd thousand houses in the borough' had been surveyed from door-to-door. The sequence as described in the planning department's latest version now appeared to be as follows. The survey had been started on Monday, February 12th 1968. Two thousand cottages in the 1965–70 clearance area, including all the houses in Mill-field, had been *internally* inspected by the health department. The results of both these surveys had been analysed and organized by the computer in various rather elaborate ways based on a system of scoring. Finally, when the results were known, the health department had resurveyed the worst streets. By October 1968 the proposals based upon these procedures were passed by a committee of the Council. That was what the planning department was now saying.

3. *When were the surveys carried out?* The secretary, however, asked if he could see the copy of the list of streets and blocks which the health department had resurveyed. Somewhat reluctantly, but given the situation rather unavoidably, the planning department passed the handwritten sheet to the secretary.

The sheet was retrieved before the secretary could note all details and it is possible that on certain small points the version below is not an absolutely accurate copy of the original. In all points of substance, however, it corresponds exactly to the minute kept of the meeting of October 6th by the planners themselves. [2]

SURVEY BY M.O.H. MILLFIELD CLEARANCE
PROGRAMME

Alfred Street: All surveyed for representation March 1967. Most surveyed
October 1968 except Cornwall Street.
27/1/69: Alliance Street area. Aa.[3] No hurry to take this as separate area,
but could be taken with North Hedley Street. 50 per cent inspected.

| | BLOCK NO. | ADDRESS | REMARKS |
|---|---|---|---|
| 28/1/69: | 15 | 34–39 Deptford Road | Very small no. of greys: 2/6?[4] |
| | 23 | $17\frac{1}{2}$–24 Deptford Road | 3/8 |
| | 24 | 7–17 North Hedley St. | 5/12 |
| 30/1/69: | | 63–80 Millburn St. | Some poor properties: 4 good out of 7 |
| | | 9–15 Deptford Road | 5 poor |
| | | 62–75 Hedley Street | 3 out of 13 |
| | | 1–4  Hedley Street | 4 out of 14 |
| 31/1/69: | | 63–80 Millburn St. | First 10 from Hylton Road fit |

At that point the planning department asked for the sheet
back. In the planners' own minute, however, dates of inspections are shown as late as February 4th 1969. (A total of 200
inspections had been carried out between January 27th and
February 4th 1969.)

There are no conceivable grounds for objecting to the health
department continuing its more detailed survey at the end of
January and the beginning of February 1969. Equally, however, it is extremely difficult to see what surveys carried out in
January and February 1969 have to do with proposals approved
three or four months *previously*, on October 8th 1968, or what
inspections carried out on February 4th 1969 have to do with
proposals presented only three days later, complete with photo-
stated maps, on February 7th 1969.

## Millfield's Scepticism

Apart from a single remark right at the beginning of the meeting, the secretary made no contribution until the very end, and none of the remarks were about the quality of the surveys, who had done them, where, or when. But other members of the committee (twenty-seven street representatives were present on October 6th, including a strong contingent from West Millfield) continued to express their grave doubts.

At one point, for example, the planning department was saying that the results based on the February–March 1968 surveys were kept up-to-date. 'If you do get an improvement grant, then I note it on the card. If the rates go up, I note it on the card. I keep it all updated. It will most certainly be kept up-to-date. We get facts from the Rate Office . . .'

A committee member burst out scornfully, 'You are kept up-to-date by the Rate Office? The Rating Officer came the other day. "Have you still got the air raid shelter in the back?" I got the government grant *ten years ago* to rebuild the whole of the back! I objected to being told that I still had an air raid shelter!'

The reply?

'Yes, there are defects in Corporation business, but that is a bit academic for present purposes.'

A representative from West Millfield asked about the relationship between the survey and the lifing of the property: 'The card survey. Does that determine the life of the houses?'

'No, it only gives priorities.'

'Then *how* do you get the lifing?'

'The Minister lays down conditions about grants. We are obliged to assess. If the Corporation will grant money, that money must be well spent.'

'Since your card survey, quite a lot of properties have been improved. I could take you to quite a lot. I really think there should be another survey. There are whole streets which have become owner-occupied and been lifted up.'

'Yes, yes.'

'I'm off sick at the present time, so I've been able to get around quite a lot I can tell you: the streets with "fifteen years" could stand for another fifteen years on top of that, and perhaps more. How do you arrive at the lives? If it was technical, then there would be quite a wrangle with the man who did it. But how is it done? How can you get the lives from the card survey? There are a lot of instances where the structure is given as "moderate" when the house is structurally perfect. And plenty of cases where, to take an example, it says "no bathroom" when it has everything there is to have!'

The reply?

'It is possible there is a card wrong. There is an error. It is only a very small percentage. It certainly makes no difference to the blocks. Yes, it *is* taken at a point in time. But we can't have a survey every six months.'

One final example closes this chapter. The chairman resurrected the old question of Granville Street and Westbury Street. 'And look! Granville Street is far superior to Westbury Street. The health department could not have done detailed surveys there.'

'The older parts of Granville Street: standard grants *if* we think a lot of people will do it. If there is only one applicant this year, and a couple next, no good—the rest getting older and older.'

'If five improved?'

'But if ten went down!'

'But they will *not* deteriorate. The families there could not be surpassed as far as character etc. are concerned. Yet they have nothing but uncertainty.'

'We've said a fifteen-year basis.'

After the meeting had concluded, a resident was weeping with misery and anger. She was pleading with the planning department, trying to make them realize that the reason so few applications for improvement grants came from Granville Street was that the cottages were already improved beyond the grant standard.

As the resident wept, there was the reverberation of the words with which the planning department had concluded its description of the surveys the department had carried out. 'So it's a little bit hurtful for you to come and say, "Prove that you've done your job!" Of course we have!' The lads at the planning office 'get a feeling about this'. The lads at the planning office 'don't like it'.[5] But like it or not, the story of Millfield's planning proposals and of the surveys upon which they were based seems to give support once more to Bentham's familiar words, that publicity is the keenest spur to exertion and the surest of all guards against improbity. 'Where there is no publicity, there is no justice.'

## NOTES

1 A block of streets of pre-1914 cottages outside the Millfield area.
2 Planning department's minutes of meeting of October 6th 1969, p. 3, section 4, paras. 1–6.
3 Aa means first class structure, first class amenities.
4 Grey means fit (pink means unfit). These are the colours used in the maps of slum-clearance areas. That note means that under the Housing Acts two of the six houses were in the inspector's opinion fit, four unfit.
5 There is no tape recording of the meeting of October 6th. On the point as to whether or not the planning department was annoyed there is, however, ample documentary evidence in a letter from the planning department to the secretary of the Millfield Residents' Association dated October 2nd 1969. 'The cause of the people of Millfield', the planning department wrote (PO 50/2), 'is not served by this kind of correspondence which in fact, now *irritates and antagonizes* those members of the Council, *my staff and the public health inspectors* who have been conscientiously working to help them.' (Emphasis added.)

# CHAPTER 11

# WERE THE SURVEYS RELEVANT?

Participation in planning will always have this as one of its functions: achieving credibility and removing suspicions. The association's resolution No. 5 had asked for valid, reliable and accurate facts. The Corporation failed to convince Millfielders that policy conclusions had been deduced from such facts. As Chapters 6 to 10 have shown, the residents' committee wanted to be reassured that plans closely and extensively affecting their lives and the future of their families were not based upon spurious information. That simple request deteriorated into a long hunt down the months for a straightforward answer to the question: 'Well, then, who did survey what, where and when?'

For very special reasons this working-class area proved obstinate in its resolve to obtain a rational answer. An important element in the stubbornness of the committee was its possession of exhaustive accounts of what was said by the planning department and others on different occasions.

This study is concerned with the link between secrecy and rationality. Secrecy can be maintained not only by refusing to disclose any information (a difficult stance for a public-service bureaucracy). Often it can be maintained just as effectively by the disclosure of partial information and by making it difficult to piece the different parts of the argument together. Anyone with a weak case, or who is under pressure of questioning from a source which he feels has no right to do any questioning but which for some reason cannot be brushed aside, is likely to feel the intuitive force of the saying, 'If you can't kid them, confuse them'.

The surveys were purportedly used for two sets of policies. First, clearance-area policy. Secondly, the policy of distributing government grants for the improvement of older houses and their environment.

1. *Clearance policies*: Whatever level of clearance private citizens or officials in their private capacity may favour and advocate, local-government clearance activities operate within a determinate set of constraints. The number and quality of dwellings actually cleared within a particular period of time depend upon the current legislative standards; the standards accepted as normal by the local Medical Officer of Health; the standards accepted by the Minister's inspectors at public inquiries; the nature and weight of residents' opinion; and the general economic and political climate, national and municipal. How important planners' views are in this network of influence is an empirical question. In some localities the planners dominate the health inspectorate. In other localities (such as, for example, Newcastle upon Tyne) the housing inspectorate is robustly able to hold its own.[1]

In this network of influence, the authoritative consideration of whether or not to represent an area for clearance is undertaken by personnel of the health department. Their decision must be formally justifiable in terms of the degree of correspondence between the quality of the dwellings on the one hand and on the other the criteria laid down in national housing legislation. Unless, therefore, surveys supposedly geared to provide information for clearance policy are predictive of the decisions which will actually be reached about representation, clearance-area announcements based on such surveys can be productive of nothing but blight; and because of the formal centrality of the standards contained in housing legislation, slum-clearance surveys which do not deal adequately with at least these are bound to be seriously defective.

2. *Lifing policies*: The second main set of policies, lifing, is a matter of deciding which dwellings and areas might receive

grants for amenities they lack; for example, an indoor w.c., a bath, a hot water supply or a wash basin.

Throughout this chapter it will be assumed that the concrete results of the surveys were themselves reasonably reliable, i.e. described the reality they were intended to describe. The examination of that assumption itself will be postponed until the next chapter. Assuming the accuracy of the data, then, to what extent was it relevant in its raw and processed forms to these two sets of conditions?

*Structural Condition*

In the planning department's survey-design each dwelling was to be given a number of penalty points for different aspects of its structure, namely, the state of its repair, stability, rising dampness, penetrating dampness and a fifth aspect which in some places was described by the planners as 'general' but in others as 'overall appearance'.[2]

If a dwelling was judged good on any of these items, it was given only one penalty point for that aspect. A dwelling which was good on all five counts therefore received the lowest possible number of penalty points, five. A house which was fair (sometimes called average) on any of the items was given a penalty score of two in respect of that item. A house which was poor on any item received a penalty score of three for that item. Dwellings in the poorest structural condition therefore received the maximum penalty of fifteen points.

Dwellings with 5–7 penalty points were then classified as good. Those with 8–10 were classified as average or fair. Those with 11–15 penalty points were classified as poor.

As an indication of suitability for clearance there are some difficulties about that scheme: it has at least to be handled carefully. For example, given the criteria of the governing legislation, the Housing Act of 1957, what is the justification (assuming it is reasonable to count dampness twice) for taking no account at all of defects of ventilation, lighting etc.? General appearance may be legitimately considered relevant for certain planning policies. But what is the justification, in terms of slum clearance, of giving it weight and amalgamating it into a single inseparable category with stability, repair and rising and pene-trating dampness?

It is therefore quite possible, indeed likely, that dwellings would be judged fair on all the Housing Act items, yet poor in appearance. It would thus fall into the general category of poor (11 penalty points). Another house may be suffering from rising dampness to such an extent that it would certainly be legisla-tively unfit for human habitation and in fact receive the maxi-mum penalty of three points. That need not prevent its overall appearance being good if the other items are all fair. Such a house then receives ten penalty points and is classified as fair or average along with dwellings which are good on two criteria and fair on the other three. These are not remote speculations. Such anomalies must have frequently appeared. Were these difficulties appreciated before the scheme was accepted? Were any adjustments made to the data to take account of them? The available evidence points to an answer in the negative to both those questions.

Also unexplained is the choice of class intervals. These are clearly fundamental to the identification of the areas suitable for clearance. The scheme resulted in Sunderland's pre-1914 dwellings being classified in the following groups: Good = 7,872; Fair or Average = 10,236; Poor = 1,800. What would the result have been if, as is on the face of it quite reasonable houses had been classified as good if they fell below the good classification on not more than one item, instead of allowing two items of the five to be fair; classifying dwellings as 'fair' in the range of 7–9 points; and regarding the rest, 10–15 points as clearance candidates? This would have cut out of the very large fair category the highest penalty-point scorers.

What could not fail to strike anyone knowing the history of

Sunderland's housing programmes is the fact that the scheme adopted by the planning department gives a figure of poor houses which is very close to the number of dwellings in the abandoned 1965–70 clearance plan.[3] The selection of class intervals was either considered by the planning department, or it was not. (It ought to have been very seriously considered.) If it was considered, did the 1965–70 figure have any influence on the choice? To the extent that it did have an influence, then the survey was not a re-examination of the 1965–70 programme, but to an unknown degree simply a replication of it.

*Amenities*

Although the Housing Act of 1957 specified certain amenities such as sanitary facilities, water supply and so forth, it did not specify any of the amenities included by the planners in their survey. None of the amenities listed in the survey, that is, were relevant to clearance decisions. Legislation did not exist which allowed a house to be acquired and demolished without the occupier's consent simply because it lacked any or all of the amenities enumerated in the survey.[4] The planning department itself made it clear that the list of amenities had been selected not from the legislation which dealt with clearance, but from the improvement-grant legislation.[5] If the information had been suitably utilized for that purpose, then no objection could be raised. It was collapsed, however, into a single category which inextricably mixed clearance data and improvement-grant data. On the other hand it was *not* combined with the relevant data on structure in order to produce useful information for improvement-grant policies.

Penalty points for lack of facilities were awarded according to the scale shown in Table 2 overleaf.

A dwelling with the complete array of amenities investigated in the survey, i.e. with the exclusive use of bath in a bathroom with a hot water supply, the exclusive use of a wash-hand basin with a hot water supply, the exclusive use of a kitchen sink with a hot water supply and the exclusive use of an internal w.c., would receive the lowest possible score, four penalty points. A family sharing all four amenities, without any hot water supply, and using an outside toilet would receive a penalty of 22 points. The categories a, b, and c were then based on the scores: a = 4–9 penalty points; b = 10–14 penalty points; and c = 15 penalty points or more.

TABLE 2

PENALTY-POINT SCALE FOR HOUSEHOLD AMENITIES

|  | Number of penalty points |
|---|---|
| Exclusive use of bath in bathroom with hot water supply | 1 |
| Exclusive use of bath in bathroom without hot water supply | 2 |
| Shared use of bath in bathroom with hot water supply | 3 |
| Shared use of bath in bathroom without hot water supply | 4 |
| Exclusive use of bath not in bathroom with hot water supply | 3 |
| Exclusive use of bath not in bathroom without hot water supply | 4 |
| Shared use of bath not in bathroom with hot water supply | 5 |
| Shared use of bath not in bathroom without hot water supply | 6 |
| Exclusive use of wash-hand basin with hot water supply | 1 |
| Exclusive use of wash-hand basin without hot water supply | 2 |
| Shared use of wash-hand basin with hot water supply | 3 |
| Shared use of wash-hand basin without hot water supply | 4 |
| Exclusive use of kitchen sink with hot water supply | 1 |
| Exclusive use of kitchen sink without hot water supply | 2 |
| Shared use of kitchen sink with hot water supply | 6 |
| Shared use of kitchen sink without hot water supply | 7 |
| Exclusive use of internal w.c. | 1 |
| Exclusive use of external w.c. | 4 |
| Shared use of internal w.c. | 5 |
| Shared use of external w.c. | 7 |

The first thing to say about the above scheme is, 'How does *sharing* amenities fit into the survey?' The problem of sharing amenities with another family is very serious for those who experience it. In a place like Millfield families in shared dwellings probably feel, subjectively, far greater housing hardship, even if they are in reasonably sound property, than families in any but the very worst single-family cottages. But it helps towards clarity on the scope and nature of neither clearance, nor improvement, nor the relief of overcrowding and shared accommodation to collapse penalty points for sharing into a scheme which is supposed to provide information for clearance and improvement-grant policies.

Secondly, is the relative importance of each item anything more than some single outsider's arbitrary opinion? Again, there are statistical techniques, if not for devising any given scheme, at least for avoiding the worst excesses of subjectivity. Where did these weights come from? What logic are they supposed to express? Who said, on what grounds, that to share an outside water closet was the 'same' in terms of housing hardship in Millfield as having no bath? Who said that the absence of an indoor toilet is a disadvantage, irrespective of personal preferences, 'four times worse' than having an inside toilet?

*The Block Analysis*

It is easy to see that if the data were valid and if the various statistical problems of class-interval etc. had been faced and more or less satisfactorily solved, combined categories of facility and structure could be devised to yield information on houses or areas especially suitable for improvement-grant treatment: namely, information showing houses in sound structural condition but with poor amenities. Using three categories of amenity and three of structure the resulting nine-cell table would show, in the Ab and Ac categories, houses which were promising improvement-grant material. Bb and Bc houses might also be suitable, but the B category would need to be subdivided further, as the range of quality in the structurally fair houses (well over half of all houses in the survey) would be wide.

TABLE 3

STRUCTURE-AND-AMENITIES GRADES

| | | Facilities | | |
| --- | --- | --- | --- | --- |
| | | Good | Fair | Poor |
| | | (a) | (b) | (c) |
| | Good (A) | Aa | Ab | Ac |
| Structure | Fair (B) | Ba | Bb | Bc |
| | Poor (C) | Ca | Cb | Cc |

As a matter of fact, the planning department did produce these categories but only as an intermediate step in the production of the 'block analysis'. No maps, tables or descriptive material of any kind was ever shown in printed form or referred to verbally in which the categories were used in connection with lifing, i.e. improvement-grant proposals.

At the meeting of October 6th 1969, the total number of pre-1914 dwellings in the whole of the borough falling into each of the nine categories was, in passing, mentioned.

$$Aa = 5{,}263 \quad Ab = 1{,}066 \quad Ac = 1{,}543$$
$$Ba = 3{,}423 \quad Bb = 1{,}314 \quad Bc = 5{,}499$$
$$Ca = \phantom{0}99 \quad Cb = \phantom{00}108 \quad Cc = 1{,}593$$

Without further comment, the explication then moved to the way in which these categories had been used in order to produce the 'block scores'.

The planning department's own minutes of the meeting confirm this. The nine combinations of A, B, C with a, b, c, are shown. Then, without giving the above figures, the minute goes on immediately to say, 'With this information blocks of property were identified so that the whole area could be compared block by block.'[6]

What was the block analysis—and what was its relevance for

clearance and improvement decision-making? The first step in the block coding was to combine the structural classification of each dwelling (the structural classification being a combination of clearance and improvement data) with the overall classification of the same dwelling on its facilities score. This gives the ninefold table, the Aa, Ab, Cb, Cc, etc. already described. Points were then awarded on the basis of this new structure/facilities classification. The structure/facilities points for each dwelling in each unbroken terrace of properties were then summed, divided by the number of properties and the figure so obtained constituted the 'block value'.

First, in terms of the relevance of the resulting data for policy-making, what was the logic of the penalty pointing of the combined categories, Aa, Ab, Ac, etc.? At the June exhibition a chart was displayed which showed the combined categories and the penalty points associated with them (see Table 4).

This being his first sight of the statistical scheme, the observer asked the planning official on duty at the exhibition how it was that a capital A and small a 'added up' to one penalty point, and a capital C and small c added up (as it appeared from the layout of the chart) to nine penalty points. So far as the observer knew he was as much a stranger to the planning official as the planning official was to him; and so far as he could judge he asked politely, an ordinary interested visitor to the exhibition. The official looked at the chart for a moment and then replied brusquely that it was 'obvious'. A little put off, the observer risked being thought rather slow and simple (it might have been obvious, he had not bothered to think too much about it) and asked if the official would nevertheless explain. The official then stared at the chart with rising blushes. After several seconds of silence the official, by his manner, terminated the conversation and the inquiry. 'I don't know', he said, 'in detail.'

What is obvious when the cross-classification is presented as a ninefold table was seriously obscured by what looked like 'addition sums' on the chart.

TABLE 4
## BLOCK ANALYSIS CODE

Penalty points have been awarded to each property ranging from 1 (for a house in good structural condition with good facilities) to 9 (for a house in poor structural condition and poor facilities). These were then averaged out for each street block and the no. of penalty points is shown.

*Block Analysis Code*

Block 1

|  | House A | House B | House C | House D |  |
|---|---|---|---|---|---|
| Structure | A | A | A | A |  |
| Facilities | a | a | a | a |  |
| Points | 1 | 1 | 1 | 1 |  |
|  |  |  | Total points | 4 |  |
|  |  |  | Total properties | 4 |  |
|  |  |  | Block value | 1 |  |

Block 2

|  | House A | House B | House C | House D |  |
|---|---|---|---|---|---|
| Structure | A | A | C | C |  |
| Facilities | a | a | c | c |  |
| Points | 1 | 1 | 9 | 9 |  |
|  |  |  | Total points | 20 |  |
|  |  |  | Total properties | 4 |  |
|  |  |  | Block value | 5 |  |

Block 3

|  | House A | House B | House C | House D |  |
|---|---|---|---|---|---|
| Structure | C | C | C | C |  |
| Facilities | c | c | c | c |  |
| Points | 9 | 9 | 9 | 9 |  |
|  |  |  | Total points | 36 |  |
|  |  |  | Total properties | 4 |  |
|  |  |  | Block value | 9 |  |

The pointing scheme was eventually explained by the planning department at the meeting of October 6th 1969. The numbers from one to nine are the order from the best of the nine categories. Aa, to the worst, Cc. An ordinal scale, that is, had been transposed without further statistical processing into a cardinal scale.

The order is:

1. Good structure and good facilities    (Aa)
2. Good structure and fair facilities     (Ab)
3. Good structure and poor facilities    (Ac)

4. Fair structure and good facilities    (Ba)
5. Fair structure and fair facilities     (Bb)
6. Fair structure and poor facilities    (Bc)

7. Poor structure and good facilities    (Ca)
8. Poor structure and fair facilities     (Cb)
9. Poor structure and poor facilities    (Cc)

The reduction of ordinal scales to cardinal scales is common practice in statistical analysis. But there are several pitfalls which must be negotiated. It is very rare that an analyst finds after proper study of the issues involved that the relationship between first, second, third, fourth etc. can be represented by weights of one point, two points, etc. This scaling says that the ninth is 'three times' the third in respect of whatever is being represented, in this case 'degree of badness of housing conditions'. It is four times worse to live in a house in poor structural condition and with fair internal facilities than it is to live in a house which is in good structural condition and with fair facilities. Why four times worse? Why not only twice as bad? Why not twenty times as bad?

It is in the abstract possible to argue that the crudest derivation of a quasi-variable from a rank order may serve a useful exploratory purpose. Of course there are instances when that would be true. The whole point about this survey was that it was claimed not to be exploratory. The planning department claimed that the process was not crude, but refined—uniquely refined.[7]

In the scheme poor structure was three times more heavily

penalized than absence of amenities. That is a not unreasonable decision, if decision it was. What raises doubts about whether it was a conscious choice and therefore could be discussed by its inventors in terms of some rationale is not only the extreme naïvety of the weighting. A far more serious source of doubt is the fact that the greater penalty weight to *structure* is purely an artifact of the *number of amenity grades* in the table. If the four grades of amenity-provision had been used instead of three (i.e. the four grades of complete, good, average and poor) that would have automatically given a fall of one grade in structure (from A to B or from B to C) four times and not three times the penalty of a fall in one amenity grade (from a to b, or from b to c). How accidental was the layout of the table in the first place? If structure had been run along the top margin instead of the side margin, and facilities along the side instead of along the top (see p. 140), and the planning department's rank ordering had run from left to right across the table again, this would have automatically meant that facilities were being given three times the weight of structure. Presumably such a bizarre result would have compelled self-consciousness about what was involved in the whole business of treating an ordinal scale simply as if it was a cardinal scale.

Even if all the data were absolutely authentic and precise and the weighting schemes had been impeccable, the block analysis would still be fatally flawed. It takes meaningful categories and combines them into a pointing scheme, the block value, which is intrinsically irrelevant to the purpose at hand, and the potentially most useful set of categories are not refined, but systematically obliterated.

Having discussed the relevance of the raw and processed data on the assumption of their accuracy, it is now time to see whether or not that assumption is correct.

NOTES

1 See the forthcoming study by Peter Norman, of the Department of Social and Economic Research, University of Glasgow.

2 The fifth item was described as 'general appearance' in the planning department's proposals booklet for East Millfield. *Millfield: Clearance and Improvement*, November 1968. Section C: 'Survey'; paragraph 4(a).

3 See *People and Planning*, p. 193; the 1965–70 programme covered 2,056 dwellings.

4 An interesting sidelight is thrown on planners' attitudes to the powerful and to the powerless by comparing their treatment of Millfielders' homes with their assumptions about the owners of hotel chains. At a meeting of the planning committee at which an outline application for the development of a site for a new hotel was being discussed, the planning department's answer to one contribution was, 'We can't tell people what to do with their own property'. *Sunderland Echo*, October 1st 1970. That remark seems to reveal something about who and who are not classified as 'people' and what and what is not people's 'own property'.

5 'Now, on the internal facilities: we took the Ministry's standard. The Ministry says, "If you don't have a bath, or a wash-hand basin, or an inside w.c.—I know that caused some trouble at another meeting—we'll give you a grant to get them." The Ministry will give a grant, therefore they are desirable.' (Verbatim note from the statement at the meeting of October 6th 1969.) The planning department's own minute of the meeting says substantially the same thing: that the department 'explained by means of the chart the checklist of facilities surveyed. The department took as a standard, the MOHLG's view that if basic facilities were lacking a standard grant would be given to remedy the deficiency'.

6 Two years after the meeting of October 6th 1969 the existence of a document entitled *Sunderland Structure Plan: 2, Pre-1914 Housing*, dated March 1969, became known.

It showed, as above, the total number of dwellings in the borough falling into each of the categories Aa, Ab, Ac, Ba, Bb, etc. (para. 28). The general point was made that categories Ab and Ac offered the greatest scope for improvement through the provisions of the improvement-grant legislation, the three C categories the least, and that Bb and Bc properties would need to be looked at more closely (para. 29). Property types were plotted, however, only on the basis of the 'block values', i.e. only on the basis of a scaling system in which the information relevant to improvement-grant policy was lost (paras. 30–2). The Millfield maps prepared by the planning department for the June exhibition showed the block analysis, three structural grades and four facilities grades of each cottage, but there was no information for either cottages or blocks based upon the combined structure/facilities system.

7 Although the secretary's minutes are much fuller than those of the planning department, covering 26 pages of typescript, as compared with the 7½ pages of the planning department's minutes (it was a committee meeting of the Millfield Residents' Association) a sentence follows in the planning department's minutes which the association's secretary appears to have missed, in spite of his notes being as far as possible verbatim. The planning department's minutes say, 'Although so far indicating "theoretical areas", it pinpointed areas in the town where conditions are suspect, *on a more sophisticated basis than has been previously tried in Sunderland or elsewhere.*'

# CHAPTER 12

# WERE THEY ACCURATE?

It was never doubted that in February and March 1968 Corporation officials had engaged in a door-to-door survey of Millfield, organized by the planning department. There were, however, many protesters who said that the planning department's data were erroneous with regard to their own dwelling. The East Millfield participation meetings were held in November and December 1968 and in February 1969, and at that time the information about the individual cottages had not been displayed. The maps showing this information were not seen until the exhibition in June 1969. Complaints in East Millfield were therefore based upon (1) anomalies (in Millfielders' eyes) in the lifing and clearance policies affecting different streets; (2) allegations that surveyors had not been to particular cottages; and (in the case of committee members of the residents' association) (3) errors in descriptions of the structure and amenities of their own cottages when these were read from the computer printouts. In West Millfield no participation meetings took place, but the details of each cottage were displayed shortly after the proposals were made known, and dissatisfaction with the descriptions was widespread, both with regard to cottages which people said were better and those which were worse than the planning department's classification. The complainants, that is, were not arguing in absolute terms. They were saying all the time, either, 'Look, my cottage has all the amenities, yet it is poor on the amenities map', or else they were saying, 'Look, the structural-condition map says that No. 8 is better than No. 9, yet No. 8 is a wreck and No. 9 is a nice little cottage.'

It would be difficult to exaggerate the anger and depth of

insult felt by many home-centred and house-proud residents when they discovered that their own cottages were described as poor. If they were poor by some obscurely comprehended national standard, something the experts knew all about but not them, they might have resigned themselves to the fact that what to them was a decent and comfortable home (one of 'the little palaces' of Millfield) was somewhat like a motor car which was unroadworthy; they could no longer use it. But very frequently there was a nearby cottage which to their untrained, inexpert eyes was in a deplorable condition (one of Millfield's 'rotten apples' which the Corporation would do nothing about because—it was widely believed—it was public policy to deteriorate the whole area) which the planning survey had classified as good. They were not now dealing with impalpable abstractions. Trained or not, expert or inexpert, they were being invited to disbelieve the evidence of their everyday experience.

In conversation with particular friends or relatives feelings were vehemently expressed. But dissenting residents were in a difficult position. They were very chary about going beyond such private manifestations of disbelief and rage. Their objections were based on local comparisons; on concrete knowledge and judgements of their neighbours' homes.

Out of kindly feelings many residents would not want to engage in any controversy which would involve them in invidious comparisons. The poorer properties which had received the accolade 'good' were most frequently the homes of old people who had not been able to do much about them. What an unneighbourly thing to do to old Mrs. So-and-so, to kick up a public row because her home had been too generously assessed!

Even where positive feelings for old friends and neighbours were not involved, in Millfield the negative sanctions against commenting on other people's domestic affairs, outside the delicate mechanisms of local gossip, were very strong and resulted in a virtual taboo on so heinous an offence against good community relations.

It would have been possible for the association or some other interested person or body to sample the gradings on the planning department's structure and amenities maps and conduct another survey to see to what extent the planning department's findings would be reproduced. The association considered this course of action. Because of the marked reluctance of the planning department in the East Millfield participation meetings to seriously consider any statement that the survey was defective, however, the association decided that any findings of their own which differed from those of the planning department would be dismissed as biased (although the association had nothing to gain by distortion; if the check proved the reliability of the planning department's findings, well and good).

Residents complain of errors as individuals. Each one can be separately excused as an exceptional case. Residents complain through their association. The complaint can be ignored as factitious.

The uselessness of producing contrary evidence which was backed by nothing but the statements of Millfielders themselves was well illustrated shortly after the June exhibition, when the secret 'suggestion box' report (the planning department's report to the July 1969 planning sub-committee) came into the possession of the association. One resident, a very able man, used one of the suggestion slips to complain that his cottage was classified as poor with regard to facilities. It was as fully equipped as he wanted it to be. If he wanted an indoor toilet he would have provided one; if he'd wanted a wash-hand basin instead of just using the kitchen sink, he could have seen to it. The planning department's observations to the committee on that particular suggestion-box contribution reads: 'Had only H/C to sink at time of survey; kitchen bath installed since but hot water carried to it. Has no W.H. basin and an outside W.C. 13 points —fair.' The cottage, that is, was upgraded from poor to fair because a bath had been added to its amenities.

Where it was appropriate, householders were approached by

the association to ask about the response to their own items. This particular resident said, with remarkable mildness, 'The bath has been there since I was a boy.' If the planning department stick to their story what can the resident do to prove his case? If his case is the true one, he is scarcely likely to have documentary evidence of the installation of a bath a quarter of a century ago. Unless a large-scale check was undertaken, it would necessarily remain anecdotal and inconclusive. So far as the general public is concerned the fictional, publicized Millfield of the planners is more real than the fragmented protests of householders.

Those difficulties existed with the identifiable, countable items such as baths and sinks. To contradict or comment in any meaningful way on the assessments of structure, to undertake a survey and produce a result which stated that so-and-so many of the planning department's poor cottages were judged by the residents' association, or by a surveyor or independent planner helping the association, as fair or good would be, experience said, a waste of effort.[1]

It will be remembered that the health department had abandoned the clearance inspections of the Alfred Street area because of 'the high degree of good maintenance'; it had reported that fact to the relevant Corporation committee on November 10th 1968. (See p. 108 above.) November 10th was four days before the first occasion on which the planning department's maps and booklet were presented to the association; the maps and booklet which described the Alfred Street area as the worst in East Millfield. (See Plate VIIIa.)

That would seem to indicate a discrepancy between the planning department's data and the data in possession of the health department. The health department said in its report, however, that the Alfred Street area 'could be taken at any time'. Its switch from Alfred Street to other areas does not necessarily constitute evidence, therefore, that Alfred Street was not as bad as the planning department said it was. While lifing or clearance announcements were only too tangible, the confirmation or refutation of the evidence upon which the proposals were based was difficult; the facts were so extraordinarily vague.

The bewildering changes in the plans between November 14th 1968 and February 7th 1969 also seemed to indicate that either the old facts or the new facts or both the old and the new facts about the structure and amenities of the areas concerned were dubious. Local opinion contradicted the planning department's assertion that Alfred Street was the worst street in the area, and their assertion that Granville Street was worse than Westbury Street. But what weight was 'local opinion' on matters such as these?

## Hard Evidence on the Accuracy of the Planning Department's Data

On September 10th 1969, a map was put on display at the Town Hall. It was of the Washington Street clearance area, part of West Millfield,[2] and it gave the results of the inspections carried out by the health department in preparation for the submission of a compulsory purchase order for the area.[3] The information given on this map constituted the first authoritative check on the planning department's findings in at least part of the Millfield area. The results shown on the health department's map could be compared with the results displayed a little over two months previously on the planning department's maps at the June exhibition.[4]

Of the four streets in the clearance area (including end properties sometimes numbered with cross streets), three contained houses classified as 'fit for human habitation' by the health department. If the planning department's data for the area had predictive value, then there ought to have been a high correlation between these fit properties and the properties described as good by the planning department with regard to structural condition and the possession of amenities.[5]

The comparison of the two sets of data for Potts Street, those of the health department and those of the planning department, are given in Table 5.

TABLE 5

ASSESSMENTS BY THE HEALTH DEPARTMENT
AND PLANNING DEPARTMENT COMPARED

| Health department fit properties | Planning department assessment of structural condition | Planning department assessment of amenities |
| :---: | :---: | :---: |
| a | Fair | Complete |
| b | POOR | POOR |
| c | Fair | Complete |
| d | POOR | POOR |
| e | Fair | Fair |
| f | POOR | Complete |
| g | Good | POOR |
| h | Fair | Fair |
| i | Fair | Fair |
| j | Good | Good |
| k | Fair | POOR |
| l | Unassessed | Unassessed |
| m | Unassessed | Unassessed |
| n | Unassessed | Unassessed |

In the eleven assessed cases, therefore, only one of the properties judged fit by the health department was graded as good on both structure and amenities by the planning department (j). Two were actually graded by the planning department as poor on both counts (b and d). Only two of the eleven fit houses were classified as structurally good by the planning department (g and j). Three were actually classified as structurally poor (b, d and f).

There were eighty-two properties in the Potts Street blocks. Seventy-seven of them were appraised in the planning department's survey. Eight were good or fair structurally and at the same time had complete, good or fair amenities. In that sense these eight were the best of the eighty or so houses. Yet only five of them were included in the eleven the health department classified as fit for human habitation. Among the top ten per cent of the properties, therefore, at the end of the range of measurement, where classification usually presents the fewest difficulties as compared with the middle ranges, the discrepancy between the two surveys is in excess of one case in three.

In the second of the three streets, Bell Street, the discrepancies are even wider. Of the eight properties classified as fit by the health department, *no fewer than six had been classified as structurally poor in the planning department's survey.* Only one of the five properties which the planning department had classified as structurally good was classified as fit by the health department.

Two of the poor properties in Bell Street which had been classified as fit by the health department were neighbours to properties which the planning department had shown as fair, but which the health department found unfit. That is, the slightly more hopeful compensation expectations of the owner of the property which the planning department had put on display as fair were not only disappointed; there was the added sense of arbitrariness resulting from the fact that poor property next door was fit while his own fair property was unfit.

This effect was rampant in the third street, north Washington Street. Of the four properties described by the planning department in their display of maps at the June exhibition as structurally poor but which were classified as fit by the health department for purposes of compulsory purchase compensation[6] all but one were next door to a planning department's fair house which the health department judged was unfit.

Although the survey has been referred to throughout as the planning department's survey, it ought to be borne in mind that to an extent which is still not clear personnel from the health department and possibly personnel from other departments (for example the Town Clerk's department) were also involved. It was, however, a survey organized, supervised and data-processed by the planning department. It is also necessary to say that the question of whose data are correct, or in which particular instances the planning department's or Medical Officer of Health's assessments are more accurate, on the basis of the above evidence is still open. All that can be said with certainty is that they both cannot be right. Somewhat less certainly, but still with a good deal of conviction, it can be asserted that the training of the health inspectors; the time spent over inspections for representation by the inspectors (as contrasted with the planning department's notorious '8,000 dwellings in one month'); and generally the much more lively prospect that the housing inspectors might face a challenge to their findings at a public inquiry ('I put my head on a chopping block') makes it likely that on the whole they would tend to produce more careful descriptions and assessments.

Certain blocks suggested by the planning department for clearance were suggested for clearance by the health department and clearance was desired also by a majority of the residents of the blocks.[7] The planning department cannot argue, however, that such examples of agreement on a block basis constitutes empirical support for the soundness of their findings, because, especially in the lifing streets, such agreement between the planning department and the people did not exist and there were no separate health department data for the lifing streets, which constituted by far the largest portion of the Millfield planning area.[8]

Logically, the argument is not available to the planning department at all. It might have maintained over the months of participation that it had a broad picture which was accurate and valid, the result not of evaluating individual properties but of obtaining general impressions of blocks, streets or localities. That is what it did in preparing the 1965–70 clearance programme and in the 'lifing' programmes of the development plan quinquennium by quinquennium. In the case of the 1967–

1969 plans for Millfield, however, the planning department insisted that the process had proceeded from the identification of individual properties to average block assessments. If the assessments of the individual properties were 'wrong',[9] therefore, then in terms of the planning department's own logic the block analysis must also have been wrong. Even when their own ultimate assessment of certain blocks agree with the ultimate assessment of the health department and/or local wish and opinion, the fact that the individual gradings are divergent means that logically the agreement for the average blocks is a random effect; the data collection, the coding and the analysis which preceded it were related to the result not as science, but by accident.

There is nothing shameful about survey errors. Errors are always being made. It is the main business of the competent researcher to remain alert to their discovery. Any experienced researcher knows that perusal of his work by colleagues means that more errors are uncovered, trivial and gross. What made participation in Millfield so difficult was the planners' determination to admit to no errors. They came perilously close to denying the possibility of errors.

Nor is there anything reprehensible about sketching in the broad contours of a problem before investing in detailed studies. Quite the contrary. Such a broad picture, however, must be preliminary not to policies which are publicly announced and which by their existence cause widespread and long-lasting distress, but ought to precede those very surveys which are revealed by the broad picture to be appropriate.

The planning bureaucracy in Sunderland (for this is obviously not a matter of personality, but of social organization and the constraints within which functionaries operate), would have had no case to answer, presumably, if all they had claimed for the Millfield survey was that they had completed a rough-and-ready questionnaire study and had rapidly and economically processed the results with no particular attention at that stage to statistical elegance. There might have been grumbles about the length of time the planning department had taken before doing the necessary first thing; but no one could complain about that belated step itself.

Instead, the administration insisted that full, detailed, accurate and sophisticated surveys had been completed, analysed, processed and used as a scientific basis for their proposals. Who would say now that the data were either correct or sensibly manipulated?

Advanced statistical manipulations all-embracing in their conception are now in vogue in the world of town planning. To apply quantitative techniques and to utilize to the full the electronic computer's capacity to add rapidly is necessary. An interest in econometrics and related disciplines and the search for statistical models of how towns and regions operate as wholes is to be welcomed. The existence and growth of such interests and efforts in some places, however, only throw into starker relief the weaknesses of statistical training and lack of awareness of elementary survey techniques among planners elsewhere (one cannot say only at the lower levels of the hierarchy), whose powers for good or evil, by what they do and by what they fail to do, by what they announce and by what they fail to announce, are formidable. When so much of practical planning takes place, and certainly when so many of its direct human consequences are felt in areas such as Millfield, it may be regarded as desirable that no planner should qualify unless he can demonstrate that he has some grasp of the difficulties of statistical analysis. There must be at least the realization (as Karl Popper is fond of saying) that 'you can't carry water in a sieve' and a feeling for what is a statistical sieve and what is not.

What is probably even more important is that planning schools and the general ethos of the profession should ensure that practitioners do not pick up from inadequate courses a cast of mind which has no other effect than to cripple their common sense or to regard statistical operations which are designed for no other purpose than those of simplicity and clarity as merely instruments with which they can conveniently lift their conjectures still further out of touch with the material facts. That the survey should have been presented as an adequate basis for policy was exasperating to the residents of Millfield. That it should have been presented with authority; that it should have been wrapped in the prestige of computer print-outs; and that comments should have been rebutted always with words of self-congratulation was symptomatic of the slackening in intellectual tone which afflicts a bureaucracy of consumption when so few of its activities in places like Millfield have had to be rationally defended in front of the people whose lives their decisions will most drastically affect.

The two issues which have arisen throughout this book arise again. First, would similar scrutiny elsewhere show that Millfield was an extremely favourable, unfavourable or average example of planners' practice? Only case studies elsewhere can produce an answer. Secondly, it is certain that in Millfield, and probable that to a greater or lesser extent in other places too, however dissatisfied in years of psychological discomfort and financial loss he might have felt about the evidence against him, i.e. the factual justification for the blight on his home, no ordinary member of the public in the ordinary course of planning procedures could possibly have ferreted through to the truth about the Millfield surveys.

Local public inquiries do not fulfil the function of bringing such grievances to light. This is evidenced by the secretary's experience at the local public inquiry into the local authority's application for the Washington Street compulsory purchase order, which was held on August 18th 1970. After two spontaneous interruptions from the public benches had been ruled out of order by the inspector, the secretary asked at what point the inspector would indicate in general or in individual cases what sort of statement he would permit. The inspector asked what statement was envisaged. The secretary outlined it in a few words, and the inspector signified that he would listen at a later stage in the proceedings. Some time later, while the local authority was making out its case, another resident interrupted, and was told by the inspector that he would not have his inquiry turned into a public meeting (of course, quite properly).

'It's our property and our homes', she replied. 'What's the use of coming to a meeting if you can't speak? It's our property and our homes, not yours.' (*Applause.*)

The inspector then said how he would conduct his inquiry so far as such contributions were concerned. 'I'm quite prepared to hear anyone, after the evidence', he said. 'I won't restrict anyone. This inquiry is held not for the public, but for objectors. After the objections, then anyone who wants to make a statement, when the local authority is finished, anyone will have the opportunity, provided it is relevant.'

The secretary was in due course invited to the chair from which witnesses had given evidence. He put the case that announcements of the intention to clear areas helped cause the state of affairs which in the end had justified clearance. It did not happen in all cases, but, he said, in the area under discussion it had certainly happened in Washington Street and Potts Street. Potts Street, in particular, had fallen into a very bad state in the past very few years. The same process was now well under way in the contiguous area of Hume Street, Booth Street and Pickard Street. The inspector listened attentively, interjecting comments in order to help the secretary make his case. He indicated that he would record them for the Minister. The secretary then endeavoured to make the crucial point that quite possibly the announcements of slum clearance which preceded the inspection by the health department were badly based empirically. There were discrepancies in the data. Actually, an objector at the enquiry was the owner of one of the health department's *fit* houses (objecting to its demolition) which had been graded as *poor* structurally and *poor* in amenities by the planning department. Even though this was the example taken

by the secretary, in order to heighten the relevance of his remarks to the particular public inquiry, the inspector courteously
disallowed the contribution, and the secretary was unable to
proceed any further with it. From the point of view of his
inquiry, the inspector was no doubt justified in refusing to
receive a statement on the general accuracy and applicability
of the pre-clearance surveys.

The *Sunderland Echo*, generally a useful journal of record,
reported the secretary's argument about deterioration, but
made no mention of what for the secretary was the main point,
the unsatisfactory factual basis of the original (and repeated)
blighting announcements.[10]

Whatever devices may prove desirable, therefore, in order to
amend public policy with regard to other features of the planning process, it seems conclusive that a system of checking
should be available to aggrieved citizens through a local ombudsman who would have the right to call in consultants suitably qualified in survey design and analysis, and who would
have the power and independence, the all-important institutional position, to investigate and remedy the sort of difficulty
which has been dealt with in the last two chapters.

Within the planning authority, no planner who undertakes a
survey of far-reaching importance to hundreds of families in a
community such as Millfield, should have less grasp of the
problems involved than would come from a workmanlike
familiarity with a standard statistical text.[11] The critic of the
planners' survey of 1968 need feel no obligation to re-write such
a text in order to avoid the accusation that he is being uncon-
structive. Discussions of survey technique have been available
for many years for any researcher who wishes to learn what he
might constructively do to produce good results or minimize
mistakes. All professions tend to suffer from lexicographical
kleptomania. Its symptoms are ransacking existing dictionaries
for blessing words over which exclusive rights of usage are then
proclaimed. The planners' urge to compile their private diction-

aries is particularly acute. For them it is 'positive' to persist in policies which cause distress and loss without any discernible benefits either immediately or in prospect. It is 'negative' to suggest, as Millfielders did, that such policies (for example, ill-based lifing programmes, especially those which never come to anything) which demonstrably do far more harm than good should be terminated until such time as there is a reasonable expectation of at least a small balance of benefit. Unless something better than the damaging policy is suggested, then the planners, in their own view, are justified in continuing with their own harmful, but positive plans. Similarly, criticism is constructive when and only in so far as it is accompanied by recommendations which will make few or no demands on planning talent, effort or stamina.

Town planning is, among other things, a communal arrangement for the rational rejuvenation of housing. In theory this necessitates the withdrawal of decision-making from less knowledgeable, self-directing families which are partial to their own interests to more knowledgeable, objective professionals who are unperturbed by any personal stake in the final results of their actions. The decisions of the trained expert are substituted for those of uncoordinated, emotionally involved and anxious householders in order to further either the felt or true interests of these householders more effectively and expeditiously. Alternatively the purpose is to meet common needs which may or may not be those of any particular body of householders. The touchstone is the improvement in opportunities for some determinate set of families to live a more satisfactory and rounded existence.

So far as knowledge is concerned, whatever is decided ultimately in the light of possibilities unknown to fragmented, anarchic and self-regarding families or out of consideration for general benefits in which these families may or may not be partakers, the basis of expert policy must be expertise. Were the claim to superior judgement based upon the notion of the town as an art form and planning policy as primarily and rightly the product of artistic intuition, the argument of this chapter would be redundant. The planning department's own claim to decision-making priority, however, was based not upon flair, but upon knowledge.

Yet the department took into consideration nothing but a miniscule corner of the matrix of relevant factors. Outside the confines of its questionnaire on structure and amenities there was a lack of interest in, for example, the other conditions of life and the aims of the families which would be affected by their decisions. When the limited information at their disposal proves itself imprecise, then the scientific basis of the planning department's decision-taking in Millfield is put in still greater doubt.[12]

So far as community interests are concerned, the planning department potentially commands a far wider conception of the cost-benefit balance of roads, industrial sites, the long-term implications of decay and renewal etc. Almost invariably these communal interests will require some sacrifices from certain sections of the population. On what basis of information may the planning department and the Council determine where these sacrifices shall lie? In practice they have had to rely on the volume of comment from the groups who stand to suffer or gain. As compared with other types of residential area, districts such as Millfield have proved somewhat more willing to refrain from collusive opposition or have kept their protests within the limits of decorum and manageability.

This book is basically an account of the way in which, when it became available in Millfield, it was not only under-utilized; by the treatment of the association's case in its report to the planning committee of August 27th 1969, this source of knowledge was systematically destroyed by the planning department.

The most striking (because the most useless) sacrifices were those which were extracted by—to use Matthew Arnold's phrase—the 'shadow durability' of ill-based planners' plans.

Clearance, improvement, and road plans which were no more than the crudest guesses were, throughout the period of their existence (which may have been a matter of months or of decades) imposed at considerable cost for Millfielders as permanent realities to which they had to adjust. This make-belief of dependability may have been expedient for the local planning department. It was of no conceivable benefit to anyone else.

NOTES

1 Such a structural survey had been undertaken in early 1968 on the association's behalf, as noted on p. 38 above, but the impact of the findings and references to them by members of the association was negligible. Late in 1969, in the week that his book *Urban Decay* was published, the free-lance planner Franklin Medhurst came to Millfield at the association's invitation. The association's idea was to have him conduct a survey of facilities and structure in the area, but even this was eventually judged to be too big an investment for a doubtful dividend.

2 The Washington Street clearance area is the western two-thirds of the Booth Street area, extensively discussed in *People and Planning*.

3 Map PO 46/2, entitled 'Map referred to in the Sunderland (Washington Street Area) Compulsory Purchase Order 1969'.

4 Maps PO 50/5/2 and 3.

5 See p. 137. The planning department's total of poor properties was almost the same as the number of properties originally in the 1965–70 clearance programme. Nearly all the properties in the 1965–70 programme had been estimated to be likely to be acquired at site value only, i.e. were unfit—actually 99 per cent in the case of the Washington Street area (*People and Planning*, p. 317). The correlation between the planners' good and the health department's fit houses ought, therefore, to have been very high indeed.

6 The Housing Act of 1969 changed the basis of compensation of unfit properties so that owner-occupiers receive market value whether their house is fit or unfit. Previously the owners of unfit houses received only the value of the site, and nothing for the property. That does not mean that to be classified as fit or unfit is no longer important from a financial point of view. The market value of an unfit house will not be the same as the market value of a fit house.

7  Bell Street and Rutland Street, in the Washington Street clearance area, are described in the author's *People and Planning* as 'slum enclaves of many years' standing', p. 193. Since 1965 the slum clearance proposals had very seriously deteriorated Potts Street and to a smaller extent north Washington Street, and there, too, by 1969 the attitude of the majority of residents had changed from one of wishing to stay to one of wishing to be rehoused. A description of this process of slum-clearance proposals acting as 'a self-fulfilling prophecy' can be seen, *ibid.*, pp. 350–1.

8  To the extent that inspectors from the health department themselves contributed to the planning department's Washington Street results to a greater extent than was the case in the lifing areas (see p. 127 above) discrepancies in the clearance areas are, of course, all the more damaging as evidence of inaccuracies in the lifing areas.

9  Whether objectively, or in the sense that they were not predictive of the results of authoritative consideration does not matter here; practically and humanly the results for Millfield were the same.

10  *Sunderland Echo*, August 18th 1970. In December 1971 the survey analysed in these chapters, the survey of all pre-1914 dwellings in Sunderland, was the evidence used to justify the extension and acceleration of the Council's slum-clearance programme, with the qualification that further deterioration had taken place. Booth Street and neighbouring streets were included in the accelerated programme. The very next meeting of the Council, in January 1972, was provided with the evidence for representing the Booth Street area to the Minister as a slum-clearance area. Of the seventeen properties classified as fit for human habitation in the evidence of January, one had been classified as having poor structure and fair facilities in the evidence of the previous month. Five of January's fit properties had been in the fair structure/poor facilities category in the evidence of the previous month. By contrast, of the four cottages in the highest grade of the survey, good structure/complete facilities, only two were fit and two were unfit. This applied also to the properties in the third of the twelve grades of the December evidence: half fit, half unfit. These facts were dealt with both in committee and Council by the author. Again, however, these points of central importance were quite absent from the press reports of the meetings: they were too statistical to be news. A case which is presented in figures, however dubious those figures may be, and indeed however simple, tends to protect the planning department from public scrutiny. In no time at all the figures can be made to appear so complicated that the media are unable to handle them.

11  For example, Paul F. Lazarsfeld and Morris Rosenberg (Eds.), *The*

*Language of Social Research: A Reader in the Methodology of Social Research*, Glencoe: The Free Press, 1955, or at least a 'cookbook' like Herbert Hyman's *Survey Design and Analysis: Principles, Cases and Procedures*, Glencoe: The Free Press, 1955.

12 For suggested reforms in planning education see Eric Reade, 'Sociology in Planning Education', *Official Architecture and Planning*, 34, 10, October 1971; see also D. M. Munchick, *Urban Renewal in Liverpool*, London: Bell, 1970.

PART FOUR

# INFORMATION CONTROL

# CHAPTER 13

# THE CONTROL OF INFORMATION
# IN EAST MILLFIELD

---

Whoever controls knowledge controls everything. Though knowledge is not in itself a guarantee of power a critic who can be deprived of the facts or even better fed with misinformation will surely be powerless. Eventually Millfield's own case was to some extent taken seriously outside Millfield, but only after intensive and repetitive newspaper, radio and television coverage. Rather than an absolute blockage, therefore, what needs to be described and explained are the barriers to communication Millfield had to surmount. Millfield's problem was largely due to the social complexity of urban civilization even within the confines of a single town—thousands of people pursuing hundreds of trades and professions, people with different tastes, levels of income and education and travelling diverse paths of life. All are subject to unresting assaults upon their attention. Why should anyone outside Millfield, including the members of the planning committee, invest more than a small fraction of their energy in the study of this particular issue—which in any case appeared to be unusually confusing and complicated? 'Nobody reads long letters.' Unfortunately Millfield's planning problems could not be presented in a three-line memo. Millfield was only noticed when, *and only for so long as* it kicked up a fuss. When Millfield made itself news and into a nine-days' wonder its position was improved and it was accorded political status— for, so to speak, nine days. At the level of local government, the barriers to communication were in part an aspect of the balance of power between councillor and appointed official: the readiness of the latter to get his way by defining criticism — even simple requests for information — as 'an attack on his professional integrity and competence', and the readiness of the former to allow him to do so.

That the planning department managed the content and flows of information is a motif which has run through the whole of the book. The present chapter and the next two chapters will deal directly with this problem, and a more appropriate introduction could not be found than a description of how, in its *Millfield: Progress Report*, it handled the complaints of the residents' association on this very point.

The letter from the Millfield Residents' Association to the Town Clerk's department dated August 9th 1969 pointed out that a full account of (1) participation meetings with the Corporation in East Millfield; (2) committee meetings in both East and West Millfield; (3) 'analyses of public meetings with full public reactions to and preparations for the Council's proposals'; as well as (4) interviews with individual householders, had all been sent to the local planning authority. The association was objecting to errors in the Town Clerk's department's previous letter and arguing that its mis-statements could not really be excused on the ground of lack of knowledge. The planning authority had the full record, 'conscientiously maintained by the association in the interests of participation', and the Town Clerk's department had received summaries of the record.

The extract from the letter selected for comment by the planning department as the 'point raised' by the association (item No. 20 of *Millfield: Progress Report*) reads in full, 'Summaries of the record have been transmitted to you. The full version is in possession of the planning authority . . . and sent to the chairman of the planning committee.' A bracketed addition says, 'This refers to the Millfield Residents' Association's transcript of their meetings with the Corporation.' The planning department's rejoinder for the benefit of the planning committee was that ' "the summaries of the record" have been sent only to the chairman, not the planning authority (in spite of his request)'. It is interesting to see that the words 'planning authority' were used as if they were synonymous with the department, to the exclusion of the elected representatives.

The ellipsis in the extract from the association's letter was supplied by the planning department. What the planning department's extract missed out was the list of the different types of record the association's information covered. To omit the list and then to 'explain' what the record was by mentioning only a single item listed was misleading. The planning department's comment was additionally misleading even in terms of its own misleading extract, for it said that only 'summaries of the record' had been sent to the planning authority. It is clear both in the original letter and in the extract that the planning authority had received full records, not summaries. It was the Town Clerk's department, not the planning authority, which received the summary of the record in the course of the July–August correspondence.

In this item No. 20 of *Millfield: Progress Report* there was, however, a deeper issue. The real purpose of item No. 20 was to deny that the association had a right to communicate through the chairman of the planning committee instead of through the planning department. 'Challenge' is probably the wrong word. It will become clear below (Chapter 16) that one of the department's major unreflective assumptions was that the association had no right to by-pass the officials and approach the elected side directly. They did not 'challenge' the association. They simply manifested their sense of having been affronted. Item No. 20 itself referred to other places in *Millfield: Progress Report* (items No. 1, 9 and 19) in which this same issue is raised in a more or less covert way. The planning department presented no case to show why information and requests should be channelled through the department. It was taken for granted.[1] The sole, repetitive argument was that the chairman of the planning committee had asked the association to communicate through the department and not through him.

Items No. 1, 9, 19 and 20 constitute what the planning committee was told about the issue. The true story of the struggle for the control of the data will be told under the various sub-headings below.


## The Interview with the Director of James A. Jobling

At the first participation meeting, on November 14th 1968, the planning department is recorded as advising the association 'to funnel its contacts with other committees of the Council through the planning committee'. This, the planning department said, would 'greatly facilitate matters for the association'. It would also lead to 'greater co-ordination of effort'. The association's minutes of the first meeting are not a transcript of a tape recording. They were based, however, on full notes taken at the meeting. The question of whether the association should send its information and requests through the department or through the Council had not been raised. That it might be raised had not been imagined by anyone on the Millfield association's committee. Its self-imposed task of keeping the record and transmitting it to the Corporation was conceived (at that first participation meeting) as an act of virtue and an unmistakable token of the association's intention to participate with energy and responsibility. It is therefore interesting that the words actually recorded, sent to the Council, almost certainly seen by the planning department, approved by the association, and challenged by no one, were 'planning committee' and not 'planning department'.

The question of the control of the data soon arose, however, though not yet in the form of Council versus planning department. The proposals of November 14th 1968 included, it will be remembered, the clearance of sixty-nine cottages in the Alfred Street area. The cleared site would be used for industrial purposes. At one place the proposals booklet said that this was 'the logical use'. Elsewhere it said bluntly, 'Clearance for industrial expansion.'[2] In the Cirencester Street area, 110 cottages would receive standard grants for improvements 'until a final date to be fixed when Pyrex expansion programme is known'.[3] The booklet says of the Cirencester Street area, 'Likely to be ultimately required for industrial expansion for Pyrex.'

At the meeting of November 14th 1968, at a public meeting on November 19th 1968 and at a subsequent committee meeting of the association, Pyrex's part in these plans was resented. Why should scores of families in the Cirencester Street area be on tenterhooks for another ten or fifteen years because of Pyrex's uncertain intentions? Why should they bear so large a psychic burden because of the possible future activities of an industrial firm in the neighbourhood? It was known that in a coal-exporting and ship-building town up the coast, Blyth, a similar residential area had been rendered derelict by the county planning authority's support of the 'expansion plans' of the shipyard. Before the shipyard was able to expand, it closed down. Not only had an unfair share of the risks that accompany the rewards of private industry been borne by the Blyth families in Dock Street and Burt Street; they had been borne to no purpose.

In both the Cirencester Street area and the Alfred Street area it was argued that if James A. Jobling wanted the land, or wanted to lay some claim to the land for its possible future use, then it ought to demonstrate how much it wanted to obtain it, as against how much the families wanted to stay, by negotiating with the residents. As it was, Pyrex was getting all the benefits of a lien on the land, and the residents were getting all the blows. That, briefly, was Millfield's reaction to this aspect of the November 1968 proposals, though put at greater length by the residents and with greater agitation.

The association therefore decided to discuss the matter with Pyrex, and a deputation was received by the executive engineering director. Because of the contents of the proposals' booklet, it was naturally expected by the association that Pyrex was ready to expand in the Alfred Street area, and had conducted some sort of negotiations with the Corporation or otherwise let it be known that it was interested in the Cirencester Street area.[4]

Not according to Pyrex. Jobling's made it clear to the deputation that although the Alfred Street area in its view would 'prove useful if it became available', probably for landscaping the entrance to the works, none of the land in the vicinity could be described as 'vital'. The executive director mentioned in particular the unfavourable impression made on visitors by Alfred Street's backlanes. Unfortunately the visitors he happened to mention were German businessmen. This had an adverse effect on some members of the deputation. They had fought two world wars, they said, to protect their homes from the Germans. If the Germans didn't like the look of their backlanes now, they regretted it, but they weren't prepared to accept that as good grounds for coercive demolition. The naïvety of such feelings in a man whose living-room wall still holds the Royal Artillery certificate showing the honours of Cambrai and Mons is something to scoff at now; old, forgotten, far-off things, and battles long ago. But they cannot be dealt with, except cruelly, by pretending they do not exist.

The firm would be reluctant to say that it would have any interest in the Cirencester Street area even if it were to become available due to slum clearance. In these streets, therefore, Pyrex completely repudiated the suggestion that families should live in insecurity, be deprived of improvement grants, and feel the acid of planning blight because 'Pyrex wanted the land'.[5]

This experience, immediately following the first participation meeting, shook the association's belief in the trustworthiness of the planning department's statements. If it had been made— and it had not—a query would have been placed over any suggestion that the department was the funnel through which information should pass to and from other participants in the planning process.

## *The Interpretation of the Association's Resolutions*

The association in its letter of August 9th 1969 had reacted against the Town Clerk's department's statement (August 5th) that 'it was apparent from the beginning that total agreement would not necessarily be reached and there was bound to be at some stage and on some points a clash of interests'.

The impossibility of total agreement and the clash of interests which at some stage were bound to arise were complex issues, the association said. 'What degree of agreement is possible, and the point at which any of the multitude of interests involved may clash are questions, however, which have not emerged.' In East Millfield the plans of February 7th were not a response to the resolutions of the Millfield Residents' Association in any intelligible sense. For that reason among others, the association concluded, 'where agreement lies and where interests clash is necessarily not known'.

How did the planning department deal with this point in its report of August 27th 1969? In its item No. 23 it roughly quoted the association's letter of August 9th: 'The East Millfield plans of February 7th were not a response to the first twenty-two resolutions of the Millfield Residents' Association in any intelligible sense.' The planning department retorted (for the benefit of the planning committee) that the accusation of the Millfield Residents' Association was, quite simply, stupid:

> The plans were not, of course, a complete response and never could be, but the statement is fatuous. The amended clearance/improvement proposals of February 7th *were* a response to the resolutions referred to.

The planning department, therefore, as recipient of the association's resolutions—as the channel of communications— had considered them in some undisclosed way and 'responded' to them to an unknown extent. That was the planning department's statement to the planning committee on the question of the association's dissatisfaction with the way in which its first set of resolutions had been treated — of the effect of Millfield's resolutions of December 13th 1968 on the plans of November 14th 1968 which had emerged as the amended plans of February 7th 1969.

The association's letter of July 30th had dealt with another question, namely, the effect of its second set of resolutions, those of February 14th 1969, on the amended plans of February 7th:

> Plan PO 50/4/2 was shown to the association on February 7th 1969. On February 14th 1969 the association commented on that plan in the form of nine resolutions. No further word reached the association about Plan PO 50/4/2 until it was seen *virtually unaltered* at the June exhibition. The association therefore has no idea whether Plan PO 50/4/2 is now the plan which the planning department intends to present to the Council (and that the recommendations of the association therefore had absolutely no effect whatsoever), or whether, after so long a delay, the association's resolutions have not been considered yet.

The letter therefore clearly said that the association did not know whether the resolutions of February 14th had or had not any effect. If the planning department intended to present the plans of February 7th to the Council *then* the resolutions of February 14th would have had absolutely no effect on them whatsoever. This was the central point of the correspondence, to receive an answer to this question of the status of the plans of February 7th.

In item No. 12 of *Millfield: Progress Report*, the planning department selected the sentence in brackets in the above letter as the 'point raised' by the association. '*Item No. 12: Point raised:* The Millfield Residents' Association have not been informed of what happened to the East Millfield plans, "and the recommendations of the association had absolutely no effect whatsoever on them".' The planning department's answer then devastatingly demolished with a mis-statement an argument which the association had not put.

'The point about the recommendations of the Millfield Residents' Association is blatantly not true. The changes made in the clearance/improvement programme had regard to the Millfield Residents' Association resolutions.'

What was the truth? On December 13th 1968 the association presented twenty-one resolutions to the Corporation.[6] On February 7th 1969 the Corporation returned to Millfield and presented revised plans. Some of the revisions, the new booklet stated (and this was repeated at the meeting by the planning department), were the planning authority's direct response to and in agreement with the resolutions of December 13th. According to the booklet and the planning department at the meeting, the association's counter-proposals had asked the Corporation (1) to 'delay clearance of Alfred Street area'; and (2) for 'immediate clearance of the area between Deptford Road and Ravensworth Street in one phase'.[7] The booklet adduced other reasons for the revisions, including the claim that 'the information collected by the survey of the town as a whole had been analysed and a more accurate picture of priorities had been obtained'. That is, the proposals of November 14th 1968 had been devised before the pre-1914 survey had been processed. Now that it had been processed, three months later, revisions in the plans were necessary.[8] 'Furthermore', the booklet said, 'following the public meetings which have been held a review of the phasing ... has been undertaken to see how far the wishes of the residents can be met.' (The only record of the public meetings was that maintained by the association and sent to the Council. This is one of the many statements by the planning department which show that they were shown the association's documents even though they were sent to the Council—with the request that they be circulated to all relevant sections of the authority.)

What the association's resolutions of December 13th 1968 said was that if Alfred Street was wanted by Jobling's, then let the residents be adequately paid for their homes and land. Its resolutions said that any clearance, 'in view of the long-drawn-out agony of Millfield' should be undertaken *immediately*, including any clearance *eventually undertaken* in the Deptford Road and Hedley Street area. The planning department's startling misreading of the association's proposals dealt a second blow to its credibility as the best communication channel.

The other resolutions of the association were presented on February 14th 1969 in response to the Corporation's revised plans of February 7th. The association did not know the Corporation's decision about the plans of February 7th until six months later, August 14th. In fact the words 'by 1978' were removed from the phasing of the Ravensworth/Millburn Street area. That was all. The deletion of the word 'by', and the date '1978' was the only alteration made in the plans of February 7th. The alteration had nothing whatsoever to do with any of the resolutions of the Millfield Residents' Association. It will be remembered, in addition, that in June 1970 an enquirer about the date of demolition in Millburn Street was told—'by 1978'. (Page 70.) Even that single change, apparently, had been quietly cancelled.

Such were the facts which lay behind the Millfield Residents' Associations' statement to the Town Clerk that it did not know whether its resolutions of February 14th had had any effect, the planning department's report that the Millfield Residents' Association had complained that they had had no effect whatsoever, and its denunciation of such a notion as 'blatantly untrue'. It is difficult to see how the Millfield Residents' Association's case and the facts of the matter could have been more thoroughly misrepresented.

NOTES

1 It is not taken for granted by all departments, even within the same local authority. A few weeks after the planning department's report was presented to the planning committee, the housing department was taking it for granted that information and requests should be channelled

through elected representatives and not through officials. See 'Housing Complaints', *Sunderland Echo*, October 8th 1969. The *Echo* is in any case a reliable newspaper when party politics are not directly involved, but the accuracy of this report was checked with the reporter concerned.

2 *Millfield: Clearance and Improvement*, November 1968, p. 5 and Table A.

3 The glassworks of James A. Jobling and Co. Ltd. (Pyrex) borders East Millfield on the west and north.

4 'Pyrex need additional land for expansion and have indicated that the most suitable area is eastwards.' *op. cit.*, p. 3; 'immediate expansion by Pyrex', *ibid.*, p. 5.

5 Minutes of meeting held in the board room, Leopold Street, November 25th 1968, and confirmed by Pyrex in their letter NWV/JL dated November 28th 1968.

6 Because of an early typing error, these twenty-one resolutions were generally referred to wrongly as the first twenty-two resolutions.

7 *Millfield Clearance and Improvement: Amended Proposals*, February 1969, p. 1.

8 At the previous meetings, those of November 14th and December 13th 1968, the planning department did not claim that the survey of all pre-1914 houses had been analysed. The Council, however, had made that claim at these previous meetings, and had not been contradicted or corrected.

# CHAPTER 14

# THE CONTROL OF INFORMATION
# IN WEST MILLFIELD

---

*The Suggestion Box*

The association had been assured that in West Millfield participation would take place on the model of the East Millfield
meetings. (See p. 198.) This was never spelled out by the Corporation. Participation 'as in East Millfield' was referred to only
in a general way. The pattern of East Millfield participation
had been, specifically, meetings between the residents' committee and senior officials of the Corporation, appointed and
elected, within the structure of an association committee
meeting. Public meetings had then been organized by the association, not by the Corporation, to publicize the plans and
obtain reactions to them.

When the parish priest in West Millfield, co-chairman of the
association with the vicar of East Millfield, told the committee of
the Millfield Residents' Association at its meeting of June 10th
1969 that the planning department had been in touch with him
and he had arranged with them that the exhibition dates should
be June 23rd–27th the discussion (to which the secretary made
no contribution) turned to the provision of a 'suggestion box'.

'Could we have a suggestion box?', Mrs. Callum asked.

'That is a good idea.'

'Will they let us?'

Mrs. Callum exclaimed, 'Make it part of our bargain!'

By this she meant that as the Corporation was using the
church hall and the association was advertising and supporting
the exhibition a suggestion box should be a *quid pro quo*. The

association's posters for the exhibition were displayed in several shops and in the windows of dozens of cottages.

'We could ask in the name of participation.'

'Perhaps we couldn't do it if it's their exhibition.'

'Perhaps we could ask them to provide the suggestion box.'

'We wouldn't see the suggestions at all!', a member said scornfully. 'The only suggestions we would see would be the ones they wanted us to see.'

A fairly strong feeling that a suggestion box ought to be available at the exhibition was combined with a unanimous view that the planning department could not be trusted to use its contents fairly. It was therefore agreed that a suggestion box should be allowed if and only if the association inspected its contents at the end of each day's proceedings.

The association took the view that so long as it had the promise of participation on the East Millfield model, for its own purposes the suggestion box was redundant; it was infinitely inferior as a method of clarification and interrogation. The association also took the view that the Corporation would not get very much out of it, because so few people used such a device; but for what good it might do the Corporation and those who deposited suggestion slips then there was no possible objection. Positively, if there was some hitherto unheard opinion contrary to the policy of the Millfield Residents' Association, the association certainly did not want to swamp it with its own suggestion slips.

The association's letter of July 29th 1969 raised the suggestion-box issue only as one example of the extent to which the association had been left in the dark. It pointed out that as a matter of policy the suggestion box had not been used by the association. It had been deliberately left to the unorganized public. The association's view that suggestion boxes were very poor instruments of public participation had been confirmed in the event. The letter quoted the very small numbers of comments which had been received on various tense and turbulent issues, such as the road proposals (six comments) and the proposals to demolish the Booth Street area by 1972 (five comments). (The association itself had as many committee members in the Booth Street area as there were suggestions about the area from the unorganized public. In the case of the areas affected by the road proposals the association's committee membership in such areas far exceeded the number of comments in the box.)

The letter demonstrated both (i) that the suggestion box had showed its weaknesses and (ii) that the association, though it had decided not to prepare an organized response through it, had in no way discouraged its use by individual members of the committee. In fact, three of the six comments on the roads had come from committee members in their private capacity and a petition deposited in the box had been organized by committee members in their private capacity. None of the five committee members from the Booth Street area had contributed or encouraged anyone to contribute, but it was interesting to see, the letter said, that two of the five contributions were the result of residents approaching the wife of the secretary for assistance in filling out the suggestion slips. (Actually, they were two of the secretary's aunts.)

All this, in the letter of July 29th, was related to the fact that on July 23rd the health and planning sub-committee had been called upon to discuss important matters affecting Millfielders—yet the only 'Millfielder opinion' with which they were supplied by the planning department had been the contents of this suggestion box. 'The association was not informed that the health and planning sub-committee would be dealing with Millfield on July 23rd. (Obviously, as the association has never been informed about anything officially and in writing)', the letter said. Yet it was against the background of these suggestion-box comments only that the compulsory purchase order for the Washington Street area was discussed, and decisions reached on the fate of south Washington Street.

The association had started the correspondence with the

Town Clerk's department to discover the date of the promised participation meeting and to find out about the status of the plans. These were the matters that the association had been told would be put to the planning committee at its meeting of August 27th. The suggestion box was a minor point, which came up late in the correspondence and was presented as 'only one example' of the general problem of lack of information.

No fewer than five of the twenty-six items of *Millfield: Progress Report*, however, deal directly with this portion of this one letter. The five items were slanted by the planning department to the discredit of the association. From the point of view of understanding the behaviour of a planning agency they are, therefore, of some importance.

1. Item No. 2 of the planning department's document gives as the association's point the protest that it had not been informed that the contents of the suggestion box were to be discussed on July 23rd by the health and planning sub-committee. The planning department's reply to the association's objections to the way in which the contents of the suggestions box had been used reads as follows:

> The comments as a whole were not then discussed (except in so far as they related to the Washington Street area). But in any case it is surely up to the committee to decide what it considers and when without the approval of the association. In this case they seem to have boycotted the suggestion box, yet are concerned with what is in it.

The letter of July 29th, basically, had not been a protest against not being informed that the health and planning sub-committee was to discuss the contents of the suggestion box. That was mentioned only in passing. The association's objection was to decisions about the Washington Street clearance area and the exclusion from it of the south end of Washington Street being reached on the basis *solely* of the suggestion box, without the association's promised contribution at a participation meeting being considered. The above comment by the planning department corrects the association on some supposed assertion

that the comments as a whole had been discussed, when in truth
the letter from the association had mentioned only this very
issue—the Washington Street area. More importantly, the
planning department's comment suggested that the association
was encroaching on the authority of the health and planning
sub-committee. An essential piece of information was missing:
the association's clearly expressed policy in relation to the
suggestion box. The planning department said that it seemed
to have been boycotted by the association. The letter of July
29th had gone into a great deal of detail, on the contrary, to
show that, although the association had decided not to arrange
any collective response through the suggestion box, it had been
used by committee members as individuals. There were not only
no grounds for the planning department's statement that the
association seemed to have 'boycotted' the suggestion box. The
letter of July 29th, which the planning department was quoting,
comprehensively disproved the accusation.[1]

2. Let us now look at item No. 3 of *Millfield: Progress Report*,
which also deals with the suggestion box. It quotes the association's letter: 'This suggestion box has been deliberately left to
the "unorganized public" and as a matter of policy not used by
the association.' The planning department's comment had no
bearing whatsoever on any policy issue, or on any matter the
planning committee of August 27th 1969 would be called upon
to decide (unless it was the decision, implicit or announced, that
participation with the Millfield Residents' Association was no
longer desirable). The planning department's comment was:
'This is presumably why there were not as many comments as
we had hoped for.' The planning department was therefore
asserting that the suggestion box, in so far as it failed, failed
because of the association's lack of co-operation. Yet, again, the
letter of July 29th which is the subject of its attack contains
the details which refute this. As a matter of fact, eight out of the
thirty-nine persons using the box (20 per cent) were members of
the committee of the Millfield Residents' Association or their

relatives. Sixty out of the ninety-three names in the box (i.e. including the petitions) were there directly as the result of committee members or their relatives (65 per cent).

3. Item No. 4 ridicules the point in the association's letter that suggestion boxes were very poor instruments of public participation. The association's principal concern was less their intrinsic demerits than their inferiority to participation meetings of the East Millfield type. As the association's letter of July 29th showed, not only was this a poor mode of communication; it had been used by very few people. In Sunderland's own recent experience, the suggestion box which had been used in connection with the whole of the north-west quarter of Sunderland (pre-1967 boundaries) brought forward a total of only thirty-six observations.[2] By the time the planning department made the above comment, the failure of the suggestion box in Millfield (though certainly much less of a failure than it had been in north-west Sunderland) was known. The department chose to ignore all the empirical evidence before its own eyes, and in its report to the planning committee refute the association with the authority of Skeffington.

4. Item No. 5: 'In the whole of the Booth Street clearance area only five comments were made. (We know this from *unofficial* sources closely connected with the planning department).' The planning department's answer was:

> There is an implication that someone has 'leaked' the comments. The committee can draw their own conclusions as to this implication and the way it is made. The document contains names and addresses of people making comments. It will be even more difficult in future to carry out public participation if people with views cannot be assured of anonymity when they desire it. If in these circumstances the document were to be released, it was certainly for the committee to decide.

The committee was once again told that the association was threatening its prerogative. Without the crucial assumption that there was a prior agreement that the association should see the contents of the suggestion box at the end of each day, the members of the planning committee were entitled to feel angry. The question of the confidentiality of committee proceedings was one on which the association was clearly in a vulnerable position. Without some expectation of privacy and loyalty to the norms of committee privilege (within which limits is a practical question) much valuable work would be rendered socially impossible. In this particular instance two factors were relevant to the use by the association of the analysis of the suggestion-box slips, which the planning department had wished to categorize as confidential. First, Millfielders believed that the association was to inspect the contents of the suggestion box. Members of the association, at least, saw that as a reason for feeling it was safe to use the device, rather than a reason for avoiding it. Secondly, the Corporation had agreed that the association should see the contents. The Millfield Residents' Association felt little compunction in violating the planning department's 'confidentiality' when it believed it had been so coolly duped.

5. The last of the five items in *Millfield: Progress Report* which dealt with the suggestion box was item No. 6. 'It was against the background of these suggestion-box comments only that the compulsory purchase order for the Washington Street area was discussed.' The planning department's refutation of this point read: 'This is not true, both the health committee and the planning and health sub-committee were made aware of the survey in south Washington Street carried out by the Millfield Residents' Association.' What was this 'survey of south Washington Street carried out by the Millfield Residents' Association'?

The association had always been careful to keep its participation undertaking within bounds of practicality. It would render, as one of its resolutions stated, 'such assistance as may be possible within its limited resources of time, finance and manpower'. As part of its realistic approach, it had insisted that surveys were a skilled job which could not be usefully undertaken by amateurs—whether amateurs in the streets or amateurs in the planning department. On May 27th 1969, however, the Council came to a meeting of the association's committee and asked for a response to the Washington Street area clearance proposals. In a letter to the *Sunderland Echo*, which was published on May 30th 1969, the secretary announced the invitation, and gave the address of street representatives who could be contacted by Washington Street families.

The street representative for the south end of Washington Street expressed the desire to carry out a questionnaire survey there. The committee encouraged him to do this, but made it clear that it was to be his own survey, not the association's. It was agreed, as a symbol of co-operativeness and good will, that the association would pass the schedules on to the Corporation. This the association did, deliberately refraining from analysing the results. A copy of the completed questionnaires was retained by the secretary.

The letter of July 30th gave the facts about this survey, which the planning department in its item No. 6 used to contradict the association's statement that 'only the suggestion-box comments' had been used as the basis of policy at the mid-July planning sub-committee. The association's letter of July 30th read in part:

> I should like to give one more specific example from many scores of examples, and perhaps an answer to this specific problem may be forthcoming. The association was aware that the south end of Washington Street, containing thirty-nine dwellings, had been inspected by the health department. Twenty-two of the dwellings had been judged 'fit' and seventeen 'unfit'. . . . On May 27th, however, the Council appeared uninvited and unannounced (but none the less welcome) at a committee meeting of the Millfield Residents' Association purely in order to offer the Millfield Residents' Association a chance to express the opinion of the people in south Washington Street on whether or not they *wanted* to be cleared. The association's committee was assured in unambiguous terms that what the majority wanted would be implemented. The survey questionnaires from south Washington Street (the work of a Millfield Residents' Association street representative) were sent to the planning

authority. Nothing more has been heard of them. (As usual, no acknowledgement of their receipt has been forthcoming.) Unofficially, one of the joint chairmen of the Millfield Residents' Association, the parish priest, has been told that as a majority of the houses are 'fit', the 'popularity' or otherwise of clearance is irrelevant. That is understandable. But what then was the status of the original proposal for south Washington Street —i.e. what effect *could* the opinions, the work, the evidence, of the Millfield Residents' Association have in altering the proposals?

The subsequent history of the survey of the south end of Washington Street is not something which finds an appropriate place in this book.[3] Here it is enough to say that the planning department's item No. 6 takes on an entirely different complexion when viewed against this section of the relevant correspondence. It chose to ignore it in its report to the planning committee.

### The Proposals Map for West Millfield

The proposals for West Millfield were announced by the planning department and the Council to the public meeting held on March 31st 1969. Subsequently, now much strengthened in West Millfield and with the parish priest as co-chairman, the association called its own public meeting for April 14th. The attendance at the association's meeting far exceeded the attendance at the Corporation's meeting in the same hall.

In preparation for the meeting the local authority was asked if the most important map from the March 31st presentation, that which showed the proposals, could be made available for the meeting of April 14th. Another chance to see and discuss the map, the association said, would help prepare the public for more effective and knowledgeable comment when the coming exhibition was staged. When the public meeting was held, however, the parish priest had to tell the audience that 'the planning department would not release this map No. 8 which we asked for—the planning committee would not do this— unless they had one of their own men to explain it'.[4] Why the map could not have come with such a man was neither accounted for nor explained away.

The planning department's first and only letter, of July 28th 1969, which was its response to the association's decision to correspond through the Town Clerk's department (crudely, it can be supposed that the planning department received a rocket) offered to let the association have this map and others. The association said in its reply of July 30th that these presumably included the map which had been asked for in the letter of April 11th, and had been verbally refused on the grounds that to supply them would be contrary to planning committee policy. The association would be extremely grateful if the Town Clerk's department would have the maps sent as quickly as could be arranged.

This matter was dealt with in *Millfield: Progress Report* under item No. 10. 'Two maps dealing with proposals (a) clearance and improvements and (b) roads, were asked for in a letter dated April 11th 1969. On April 14th there was a verbal refusal.' The planning department, in its comment on this, said that it had received no such letter. The planning department added, 'In any case the exhibition material was still being prepared at this time [April 11th–14th] and was not completed until mid-June.' It is true that the exhibition material was still being prepared: material *additional to* that shown on March 31st. But the implication of that statement, that the maps of March 31st could not be made available because they were being altered, was false. The maps of March 31st were displayed in June unaltered in every particular.

On August 8th the association again wrote to the Town Clerk's department. 'You will remember', the secretary said, 'that certain maps were exhibited by the planning authority on March 31st 1969.' Because of their small scale they had been inappropriate for display from the platform and members of the audience were unable to see how the proposals affected their particular property. The letter then repeated the story of the verbal refusal by the planning authority of the request contained in the letter of April 11th.

> After your intervention the planning authority wrote on July 28th offering the maps to the association. The offer was accepted, through you, by return of post. I regret to say that I am still without the maps in question. The committee had expected that at its meeting of August 7th several outstanding details could have been cleared up—more than four months after the original display. . . . This is, of course much more than four months after the maps were originally promised 'by the Autumn of 1968'.

A letter was written on August 9th. It was not sent until August 13th, in the hope that the promised maps would after all appear and a postscript explained this to the Town Clerk. On August 14th the maps were delivered by hand to the association's secretary. They were immediately put on display in the window of Mrs. Callum's newspaper shop in West Millfield and shortly afterwards in Carpenter's window in East Millfield. 'Now They All Know',[5] said the headline in the *Sunderland Echo*. They did not know before because the planning department was the controller of the channels of information and the manager of information flows. Neither the letter of August 9th, nor any part of this account, was referred to at all by the planning department's report of August 27th. Perhaps the planning department was not shown the letter; it certainly knew the rest.

### NOTES

1 Indeed, so far as its committee was concerned, the association had not refrained unilaterally from organizing a response through the suggestion box. It was clearly understood that the Council had been asked to allow the parish priest to see the contents at the end of the day, 'as part of the bargain' (see above p. 178). Many members of the committee, at least, believed that the request had been granted, and that the agreement had been broken—the box had been permitted, but then the contents had not been shown. The planning department, however, might have been unaware of this particular aspect of the affair.

2 See County Borough of Sunderland, *Southwick: A Plan for the Future*, 1967, and *Sunderland Echo*, October 27th 1967.

3 It is dealt with at length in the *Sunderland Echo*, August 21st 1970 — briefly, this sore thumb was to remain as an exclusion from the clearance area, to every Millfielder's intense puzzlement. The street representative's survey, which the secretary subsequently analysed, showed that just half wanted clearance and half did not in a 75 per cent response. Conclusively and unequivocally, however, the vast majority wanted the south end of Washington Street to be cleared if the surrounding streets were to be cleared — which was what was going to happen. Yet this survey was always presented by the planning department as 'the association's survey' which proved that the residents of the south end of Washington Street were opposed to clearance.

4 Tape transcript of public meeting of April 14th 1969.

5 That is, the people who had not attended the public meeting or the exhibition, as well as those who had.

# CHAPTER 15

# DELIBERATE
# MISUNDERSTANDINGS

As one writes about planning in Millfield, one is depressed by
something Melville wrote in *Moby Dick*. 'To produce a mighty
book, you must choose a mighty theme. No great and enduring
volume can be written on the flea, though many there be who
have tried it.' Yet it is necessary that someone, some time, should
make public the treatment Millfielders experienced at the
hands of the experts, which was certainly not less squalid than
the housing and environmental conditions which were supposed
to be the experts' concern. Two further examples of juggling
with data will be given.

### The Status of the Plans

This subject has been dealt with substantively in Chapters 4
and 5. Here, quite shortly, is the way in which it was reported to
the planning committee. When this question of the status of the
plans was put to the Town Clerk's department in the correspondence of July 1969, the planning department's reply to the
association had said that the status of the plans was exactly the
same 'as the first proposals prepared in relation to Millfield
(the area east of the Durham railway)'. The association replied
that it was scarcely a clarification of the status of the plans for
West Millfield to say that it was the same as the plans for East
Millfield. 'It is precisely because the association has been left so
completely in the dark about the East Millfield plans that the
question arose. On February 14th 1969 the association com-

mented on that plan in the form of nine resolutions. No further word reached the association until it was seen virtually unaltered at the June exhibition. The association has therefore no idea whether it is now the plan which the planning department intends to present to the Council or whether after so long a delay the association's resolutions have not been considered yet.' The status of the plans was a question of tremendous importance, the association repeated. 'It is clearly not answered by the planning department in its letter of July 28th 1969.'

The issue raised by the association appeared in *Millfield: Progress Report* in this form: 'In particular we are puzzled by the planning department's reference to the East Millfield plans as a model of the status of the West Millfield plans.' The planning department's comment was: 'This must be a deliberate misunderstanding as the letter to which this is a reply clearly stated "the proposals have exactly the same status as the *first* proposals prepared in relation to East Millfield".'

On this central issue, therefore, the planning committee had only a few words of the association's query to consider. That is the main point. But look at this silly detail.

The planning department's letter of July 28th 1969 had said that the proposals for West Millfield were exactly the same 'as the first proposals prepared in relation to Millfield (the area east of the Durham railway)'. The Millfield Residents' Association had taken that to mean that the status of the proposals for West Millfield (the second set of proposals for Millfield) were the same as those for East Millfield (the first set of proposals for Millfield). That seems to be the most reasonable interpretation of what is admittedly, once it is pointed out, an ambiguous statement. The reply from the Millfield Residents' Association was not ambiguous. It made it quite clear that it objected to being told that the West Millfield proposals had the same status as the *current*, i.e. February 7th, East Millfield proposals, the status of which was a parallel mystery. The planning department, which presumably realized that the association had chosen the wrong meaning, could therefore have written to point out this error.

The planning department chose instead to use this item, not to help the planning committee to reach the only relevant decision, namely, in what light should the proposals be viewed by the participants, but to discredit the association in its absence and without its knowledge. The association had deliberately misunderstood, the planning department said, something which was perfectly clear. The planning department demonstrated to the planning committee this perfect clarity by quoting what it had written to the association: except that the quotation was not what had been written, but a new version. The point was then indeed clear, for by rewording—changing the actual quotation 'the first proposals prepared in relation to Millfield (the area east of the Durham railway)' to 'the *first* proposals prepared in relation to East Millfield'—and by added and unacknowledged stress on the word 'first' all ambiguity had been removed, so that it could only mean, not East Millfield = 'first', West Millfield = 'second', but East Millfield proposals of November 14th 1968 = 'first', East Millfield proposals of February 7th 1969 = 'second'. What chance was there that anyone on the planning committee would see that the accusation levelled at the residents' association of *deliberately* misunderstanding the correspondence was based on fabricated evidence?

### The Date of the Promised Participation Meeting

The meeting of February 14th 1969 with the representatives of the Corporation (the chairman of the planning committee, the chief planning officer, his deputy, other senior members of the planning department and others) ended with the association's committee trying to arrange another participation meeting or, alternatively, to discover what form future participation in planning would take.

A resolution submitted by the Millfield Residents' Association had asked the Corporation to invite representatives of the residents' association to meetings of the borough planning committee when items affecting the objectives of the association were under discussion. The local authority representative said it was not legally possible to allow this and there were practical difficulties. In any case it was better for the Millfield Residents' Association not to attend planning committee meetings, even if it had been possible to allow such a thing. 'Well, this method of doing is, where you are talking to us, and we will represent you, and put your representations to the committee is, I think, a better way, because it gives a better feeling of what you mean. You know, you may say something, and you may say something different to the secretary and we've got to take this into account.'

The chairman of the association was very sceptical of this point. 'The only thing that we can say here', he said, 'in the light of what has gone before, and what follows now in the next resolution is this: That what is reported as coming from the Millfield Residents' Association committee be as printed. Then, I think, it is not simply a matter of the feeling attached to it. It is something which has been thought out and approved by the committee.'

This having been said, the discussion was taken no further, and so far as the association could tell at that juncture, participation would not, nor could it, include any invitation to a planning committee meeting.

The association's committee therefore turned to the question of how, as the next step in participation, the resolutions should be put to the planning committee. The secretary of the association said that the resolutions—as the final resolution, resolution No. 31, itself stated—had been carefully thought out after many public and committee meetings. 'They may be wrong and badly phrased and wrong in law and might strike some experts as being amusing even', he said. 'But nevertheless the point, that all of these things have to be considered, stands.' Resolution

No. 31 had been included after the meeting of February 7th, the meeting at which the planners had represented the plans as being in accordance with the earlier resolutions of the Millfield Residents' Association—when in truth the changes, as we have seen, bore no relation to the association's resolutions whatsoever.

The Council's answer was that it would be impossible to present the whole document (the thirty-one resolutions) to the planning committee: 'I would not dare put this fully as it is now to my committee. They might have twenty or thirty items on their agenda before this, and I would get hounded out if I were to do this. But you can rest assured that your points will be put as the points you've put them—without all the long wording on. But the points will be put. I cannot promise, and I will not promise to put it verbatim to the committee. It is more than I would expect.'

The vicar asked that, even if the resolutions were presented in a condensed form, the Corporation should nevertheless circulate the full version in writing to members of the planning committee.

The planning department answered that the committee members were 'very adamant' that they did not want 'a lot of paper'. 'They feel strongly about this. As I see it, the document will be précised, Mr. Chairman, for the committee. I think that is the only practical way of doing it.'

This insistence on the part of both the elected and appointed sides of the local planning authority led the secretary and the chairman of the association to point out that if the Corporation would not circulate the document, the association was free to do so.

> *Secretary:* Well, of course, there is nothing to stop the Millfield Residents' Association itself circularizing planning committee members themselves. Councillors. Or M.P.s. And so forth. That's . . .
>
> *Chairman of the association:* Yes. That's entirely up to us.
>
> *Planning department:* Well, that's sort of assuming that we're going to mis-précis it or something. I mean . . . I suppose that is your privilege if you want to do it.

*Secretary:* It is not 'a privilege'. It is a duty—and a right.

*Council:* Well, I hate this attitude you're taking. There is no such thing as 'a right'. We have been very co-operative here, and trying to help you. We come here with the goodest of intentions. We haven't come here to stop you doing anything you want to do. We are trying to help you in any way we can, and we want to put your points of view to the Corporation. That is what participation is. But there are limits to what we can do with the committee. I'm only the chairman and I have to be careful that I don't upset the committee, because they've got feelings as well. I know for a fact: you can circularize numerous papers to the committee and I doubt if they read *any* of them.

The future of participation in East Millfield was left rather vague. All that was said was that the Council was sure that the Millfield Residents' Association would 'take well account of itself in the future'. In the last moments of the meeting the chairman of the association tried to obtain some statement about the next steps, 'Well, anyway, ladies and gentlemen, we must conclude there. But . . . I should have asked before: Is this being put before the next planning committee?'

*Planning department:* I think so, yes. If we can get the stuff ready and done, I think we will.

*Chairman of the association:* That's your intention? [Inaudible section on tape-recording.] Well, it will be put to the press?

*Planning department:* Well, the press will be at the meeting.

*Council:* We can't control the press, unfortunately. They print what they consider is news value.

*Chairman of the association:* And then it would be discussed at the next Council meeting?

*Council:* It will have to go to other committees as well.

*Planning department:* I can't think it will go to the next Council meeting.

*Council:* It will have to go to the housing committee, to the finance committee.

*Chairman of the association:* Secondly, then, I should have apologized for the coldness here . . . Anyway, thank you very much. Thank you.

That was the end of the meeting of February 14th 1969. No new date of participation in East Millfield had been promised. The only indication of what would be happening was in these final remarks: after being considered by the planning committee

(perhaps, but not certainly, at the end of February) the proposals for Millfield would be passed to other committees of the
Council before coming to the Council itself for decision.

The meeting of February 14th 1969, however, was more
explicit about West Millfield. A member of the committee who
lived in West Millfield raised the subject, and the Council
answered in some detail:

> 'We are going to have a big meeting and give all the information that
> we can possibly get—every bit of information that we can possibly get
> we'll present to a general meeting. We will then obtain a room of large
> size and mount an exhibition, and in this exhibition I'm hoping that
> everyone will be able to contribute. There'll be questions which they can
> answer, and the sort of thing they want to see—and this sort of thing.
> And we can get an analysis from everyone who is interested enough to
> go to the exhibition. And then we will assimilate all this.'

From the point of view of the association's query in its first
letter to the Town Clerk's department (July 21st 1969), and
subsequent correspondence dealing with 'the date of the
participation meeting in West Millfield' the next words are
particularly significant:

> 'And then we shall assimilate all this. *And then we will start our meeting
> and get down to the brass tacks of the things*, having told everyone . . . So
> we'll start that way, and then we'll break into this when the stuff we
> receive from the exhibition is assimilated (we can get a line of thought
> there).' (Emphasis added.)

*Participation in East Millfield subsequent to the meeting of February
14th*: In view of what had been said about attendance at
meetings of the planning committee, it came as a pleasant
surprise to the association to see the newspaper report of the
February meeting of the planning committee. The association
would not meet the planning committee itself. But (according
to the newspaper report) after the Millfield clearance and
improvement proposals had been submitted to the health and
housing committees, a special meeting would be called and
representatives of the residents' association would be asked to

attend and give their views on the new plan.[1] It was known, therefore (if the newspaper report was accurate), that the deliberations of February 14th and the planning committee's decisions of February 26th were being passed through other committees, and there was therefore no particular anxiety about the inevitable and expected pause in participation in East Millfield.

As a matter of fact, the residents' association would have been even more surprised if they had been told what the planning committee's decision precisely was. In spite of all that had been said by the Corporation's representatives at the meeting of February 14th, the planning committee's resolution 7 (f) of February 26th stated that 'at the appropriate time, representatives of the Millfield Residents' Association be invited to a special meeting *of this committee*, the date and time of which to be fixed by the Council in conjunction with the Town Clerk's department'. (Emphasis added.) The association, however, did not see this document until eight months later, August 15th 1969.[2] At the time of writing (May 1971) East Millfield still awaits a summons to the meeting referred to in that two-year-old minute. The people of Millfield, distressed by uncertainty, could well say, not once but twice, 'The harvest is past, the summer is ended, and we are not saved.'

*The date of participation in West Millfield:* In West Millfield the first two of the three steps in the sequence outlined by the Council were taken. A public meeting was held by the Corporation (that of March 31st 1969). At the public meeting the intention to abide by the promised sequence was reiterated in the first words of the Council: 'In our wisdom we decided that it was best to have first hand information, to take your views and if possible to help you where we can. You can get information from the wrong places too much. You may not agree, but you know where you stand. Then there will be an exhibition. We will get your views. (The people on the other side of the bridge have had experience of this.) Hope you'll form some sort of committee, perhaps one from each street, so that we can get your ideas—meet from time to time for discussion. And I mean discussion. This is the second attempt. The first attempt was the other side of the bridge.'

In a letter from the chairman of the planning committee dated April 27th 1969 (shortly before he stood for re-election in one of the Millfield wards), this sequence was once again outlined:

> On completion of the municipal elections, an exhibition will be mounted . . . On completion of the exhibition we will start a dialogue with the Millfield Residents' Association and anyone else who wishes to put their ideas and suggestions forward, but I must admit that I personally would much prefer them to come through the Millfield Residents' Association committee. . . .

These statements, verbally and in writing, were a repetition of what had been said on February 14th.[3] The planning department itself put in writing the three-step programme of 'public meeting—exhibition—participation meetings with the association'. In answer to a private inquiry from a West Millfield member of the committee about her own street, the planning department, in a letter dated April 28th 1969, i.e. after the public meeting in West Millfield on March 31st but before the exhibition, wrote:

> I understand that the Medical Officer of Health has indicated that properties in this street may have a life of 25 years (in the case of number 11) or 30 years (in the case of number 35). This position will of course be regularized during public participation meetings which will be held in West Millfield, *as was the case with the Millfield area west* [obviously a mistake: read 'east'] *of the Durham railway line*.[4] (Emphasis added.)

This was the background to the association's letter to the Town Clerk's department, dated July 21st, which asked for information on when participation would begin in West Millfield.

> In connection with the plans for West Millfield, the association assisted the Council in every way it could in publicizing the public

meeting of March 31st and in publicizing and in other ways helping with the exhibition in June. In spite of diligent enquiries over many months the association has been unable to discover when 'participation in planning' will commence. This is a matter of crucial importance to everyone in Millfield. As the association has always stressed, no one in the area itself benefits from delays. 'Blight' has already bitten deeply into the area as a result of the plans to date, and bites deeper with every additional day of uncertainty. We therefore ask you, as a matter of great urgency, to expedite, in so far as it is within your power to do so, the Millfield plans and, as part of this, the consultation with the public which has been promised for so long, but which is still awaited.

Not only did the history of the affair make it impossible for this to mean, 'When does participation, including a public meeting and an exhibition begin?' and that it could only mean 'When would the third step in participation in the sense of the promised participation meetings of the East Millfield type begin?'; the letter itself was also quite explicit on this point.

When it was known that the Town Clerk's department was to put the letter of July 21st to the planning committee the point that it was referring to the third step in the promised participation was repeated by the association in its letter of July 25th.

> The Millfield Residents' Association had been under the impression, I think understandably, that ... questions raised in our letter of July 21st could be answered immediately—that there had simply been an administrative delay or an oversight in letting us know things which had been long since settled. ... As our original letter is to be put to the planning committee, I should like the opportunity to clarify one or two points which were only implicitly dealt with in the letter of July 21st. ... Our second request is simply to be informed of the date, or at least to be given some indication of the date, on which it is intended that 'public participation in planning'—*following on the June exhibition* ... —should take place. (Emphasis added.)

The planning department's reply to these letters simply confirmed that among knowledgeable people this was the unambiguous understanding. The same sequence of (1) public meeting; (2) exhibition; (3) meeting(s) with the association, was once again clearly enunciated by the officials. As announced by the Council at the public meeting, the views of residents would be elicited at an exhibition, followed by discussions with the Millfield Residents' Association.[5]

Two sentences in the letter of July 28th (as it subsequently transpired) introduced a new element into the discussion. They read: 'So far I have received no communication from you regarding the plans, only two letters regarding their status. I can hardly believe that this is the only comment of the Millfield Residents' Association?' This was the first hint that the 'explanation' for the delay in the participation meetings was to be that the planning department were awaiting a response from the Millfield Residents' Association to the plans displayed at the exhibition. The hint in the letter of July 28th was so obscure, however, that it was not recognized as such at the time.

On August 5th 1969, the Town Clerk's department wrote again to the association. The letter dealt in part with the question of the date of the participation meeting. It contained the amazing assertion that the participation meetings in question *had already been held*. 'The Council and the officials concerned have certainly during the past months', the Town Clerk's department wrote, 'got round a table to discuss matters with your association.' The letter concluded by stating that 'every attempt seems to have been made to involve the residents in Town Planning'.

Here we have again, then, a comparatively trivial matter. How was it dealt with by the planning department in its report to the planning committee of August 27th 1969, the committee meeting which was to have given the association an answer to its query about the date of the participation meeting?

Other chapters have shown that on questions of importance such as lifing, demolition and the status of the plans the planning department told the planning committee next to nothing. By contrast, of the twenty-six items extracted from the association's correspondence and presented to the planning committee as points raised by the association no fewer than six were on this subject. The subject was also given special attention in the planning department's introductory remarks to *Millfield: Progress Report*. The planning department itself, that is, did not treat it as a minor question, but went to great lengths, not to give or get a simple answer on the date, but to demonstrate the association's errors and, in fact, to argue that Millfield had had all the participation it was going to get.

The planning department was able to show the planning committee beyond a shadow of a doubt that on the question of the date of the participation meeting the Millfield Residents' Association was aggressive, tendentious and obstructive, and that participation was a failure. It was able to do this by misquoting and quoting out of context. It then demolished its fabricated evidence with invented history. For the planning department everything depended upon its success in violating the old rule, *audi alteram partem*. Whether the above items constituted a fair case against Millfield's request for the participation date can be judged by the reader by looking up the full evidence—items 17, 18, 21, 22, 25 and 26 of *Millfield: Progress Report* (Appendix III), the Millfield Residents' Association's correspondence (Appendix I) and the actual course of the events with which they deal.[6]

## NOTES

1 *Sunderland Echo*, February 27th 1969.

2 It was sent under cover of the Town Clerk's letter dated August 14th 1969, and was one of the fruits of corresponding with the Town Clerk's department instead of with the local planning authority.

3 These are examples, not an exhaustive account. On May 27th 1969, the Council emphasized the importance of East Millfield type meetings, which were to be undertaken in West Millfield, in perhaps the most extreme form ever: After the exhibition the 'real' participation would begin, in meetings which would include the planning department. 'I'm only the chairman', he said to the committee of the Millfield Residents' Association. 'The officials will give the *right* answers.'

4 L 2C (140)—GP.

5 PO 50—GP, dated July 28th 1969.

6 The letter which the association was originally told would be put to the planning committee, that of July 21st 1969, was not analysed in *Millfield: Progress Report*. The analysis in the report begins with the association's letter of July 29th.

# CHAPTER 16

# OFFICIAL CHANNELS

In its answer to the association's complaints about lack of communication the planning department said that it had received no letter asking for the map of the West Millfield proposals. That was an ambiguous statement. Its ambiguity lies at the heart of the matter. Who should control the channels of communication? Was comment and information to pass only through the planning department? Was the association entitled to decide for itself whether communications should be routed through the planning department or through the Council?

The planning department knew that the association habitually prepared detailed records of participation meetings and sent them to the Council. The records were intended to acquaint the Corporation with the views of the committee members of the association, who were also representatives of their streets. These were the purposes of the records. The light they happen to shed on the ideas, activities and values of the planning bureaucracy became a secondary use of the material. The planning department saw and physically handled these accounts at participation meetings. The department also knew that the association prepared and transmitted to the Council accounts and analyses of public meetings, again to give the Corporation the most direct and clearest possible picture of the state of local opinion. In the early days of participation, letters to the Council were the subject of messages over the telephone from the planning department to the vicar. The single letter received from the planning department referred to a letter dated July 16th which had been addressed to the chairman of the planning committee. At the meeting of October 6th 1969 the planning department carried a file, it said, containing dozens of letters from the association to the Council; and the planning department perhaps referred to others in its possession but which did not happen to be in the file. At the public inquiry into the Washington Street compulsory purchase order, held on August 18th 1970, the Town Clerk's deputy was able at a moment's notice to produce a letter from the secretary of the association to the Council dated June 6th 1969. The planning department could therefore truly say that it did not 'receive' letters from the association (and may indeed not have seen the letter of April 11th at all, that will never now be discovered). But there is ample evidence that in general letters and all other documents were seen by and were well known to it.

The association's records were constantly mentioned by the residents' committee from the very first participation meeting in November 1968. There was no attempt by the planning department to keep equivalent records. Before October 6th 1969 neither pen nor pencil, literally, was ever put to paper by the planning department within sight of the secretary at any meeting he attended. There was no reciprocation from the planning department beyond its attendance at the participation meetings (with maps, booklets on two occasions and its verbal contributions). The public meeting of March 31st and the June exhibition, before they were finally held, were the subjects of frequent unanswered requests for some indication of possible dates. No attention was paid, beyond vague verbal undertakings, to the association's repeatedly expressed wishes that the committee should be kept informed; nor was any attention paid to the resolution specifically dealing with this.

Communication, that is, was almost entirely a one-way affair. Information, fact and opinion flowed from Millfield to the Corporation. Hardly anything came from the other direction. Millfielders were dissatisfied with this state of affairs; so was the secretary. For many months they all accepted this as more or less normal, however, and did what they could with the information which was squeezed out of the reticent department.

It was not until May 1969, eighteen months after the formation of the residents' association, that channelling of information through the Council instead of through the planning department was raised at all as an issue. On May 27th the chairman of the planning committee arrived at a committee meeting of the association. He was accompanied by his vice-chairman. His main purpose in attending without waiting for an invitation was connected with the Washington Street clearance. At the meeting he raised another matter, that of the pattern of communication between the association and the Corporation. Instead of communicating through him, he asked the association to write and send its documents to the planning department. In that way, he said, the association could be sure of a direct reply. He also said that the officials could give the right answers. He was only the chairman of the planning committee.

The request from the chairman of the planning committee did not appear to be highly charged. He had simply asked the association if it would write through the officials. It was just one comment among hundreds, on the tape and in the transcripts. The reply was given by the secretary. He did not agree with the suggestion. Nor did he agree with the chairman of the planning committee's own estimation of his position *vis-à-vis* the appointed officials. He said he was sorry to hear the phrase 'only' used by the chairman, with the implication that the officials occupied a superordinate position. That was not so. The chairman was the man with the power, not the official. We were ruled not by the officials, the secretary said, but 'by people we ourselves elected'. If they did not do their job, ordinary people could vote them out. 'That was the meaning of democracy.' The secretary concluded by saying that he would continue to write to the elected representative, who was chairman of the planning committee — who was actually the secretary's and West Millfield's newly re-elected own local councillor—one of three Conservatives.[1]

No vote was taken after the secretary's statement. What he said appeared to be accepted by everyone present, including the chairman and vice-chairman of the planning committee. It was a straightforward committee situation, where a suggestion had been made that policy should be altered in some way, and it had failed to carry conviction. It was taken for granted, and very little additional thought was given to it, that the custom — scarcely even the policy — of transacting business through the chairman of the planning committee should continue. It was the chairman of the planning committee's own request which stimulated the secretary's contribution, the upshot of which was, that if the question were to be raised in the future, then there were, after all, reasonably important policy considerations connected with it.

In the planning department's letter of July 28th there was an extremely obscure hint, unnoticed at the time, that the valid reason for the pattern of one-way communication was the association's error of channelling its letters and other material through the chairman of the planning committee. It was not until the document *Millfield: Progress Report* was seen that the full enormity of its deviation from bureaucratic rectitude was brought home to the association.

The letter of July 29th from the Millfield Residents' Association had pointed out that the association's rule until July 1969 had been quiet consultation, only occasionally broken ('on extreme occasions') by letters to the *Sunderland Echo*. The association had sent 'many, many letters' to the planning authority; it had sent hundreds of pages of accounts of participation between Corporation representatives and the association; it had sent accounts of public meetings; it had sent detailed resolutions.

Not a word of this appears in item No. 1 of *Millfield: Progress Report*, in which the planning department dealt with this point. The association, the planning department told the planning committee, was complaining of 'lack of communication' and 'one-way communication'. The planning department's reply was that four meetings had been held with the association and two proposals' booklets had been circulated. After mentioning the participation meetings and the booklets the planning department said, 'the last letter addressed to an officer of the Corporation before the present series (commencing July 21st 1969) was in April 1968'. That was the reason for lack of communication. That was the planning department's case. The fact that there had been a large body of information flowing from the association to the Corporation was completely hidden. In its place there was the criticism that letters had not been addressed to officers. The false impression was also conveyed that no letters at all had been received from the association since April 1968.

The association's letter of July 29th had also said that its patience had at last broken so far as its hitherto exemplary forebearance was concerned. It was only when it had decided that it was fruitless to pursue matters any longer through the local planning authority, when it had decided to make the record public, that a letter had been received for the first time from the planning department. This was on the very day of the publication of the Skeffington report (July 28th 1969). In its item No. 9 of *Millfield: Progress Report* the planning department repeated two points it had made elsewhere: (1) that there were no previous letters to the council officers to reply to; and (2) that the chairman of the planning committee had asked the association to address its comments to the planning department. There was nothing to indicate that there were in truth dozens of previous letters to reply to, well-known to the department, and that the words 'to council officers' were crucial; there was no indication that the problem antedated the chairman of the planning committee's request by many months; nor was there any indication that when the chairman's request had been heard it had been turned down on grounds he was unable to, or at any rate did not, challenge.

*Millfield: Progress Report* of August 27th 1969 was not seen until six or seven weeks later, October 9th. But at the meeting of September 15th at the Town Hall between the planning sub-committee and the representatives of the Millfield Residents' Association the planning department's insistence that communications should come through the department and not through the chairman of the planning committee was very strong, and this insistence was shared by the elected officials who were present. Still not knowing on September 15th the full extent of its delinquency, the association as a gesture of conciliation decided at the next meeting of its committee that in future a copy of all material sent to the chairman should be sent also directly to the planning department. The secretary's letter of September 18th therefore said: 'As I understand you have some difficulty in passing the correspondence of the Millfield Residents' Association to the officers you would want to instruct to deal with it, I am glad to attend to this matter myself in future, and copies of this letter will therefore be circulated appropriately.'

On October 6th, three days before the report was leaked, three planning officers came to Millfield and held what turned out to be the final meeting with the association. The meeting was a result of promises made at the Town Hall by the planning department, that it would come and show that it had 'done its homework' in Millfield. (The other and more important promise of at least one further participation meeting on the East Millfield pattern was not kept.) There can be no doubt from the evidence of that meeting that for the planning department the association's 'misrouting' of the data was the source of bitter feeling among planning officers against the association. As the meeting was being closed the secretary spoke. He had not otherwise contributed except for a single sentence at the beginning. He corrected a mistake made in the course of the meeting by the planning department. He then added that he was pleased to observe that the planning department had for the first time made notes. In response the planning department repeated some of its fallacies about the association's policies (delay in the clearance of Alfred Street etc.) and the secretary said, 'We have written and written and written on all these matters, and the same mis-statements come back from you— verbally.' The planning department had never dealt with any point in writing, he said, except in its letter of July 28th 1969.

The planning department replied, with some sharpness, that the secretary had only himself to blame for that. 'I have his file here. There are dozens of them you know, and I must say they aren't helpful at all.'

'And I haven't an acknowledgement of one of them.'

'Look, the proper and decent thing to do is to write to the planning department. The chairman has asked you to write through the paid officials.'

The secretary's reply was a repetition of the point made many times before, verbally, in letters, and in minutes, that although the chairman had made that request, 'The fact that the chairman asked on May 27th this year doesn't explain on those grounds why we received no acknowledgement and no reply in the eighteen months and more before that.' But what was more important, the secretary said, the chairman had received his answer. 'It was no. It is in the minutes, which you have.' The chairman had been told this, and there the matter lay. 'And now I am scolded by you for not doing as the chairman told me!'

'Any normal, decent transaction should be done through the officials. The officials advise on policy. The councillors generally, not always but generally, accept the advice of the officials. Not always, but 99 per cent of the time. In any normal organization, any normal, decent transaction goes through the officials. If you are dealing with an industrial firm, you don't write to the managing director. You go through the officials.'

The planning department's frequent use of the word 'decent' throughout this contribution was very striking, as is its assimilation of local government to industrial practice, i.e. of democratic to non-democratic institutional arrangements.

'You've made grave mistakes!', the planning department continued.

The planning department then said that there was a technical reason why it was inappropriate to write to the chairman of the planning committee. 'If everybody wrote to the chairman, he'd have hundreds of letters. He would have to be paid for the job.'

'We've never at any time said the chairman had to write the answers', the secretary replied. 'But we have written to him as the elected representative. He is the man who is accountable to us. What you say about "hundreds of letters" applies equally well to the chief planning officer himself. He passes them on, but within his province he takes responsibility for what is written. That is the administrative arrangement. The democratic arrangement is for the responsibility, the power and the accountability to rest with the elected representative.'

Once again the planning department used the word 'decent'. 'The chairman asked you to write to him. The right and decent thing to do is to write to the officials. You have only yourself to blame.'

The vicar intervened to say that it had been a committee decision to do it through the chairman of the planning committee. 'You see we thought this was the best thing to do.'

The secretary said: 'The chairman of the planning committee has no right to say, "Because you have written directly to me, your letters will not be answered, and your written submissions and information will be ignored".'

'I have all the letters here. Look at this one!', the planning department expostulated. ' "Thank you for your letter of September 29th 1969, written, I assume, in accordance with your directions by the chief planning officer, who has delegated the writing of the actual letter to the officer initialling himself X.Y." And then it goes on. That is no way to address the chairman of the planning committee! It just antagonizes all of us. It antagonizes all the staff that have to deal with this.'

By the time that letter had come to be written, it was clear that none of the July–August correspondence, about which there had been such a turmoil, was going to be answered, and it was obvious that the Corporation intended to terminate participation. It was not known at the time the letter was written, and it was not known at the time of this exchange between the secretary and the planning department, that the explanation for the end of participation was the planning department's fatal document, *Millfield: Progress Report*, which had been presented to the planning committee more than a month previously, but was not passed to the association until October 9th, three days after the meeting of October 6th.

'Officials have no entitlement to be antagonistic towards individual citizens who transact business with them. I am entitled to be irritated and annoyed as a private citizen. Officials aren't!', the secretary said.[2] 'What is wrong with that paragraph? Don't just quote it as an obvious example of bad behaviour and in a tone of voice and with gestures which say it is heinous. I'll tell you why I did say it. It is because you have made an issue of who the Millfield Residents' Association may or may not deal with in the Corporation.'

'We have not made an issue of it! It is you who've made an issue of it!', the planning department retorted.

'You have all the correspondence and reports there. None of it has been dealt with. Why not? You say, "Because we don't like the fact that it's gone to the chairman of the planning committee". It's no good you saying the chairman told me not to do it through him. He didn't say that until May 27th, and that doesn't explain the eighteen months before that. It's fantastic. The correspondence is all in the file there . . .'

'It's not all in the file. Not all the letters are here. You have dogmatically insisted in going through . . .'

'That doesn't explain why the letters that are in that file

aren't answered and the reports acknowledged and dealt with. If the chairman had some letters that he has not passed to you, is that my neglect and oversight? By what constitutional doctrine or practice may a chairman say, "Do it through the officials, or it won't be done at all?" ', the secretary said. 'What a waste of the time of the association! All that work ignored! By what constitutional right may officials receive letters and documents and turn round and say, "It's your fault we haven't dealt with them"? We've done it through the chairman. That is what democracy is about . . .'

At this point there was a laugh from the planning department.

The secretary continued: 'That is what democracy is about, having people accountable and responsible for what is said and done. The officials are not accountable in this sense. The officials do not have authority in this sense.'

'The planning officer is responsible for planning in the town', the planning department said. 'I appeal to the vicar! As a reasonable and sensible man!'

'There were questions we wanted answering', the vicar replied. 'What we are doing could then become much more relevant. Answers have not been given. We had a jolly good meeting on September 15th. We went there to get answers to our letters. It was a jolly good meeting, I'm not saying that. But we still haven't got answers to those questions. The feeling was that we were being pushed to one side.'

The vicar pointed out that all the letters from the association (which at this juncture the planning department knew they had assassinated, but the residents' association did not) had been written with the approval of the co-chairmen—the vicar himself and the parish priest of West Millfield.

'Written with the approval of the joint chairmen!', the planning department cried. 'I am *very* surprised to be told that.'

The meeting was closed. That was the end of participation in Millfield. Three days later, *Millfield: Progress Report* was leaked and the association found out why and how it had been ended.

Millfield benefited greatly from the termination of public participation in planning. In the year that followed October 6th 1969 the association used the ordinary machinery of the local councillor and the press to disseminate fact and opinion.

By July 2nd 1970 a *Sunderland Echo* editorial was able to say that 'seldom has any local issue so dominated the correspondence and news columns of this newspaper as have the proposals and counter-proposals for the revitalization of Millfield during the past few years'. Nearly all the publicity was concentrated in the months which had elapsed since October 6th 1969. The Millfield Tip, derelict since the turn of the century,[3] received in August 1970 its first tons of soil. New street lighting was installed. The Corporation was forced by public pressure to devise for the first time a scheme which allowed householders to take advantage of borrowing power granted to the Corporation by the central government for mortgage loans for the purpose of house purchase and improvement.[4] The success of Millfielders in attending to their hitherto notoriously neglected interests led other disprivileged groups to turn to the association for assistance, and as a result the Corporation was obliged to improve substantially its provisions for the community care of mentally and physically handicapped children whose disability placed them outside the care of the education authority.[5]

Streets, which the planning department had sworn had 'maximum' lives of under fifteen years, were in late 1970 being allocated, in practice, grants which the Corporation was associating with lives of twenty and thirty years. In such streets there was a slow but eventually steep rise in morale, and extensive improvements proceeded apace. Improvements were, however, the result of knowledge spread by gossip about which particular individual had received a grant for a fifteen-year life or a thirty-year life. The association's desire that an authoritative announcement should be made so that Millfielders would know how they stood was never met.

The final word of the case study must lie, however, with the planners, first in terms of a particular project of theirs, secondly in terms of their summation of the Millfield project. In June 1970 the families in the ninety-three cottages in the Close Street and Westbury Street area received a letter from the Town Clerk's department. This was an area which in the plan of 1965 had been authoritatively and publicly approved for demolition by 1968–9, but which had been given a reprieve—not authoritatively announced—until 'at least 1990' in the plans of problematical status of November 1968 and February 1969. The letter said that a pilot scheme was to be launched to see whether the cottages in the area which were already (the letter said) 'likely to last for at least fifteen years', could be given lives of at least thirty years, dating from the early 1970s. [6]

By the middle of 1970 Millfield had had its share of publicity. The victories of the Millfield Residents' Association had lowered the temperature in many streets. The united mass of opposition in Millfield to the planners had somewhat shaken loose into diverse component interests, some of which had now been met. But the planners, of course, remained—and they remained incorrigible. No pilot scheme was launched in Close Street, Hadrian Street and Westbury Street. Instead, the planners carried out a survey to determine whether or not the streets ought to be designated a General Improvement Area under the provisions of the Housing Act of 1969. In a thirteen-page document the planners proved that they ought not to be so designated, and that therefore the plan of February 7th 1969 should stand. One of the main arguments *against* giving the streets a longer life was the *high* level of satisfaction among the residents with their unimproved homes. Out of eighty-four families, only fourteen were dissatisfied. [7] A second major reason was that the low cost of providing a new dwelling of similar type and size (one side of Close Street is composed of **two**-storey houses, the rest are terraced bungalows) would be, so the planners said, £2,500. [8] This figure was given at a time

when actually the average cost of new dwellings built by
Councils was almost twice that. The calculation ignored,
furthermore, the completely different financial impact of Close
Street residents improving and maintaining their own homes
out of current income or small loans and grants as compared
with the fact that when interest had been paid on a Council
dwelling costing £5,000 the total cost was £29,730.[9]

The third of the three main reasons for depriving the Close
Street area of the status of a thirty-year-plus life was the high
cost of improvements. The repairs and facilities required were
listed in the planners' report. They included the following
requirements: 88·5 per cent of the back yards to be hacked up
and relaid with concrete; 82·8 per cent of the dwellings to
have ceilings replastered; 95·4 per cent to have the cooker
repositioned; 93·1 per cent to have new electrical installation,
and so forth.[10] Not surprisingly, long lists of such arbitrary
requirements when costed meant that in Close Street, a sound
and solid area of contented, home-centred families, the cost of
improvements ran up to £890 a house (average £459) and the
cost of repairs up to an additional £739 a house (average
£269).[11]

In June 1971 the planning department issued what it called
an information booklet. In it, the department included a
paragraph on the problems raised by the participation provisions of the Planning Act of 1968. Its only experience of participation between 1968 and 1971 had been in Millfield.

> While planning is concerned with shaping our towns to meet techno-
> logical changes and social demands, it should not be forgotten that plan-
> ning is for people. The part that people have to play in the development
> of their town or community has been underlined in the report of the
> Skeffington committee on public participation in planning, on the
> hypothesis that the more the general public, community or other associa-
> tions can be informed of what is being done, and responsible opinion
> taken into account, the more likely it will be that the resulting plan will
> be both suited to and acceptable to society. It was not expected that
> public participation, certainly in the early stages, would be an easy

process. There are many diverging views, and the danger always exists that vociferous minority opinion can take precedence over the majority. But under the 1968 Planning Act, participation is now part of the planning process and as people become more involved in, and more used to helping to plan their own environment, we should be able to look forward to positive public contributions in plan making.[12]

This, for the planners, was the lesson of Millfield. Participation was naturally difficult in its early stages. The public was not used to it. The danger selected for special mention was that the vociferous minority might have its view accepted, to the neglect of the majority. But as people—laymen as distinct from professionals—gained experience, *positive* contributions could be looked for. *Responsible* opinion might find expression, and such responsible opinion would be taken into account. In the dialogue between planners and the public the future is not entirely gloomy, for the public might eventually gain in enlightenment: this was the planning department's conception of the blockages and hazards of participation.

At the end of the day, therefore, the Millfield Residents' Association had achieved something; but the problems of Millfielders faced with planning expertise and professionalism were basically untouched.

It is possible to think of at least two grounds on which these data might be dismissed as peculiar to Sunderland and of little general importance. First, in relation to the Planning Act of 1968, both the Council and the planning department made it quite evident at the first meeting of November 14th 1968 that participation had superseded all other citizen safeguards. That was nonsense. Neither the Act nor any of the documents or debates associated with it suggested in any way that its provisions for publicity and consultation replaced other democratic procedures. The Act conferred no new rights on the citizen. He had been as entitled to make representations to the local planning authority before the Act as he was after the Act was passed. What the Act did was to place a new legal obligation, much hedged around, upon the local authority to encourage such representations if they were not forthcoming within the existing framework of local democracy. Only in the sense that the authority was also required to consider representations were the rights of the citizen fractionally extended. It might be said, therefore, that other local authorities would not misunderstand the provisions of the Act in the way in which this local planning authority had misunderstood them. 'The fastnesses by the banks of the Wear' are almost bound to be exceptionally backward and really need not bother too much the citizen in the mainstream of British life.[13] In answer, it can only be noted that Sunderland was quite tenacious in what it took for granted about the meaning of the Act, and whether or not other local authorities would differ from Sunderland in this respect is a matter to be investigated, not assumed.

The second way in which these Sunderland data might be dismissed as merely deviant is to say that the participation was pre-Skeffington. It is true that the chairman of the planning committee had been a member of the Skeffington committee, and that the Council and the planning department had always presented the rules of the participation game as the Skeffington rules. But, it might be said, the report of the Skeffington committee was not published until July 28th 1969. This was at the mid-point of the July 21st–August 9th correspondence which the planning department used to terminate participation. Participation, therefore, had all-but ended when the Skeffington committee reported. The rules of the game from November 1967 to August or October 1969 were not those of the Skeffington report, but garbled Skeffington. The Skeffington report, it might be argued, has transformed the situation for other participation groups in other localities.

Where, to what extent and for whose benefit the Skeffington report in fact facilitates public participation are empirical questions. It is necessary, therefore, to examine its recommendations to see how likely it is that they would have strengthened the citizen in Millfield and given him a remedy against the injustices he had suffered or a prophylactic against their repetition.

## NOTES

1 In May 1970 the swing against the sitting Conservative representing the ward of which West Millfield forms a part was almost twice the average for the town (14 per cent as compared with 8 per cent). In May 1971 the ward voted in its first Labour councillor since 1958, with the biggest Labour majority since the ward was formed in 1950. The Labour candidate in 1970 was not connected with the residents' association. The author was the Labour candidate in 1971.

2 The planning department's version of the meeting says, 'The secretary said that public servants had no right to be antagonized but he had.' (Planning department minute dated October 9th 1969.)

3         *Deptford's reward for docility;*
          *Millfield's for not having its say,*
          *Sixty years of silence—*
          *Six decades of decay.*
                    Verse from 'The Ballad of Millfield Tip'.

4 See, the Reverend Jim Taylor, 'Mortgages Not Available', *Challenge in Industrial Millfield, The Magazine of St. Mark's*, February 1970 and *Sunderland Echo*, February 4th, 5th, 6th, 9th, 10th (editorial), 11th, 12th (editorial); *The Journal* (Newcastle upon Tyne), February 6th (editorial), 7th, 11th, 12th, 13th; and *Northern Echo*, February 7th, 12th.

5 See, the Reverend Jim Taylor, 'Council Refuses Site for Handicapped Children's Centre', *op. cit.*, May 1970, and *Sunderland Echo*, March 5th, 18th, 20th, 21st, 25th, 26th, 28th, April 10th, May 4th, 6th, 7th, 8th, 9th, 12th, 13th, 14th, 15th, 20th, 21st ('Wear Group to Discuss Needs of Mentally Handicapped' and 'Minister Gives a Promise'), 22nd, 23rd, 27th, 28th, 30th, June 1st, 2nd, 3rd, 5th, 6th, 10th, 11th ('Council Acts to Solve Problem of the Mentally Handicapped'), August 20th ('Town Start Move to Provide Mental Care Centre'). See also *The Journal*, March 23rd, May 4th; and *Northern Echo*, May 4th.

6 *Sunderland Echo*, July 1st 1970 ('Plan to Keep Millfield Homes Until Year 2000') and July 2nd (editorial). See also letters of Town Clerk's department TVL/13410 dated June 16th and June 30th 1970.

7 *Report of the Lower Level Officers Working Party on Surveys Undertaken in Connection with the Proposed Designation of the Close Street/Hadrian Street/ Westbury Street Area of Millfield as a General Improvement Area*, August 1970,

pp. 7, 8 and 13. (Mimeographed.) It goes without saying that no Millfielder was supposed to see this document.

8 *Ibid.*, p. 11.

9 *Hansard (Commons)*, Vol. 809, No. 61, Col. 80, January 13th 1971.

10 *Op. cit.*, Tables 1 and 2.

11 *Op. cit.*, p. 4.

12 J. E. Barlow, M.T.P.I., A.R.I.B.A., Dip. T.P., *Sunderland Planning
Information Handbook*, Publicity House, Streatham Hill, London: Pyramid
Press Ltd., 1971, p. 26.

13 The quoted phrase is that of Professor Peter Hall, who appears to take
this view exactly. See *New Society*, February 12th 1970. That Professor
Hall is not unaware of the problem itself can be seen in his article 'The
Rise and Fall of the Professional', *New Society*, February 5th 1970.

# CHAPTER 17

# SKEFFINGTON AND PUBLIC
# SCRUTINY

The chairman of the committee on public participation in planning was Arthur Skeffington, joint Parliamentary Secretary, Ministry of Housing and Local Government. The chairman of Sunderland planning committee was a member, as we know. Its twenty-four other members included a past president of the Town Planning Institute, two other M.T.P.I.s and two A.M.T.P.I.s. In its early days it also included Sir Mark Henig, who resigned to take up an appointment as chairman of the East Midlands Economic Planning Council. The report was largely drafted by a career civil servant at the Ministry. In discharging its duty of examining one of the most important aspects of the White Paper on planning and one of the most important sections of the new Act, namely 'safeguarding the interests of those affected', the committee was not one which was likely to neglect the practical problems of local planning authorities. Nor was it bound to be unsympathetic to the ideals in the evidence which stated that what was wanted was a planner's Hippocratic oath. This would require him to consult the public and 'heal its ills'. The oath would mean he must override the wishes of politicians. The planner would be related to citizen as doctor is to patient, without the intervention of elected representatives.[1]

The report defined participation as the act of sharing in the formulation of policies and proposals. Participation involves doing as well as talking. Full participation takes place, the report stated, only when the public are able to take an active part throughout the plan-making process. But the responsibility for preparing the plan 'is and must remain' that of the local planning authority. The report distinguished the preparation of the plans from the completion of the plans. The completion of the plans, the setting into statutory form of the proposals and decisions, lies with the professional staff, because it is a task demanding 'the highest standards of professional skill'.[2]

The sentiments of the report, when expressed in general terms, invariably had the ring of liberality. When illustrated in detail the local planning authority was always put in a strong position and the member of the public in a weak one. Publicity, for example, was defined in general terms as 'the making of information available to the public . . . fact, argument and explanation'. When particularizing the committee was less helpful. What is proposed for a man's home is of the very greatest importance to him. Ought he to have the right of individual notification? That is 'impractical and unrealistic'.[3]

Again, in general terms, its recommendations for publicity through exhibitions, surgeries, the press,[4] community forums[5] and the community development officer[6] were beyond criticism. But when the report turned to the details of what the public needed to know, what may be the subject of active and discussive consultation, who should participate, who should control and convene meetings, how conflicts should be resolved and so forth, then it becomes extremely difficult to see the rules as being in any sense a functional equivalent to local representation, the courts, tribunals or public inquiries. Some of the most important issues taken up by the Skeffington committee will be discussed under appropriate headings.

*What the Public Needs to Know*

The key document for the ordinary member of the public as Skeffington rightly says, is the statement of proposals of the local plan. In paragraph No. 193 the report suggests ways in which the planning authority might endeavour to publicize it and secure public discussion. What it says about this, however, is far exceeded in volume by its recommendations for educating the public in order to ensure full understanding of the proposals and permit informed comment on them. For that, 'a better public knowledge of planning is necessary'. (Paragraph No. 230.) People will need to distinguish, for example, between the opportunities to contribute at the formative stages and the opportunities to object at a later stage. They will need to know about the extended scope of development plans and the devolution of responsibility to the local planning authority. A film should be made by the central government covering these matters. The public, that is, should be thoroughly acquainted with the planners' point of view.

'The same authority will often be both the local planning authority and the local education authority . . . responsible for controlling the curricula of most schools.' Knowledge about the physical planning of the community should therefore be made available as part of 'outward-looking' syllabuses, such as have been 'recommended in several reports on education'. Senior classes should be encouraged to attend planning exhibitions. Children in all secondary schools should thus be made conscious of their future civic duties. (Paragraphs No. 244 and 245.)

Co-operation between the planning department and the education department should extend beyond the school into institutions of further education. 'This would, in fact, help to implement the policy of the Department of Education and Science, who actively encourage the introduction of a liberal element into technical education.' (Paragraph No. 246.)

The B.B.C. and I.T.V. could do much to help inform the public by putting out more programmes of an educative kind about planning matters. These might deal with 'the fundamental characteristics' of the new planning system, the kind of planning research that has to precede any new proposals, 'the considerations which professional planners have to take into account', and 'how the public can help'. (Paragraph No. 250.)

Members of the press 'need basic information about the nature and purpose of the planning process'. This is 'a prerequisite of their informed comment and discussion'. (Paragraph No. 249.) The National Council for the Training of Journalists should be approached about providing trainee journalists with 'adequate instruction about planning'.

There can be no objection to these suggestions for favourable publicity as such. Public relations is a function the importance of which is appreciated by any 'strong and persuasive' bureaucracy, corporate or public. As contrasted with outlays on salesmanship by private industry and the stimulation of consumption of what William Morris termed 'illth' similar processes ought to be encouraged in unpersuasive and backward industries and among the producers of public wealth. The problem put to the Skeffington committee, however, was not that of private affluence versus public squalor, but bureaucratic dominance versus public weakness. Its task was to find ways of strengthening the citizen's, not the administrator's voice. What is conspicuously lacking in the Skeffington report is any sign that there might be other points of view which are equally entitled to this sort of authoritative airing when planning proposals are under discussion. 'What the public needs to know' is weighed down with complacency. Basically, all that needs to be done is to let the public know what the given structure of the planning process is and what planning proposals are at any point of time. This will constitute a liberal education; it will be a training in future civic duties; it will authorize journalists to write on planning matters. This attitude is seen even more clearly when 'what the public needs to know' is compared with 'what the planner needs to know'.

*What the Planner Needs to Know*

In a way the whole of the report can be represented as what the planner needs to know. It contains very little, certainly, that he will not be glad to read.

Directly, however, 'the education of the planner' occupies six half-lines. 'Just as there is a need for the public to be better educated in planning matters, so there is a need for planners to be more aware of the importance of public participation in their initial training and refresher courses. No doubt the Town Planning Institute will give the matter consideration.' (Paragraph No. 251.)

## The Objectives of Participation

Surprisingly, nowhere does the Skeffington report discuss in a systematic way what participation ought to achieve, what tests might be applied to determine its effectiveness or in-effectiveness in general or in a particular instance. The report contains, however, various passing remarks on the subject. They point to one criterion only: success in reducing the number of public objections and in shortening the process of decision-taking for the planning authority.

> We have found little by way of systematic appraisal of the results and costs. . . . Opinions about results have been diametrically opposed; some people argue that good advance publicity can reduce objections to a plan, others that it will only lengthen the planning process by stimulating them. (Paragraph No. 238.)
>
> Unless people are involved in formulating the local plans there is the prospect of far greater antagonism than when the general principles of the structure plan are discussed. (Paragraph No. 175.)
>
> Giving publicity to this report the Statement of Choices of the local plan will . . . serve to eliminate doubts and suspicions that would other-wise arise during a plan-making process which may last many months. (Paragraph No. 191.)
>
> The public should be told what their representations have achieved. Where suggestions have been accepted people will be glad to know this; where they have not, they should be told why. This . . . offers real hope of reducing objections at the later formal stages. (Paragraph No. 174.)
>
> It was feared that the community forum would become the focal

point of opposition to the authority. But this assumes—wrongly, we think—that people who are the driving force in their own groups will allow their judgment to be submerged by representatives of other groups. (Paragraph No. 70.)

It was feared that the forum might become the centre of political opposition. We hope that this would not happen; it seems unlikely that it would, as most local groups are not party-political in their membership. (Paragraph No. 70.)

These quotations raise the obvious question: What if Skeffington's continuous assumption, that the local planning authority has nothing to present but a case that any reasonable man of good will can accept once he is clearly aware of its contents, did not apply in every case of public participation?

What are the rules of the participation game when greater knowledge of planning proposals exacerbates and does not diminish conflict between groups within the community? What happens when information about planning processes multiplies objections instead of reducing their number? What happens when the facts of the situation are not that of inadequately publicized virtue on the one side and an unfulfilled readiness to accept whatever is announced on the other? There is not the slightest hint anywhere in the Skeffington report, apart from the above references to fears which proved unjustified, that these possibilities could emerge from participation.

*What Shall Be at Stake in Active Participation?*

Appendix No. 5 of the Skeffington report lists twenty-three examples of suitable vehicles for active participation. The most important of these is the social survey. The report distinguishes between surveys of fact and surveys of opinion. Normally, only surveys of fact should be undertaken by voluntary organizations, which should be invited to do so. But if the survey is undertaken by voluntary organizations to provide part of the material upon which the plan will be based, then 'the framework of the survey will need to be approved by the authority'. The authority has a statutory duty to make the survey and must satisfy itself that the work has been 'efficiently and comprehensively performed'. (Paragraph No. 184.)

Again, these reflections offer no grounds for criticism. The criticism must be not about what the report says, but what it fails to say. Is there no possibility that a voluntary organization should see the control of the data as itself an issue? Is it not possible that the definition of the situation may depart in one way or another from that of unpaid surveyors working at the direction of the local planning authority for the sake of nothing but the satisfaction of a civic duty conscientiously discharged? It may be that this definition of the situation is generally the most meritorious and may factually be the one most commonly found. It is not likely, however, to be unique.

The survey of opinion, as distinct from the survey of fact, is a highly specialized technical exercise, the report says, and therefore should be normally carried out by the authority or by consultants appointed by the authority. When should it be carried out? It should be carried out only after the authority has presented its case. 'The aggregate of individual opinion may, at times, fail to realize the full opportunities that are available. Unless the authority have done a great deal to inform the public, their opinion may be based on an inadequate knowledge of what is possible by way of change and improvement.' (Paragraph No. 188.)

The local authority no doubt ought to survey opinion after it has presented its case, though not necessarily only then. What is so striking about the report is its complete obtuseness over the question of how surveys of opinion might be related to the presentation of the case of other interested parties, and of the pitfalls of ignorance and inadequate knowledge which lie in the path of the planner in designing and carrying out a survey as well as in the path of the member of the public in responding to it.

There is only one single sign that the interests of anyone but the planning authority should be taken into account in carrying out a survey. 'Local authorities will, no doubt', the report says on p. 35, 'seek the prior cooperation and consent of landowners when schoolchildren undertake survey work in the countryside.'

## What Shall Be at Stake in Discussive Participation?

Fundamental to the new planning legislation is the distinction between the structure plan, which still requires Ministerial scrutiny, and the local plan (district plans, action-area plans and subject plans) which do not. The structure plan is one step below the plans for whole regions. It deals with social and physical influences susceptible to planning control. It is concerned not only with land-use. Planning's new deal under the Act of 1968 means that economic factors must be considered. Techniques of economic analysis are to be utilized in order to create the right conditions for economic growth and change. The structure plan will be concerned with 'the ways of living of people' and changes in those ways of life over time. It will be concerned with the balance in housing between new development, redevelopment and the improvement of the existing housing stock. It will deal with schools, parks, shopping facilities and so forth.

The structure plan must show how these interlocking proposals can be brought to fruition in a comprehensive and not a piecemeal way. Account must be taken of national plans for, for example, long-distance railroads and of regional plans for roads and migration.

The structure plan will not predict rigid end-states and will not be related to a fixed end-date. But this flexibility will not be an excuse for woolly thinking. The structure plan will be tested through mathematical techniques where these are available. It will be examined in the light of economic criteria. It will have to prove itself satisfactory in the social results it will achieve. The Minister will have to be satisfied that the methods of forecasting trends are sound, and that the aims of the plan are not out of line with financial possibilities.

The above is the description of structural planning given by the chief planner of the Ministry at a seminar held at the University of Newcastle upon Tyne on February 2nd 1970. It will be apparent that these data lack immediacy for the man in the street.

This is best seen in the Skeffington report. In illustrating the part the public can play in the decision-making process of the structure plan, the committee takes its example not from this country, but from the United States. Presumably, therefore, the whole world had been searched for a striking and effective case. An appendix shows the 'Statement of Choices' which might be considered by the public in stage three of the structure plan:

> The Los Angeles planning department sought to involve the public in determining what the city should look like in the twenty-first century. ... The authority produced a simple leaflet illustrating four ways described as four concepts, in which Los Angeles might develop.

The centres concept involved large regional concentrations. The dispersal concept involved an even distribution of activities throughout the urban area. The corridor concept and the low density concept were the other two 'choices'. 'These issues and relevant facts were put to the public who were invited to comment on them', is the Skeffington report's terse concluding paragraph of its appendix No. 8.

It need not be said that such choices are somewhat unlikely to stimulate a frantic search for relevant information and anxious and urgent thought among members of the general public. (Skeffington did recognize this, but only in so far as it applied to the public—not the planner.)

Participation, realistically, will tend to occur only when the plans more clearly identify effects in the foreseeable future which touch in some discernable way the well-being of the potential participant. Another condition must be present: the possibility that participation will have some effect. Only a mentally-ill person would expend his energies for any length of time on an activity in which the prospects of a pay-off were negligible or nil.

Relevant participation in most cases, therefore, will only appear when the local plan is to be discussed. Skeffington described four stages in the process of making the local plan. Stage one consists of the local authority's announcement of its intention to prepare it. The proposed programme of work is outlined by the local authority, including the programme of the opportunities for participation. At stage one the local planning authority should, in Skeffington's words, 'publicize the relevant decisions in the structure plan which establish the context of the local plan'. (Paragraph No. 182.) The corollary not dealt with in the report is that the planning authority by implication publicizes the options which the pre-existing structure plan has closed.

Stage two enables the public to participate in survey work and the survey results should be made available to the public as a popular summary. They should be available in greater detail for those who wish to explore them. (Paragraph No. 189.)

Once the general wishes of the public have been ascertained by means of survey, the local planning authority should set out in more detail what choices are available. (Paragraph No. 190.) These choices are announced. Participation at this stage, stage three of the local-plan process, is dealt with in nine words in the Skeffington report: 'time should be allowed for public discussion and comment'. (Paragraph No. 192.)

Stage four of the local-plan process, the last of the eight stages (four in connection with the structure plan, four in connection with the local plan), produces 'the first document', as the report points out, 'to show the local community in detail how they would be affected'. (Paragraph No. 193.) The statement of proposals should be clearly marked 'statement for discussion' to show that it is open to public influence. (Paragraph No. 193.)

The report then says no more than this about participation: that the proposals should be covered in the press, and that a public meeting should be held in the area for which the plan is prepared, more than one meeting where the area is large. (Paragraph No. 196.) The planning authority, it is remarked in the same paragraph, 'should have a wide discretion on the localities for which meetings cater'.

## Who Shall Participate?

The Skeffington report dealt only cursorily with its terms of reference, which were to find ways of securing the participation of the public at the formative stages of the planning decisions which will affect them. It was primarily concerned with defining the relationships which will subsist between the local planning authority and citizens. This includes the question of who shall participate. On page one the committee sets out its definition of the public and a community. 'We do not think of the public solely in terms of the community as it shows itself in organized groups. We regard the community as an aggregate comprising all the individuals and groups within it without limitation.' (Paragraph No. 5.) This definition has one outstanding merit for the local planning authority. It gives it the freedom to over-ride the views of any specific individual or group in the name of the wishes whether expressed or not of any other individual or group. In the absence of controls over the planning authority there would naturally be a danger that it would more easily see those who 'co-operate' (Paragraph No. 61) and those who 'work creatively' (Paragraph No. 62) as the dependable spokesmen for 'the aggregate of individuals and groups without limitation'.

The report suggests, in line with its terms of reference, that the initiative for the creation of certain key participation groups should lie with the local planning authority. What, however, is the report's idea of a key participation group? The authority should call a meeting of representatives of bodies such as churches, civic and amenity societies, residents' associations, trade unions, chambers of trade, youth organizations etc. to form a community forum. (Paragraphs 63–4.) Appendix No. 4 of the report lists the constituents of such a forum which met at Eldon Hall, Croydon, on May 10th 1968. (The appendix consists of nothing but the names of the organizations.) Forty persons were present, representing twenty-three bodies, including the Rotary club, the trades council, Toc H, the Salvation Army, the Croydon Auctioneers and Surveyors Association, several tenants' associations, and so forth.

Sociologically speaking, fears that, even if it were the appropriate response, such a meeting would organize effective opposition to planning proposals or anything else were quite unfounded. It is surprising, however, to note that for Skeffington this is the community forum's principal virtue. Its task was, after all, to stimulate consultation, not to find ways of making disagreement ineffective.

## When Does the Public Participate?

In every detail Skeffington structures the situation to grant control of information channels to the planning authority, instead of exploring methods of overcoming indifference, apathy and public disbelief that any influence it might have on the eventual shape of the plans would repay the effort of participation.

The programme of participation too, the report states, ought to be prepared by the local planning authority. 'This sets the perspectives both for those who want to debate too long and those who expect changes overnight.' (Paragraph No. 208.) The time available should be made clear, and Skeffington mentions particular periods of time within which the local planning authority should permit representations to be made.

*How Will Conflicts Be Resolved?*

There is little to be said about this fundamental issue, for the Skeffington report, not regarding it as a problem, deals with it only briefly. The local planning authority is the adjudicator. 'Once the public has expressed its choices and these have been tested against one another, and in the light of what is possible as shown by the facts of the survey and other constraints, the authority will be able to prepare a statement of proposals.' (Paragraph No. 193.) A blander sentence to conceal greater problems could scarcely be imagined.

In the 1950s the Franks report and the Tribunals and Inquiries Act sought to develop or improve certain instrumentalities for the protection of the aggrieved citizen. In 1967 Parliament created a Parliamentary Commissioner for Administration. Planning remained relatively immune from these developments, and independently developed a system of public participation as its own way of coping with the problems which elsewhere had led in the opposite direction, that of stronger, independent, impartial scrutiny and control, or at any rate attempts at these.

The absence of effective scrutiny of planning practices and of the methods by which a citizen can be given a reasonable opportunity to obtain redress when he is at the receiving end of administrative incompetence or has suffered injury, outside the protection of his legal rights, as W. A. Robson said ten years ago and things have not improved, is an unhealthy state of affairs: bad for the administration, bad for the individual, bad for the public and detrimental to good government.[7]

## NOTES

1 A clear restatement of this position can be read in, 'Let the Public Share in Planning', *The Times*, September 4th 1970. Understandably, to a proficient and public spirited planner the elected representative when he is not completely redundant is too often just a nuisance. Social mechan-

isms, especially those designed to protect the weak cannot, however, be wisely based upon examples of good practices; their *raison d'être* is the existence of bad practices.

2 *People and Planning: Report of the Committee on Public Participation in Planning* (the Skeffington Report), London: H.M.S.O., 1969, p. 1.

3 *Ibid.*, p. 33.

4 *Ibid.*, pp. 36–7.

5 *Ibid.*, p. 14.

6 *Ibid.*, pp. 16–17.

7 William A. Robson, 'Administrative Law', in Morris Ginsberg (Ed.), *Law and Opinion in England in the Twentieth Century*, London: Stevens, 1959, p. 213.

PART FIVE

# CONCLUSION

# CHAPTER 18

# THE IMPERMEABILITY
# OF PLANNING

The main problem for Millfielders both in participation and in the ordinary processes of planning was their inability to get messages through to the institutions which were influencing their lives. Protection and redress centre round this fact, and it is necessary to understand what lay at its origin.

In the current system of English local government elected representatives carry out certain duties of control and public provision. Power and responsibility formally reside in them. They in turn are responsible to the electorate. Obviously, if bad advice is accepted by councillors, the councillors are at fault. If citizens re-elect councillors who are failing to supervise on their behalf the machinery of local government, they have nobody to blame but themselves.

The question of relationships between politicians and officers is an important one. By comparison with members of parliament, who set guide-lines of principle, local councillors are to a far greater extent directly implicated in administration. When a policy is attacked by a citizen or a councillor it is the policy, down to quite fine detail, of the appropriate committee and of the local ruling party. In practice the councillor has far less scope than the M.P. to act as ombudsman, calling the administration to account. But in Sunderland any councillor could ask any question in the Council chamber on any matter affecting the town and had the right to consult any document considered by any committee.[1] The meetings of the full Council were by no means a rubber stamp for committee decisions. They were a lively forum of debates which were informative to the public through the town's strong daily newspaper. The Labour group on the Council, in power for a score of years up to 1967 and with good prospects of return to power before the mid-1970s, not only denounced the faults of the administration, but actually allowed the press into its own pre-Council meetings of the Labour group of councillors. An examination of the relationship between appointed and elected officials in power and in opposition would therefore have been exceptionally interesting in Sunderland at this time. The relationship between Millfielders and their own councillors is also theoretically interesting and practically important. Yet the councillors have hardly appeared in this study. In part this is a matter of arbitrary choice, a decision to focus on only some of the actors in a complex situation. The systematic study of the relationship between planners and politicians and between politicians and planned-for ought to be undertaken; it simply was not undertaken on this occasion.[2] Focusing on the role of the planners in the Millfield experience was, however, arbitrary only to a small extent. The book concentrates on the planners because the record is weighed with their contributions. They rather than the politicians described and justified the proposals for Millfield. In eighteen volumes of field notes there is not a single expression by a planner of the perfectly sound case (and complete exoneration for themselves if it had been true and they had chosen to put it) that they were the servants of their elected masters, and had to do their best to bring to fruition whatever their masters insisted upon. On the contrary they always insisted in public that what was proposed (each successive contradictory policy) was on inviolate technical planning grounds and on the basis of impeccable factual data. In private the officials, far from using their advisory and executive constraints as an excuse, expressed only contempt for councillors. Not only did the councillors know nothing; a more serious matter altogether, they were not entitled to know anything.

Certainly the concrete proposals of the local Conservative administration after May 1967 differed markedly from the local Labour proposals. The changes have been fully described. What justifies a particularly close look at the planners' own role is, to a minor extent, that much of the avoidable distress of the widespread 'by 1972' blight under Labour was a direct result of the failure to introduce realism into the proposals at the successive quinquennial reviews. Much more important in justifying it, are the findings of this book on the relevance and accuracy of the planners' surveys and their control of channels of information. What it all came down to in Millfield was this. Under a Labour administration the so-called technical information which supported their professional preference for clean-sweep planning buttressed the local Labour party's policy of vigorous slum clearance and Council re-housing. Under a Conservative administration the planners' technical information still demonstrated Millfield's wholesale unfitness. Then Millfielders were caught between the planners' surveys on the one side, which stressed always short lives to the properties, and on the other the fact that the Conservatives would approve the clearance of only a small fraction of the properties. The planners were strong enough to cause blight, but not strong enough to bring about comprehensive redevelopment. What made the position worse for Millfielders, was that fact that the Conservative Council cut the house-building programme to the bone, so that such demolition as did take place inevitably meant the dispersal of the community into council-house re-lets all over the town.

The two main sources of grievance in the area were useless lifing—'hope ground to dust and mortared in the soul' (Melville)—and the consequence of slow slum clearance. It is not surprising that a bureaucratic structure should remain unaware of the disquietude which was the only product of lifing proposals and plans which come to nothing. Ignorance of the results of long-delayed slum-clearance proposals showed a more serious insensitivity. Of course blight in its different forms may be in some cases simply the unsavoury accompaniment of a fundamentally sound policy. In other cases it is not. That a particular street or area falls into the former category cannot be postulated; it has to be proved. In Millfield it never was.[3]

How far Millfield reflects a general malaise in modern British town planning is for further investigation to determine.[4] But clearly the first step in correcting the faults of planning in Millfield is to recognize that they exist. On November 10th 1966 'just a simple love story' by Jeremy Sandford was shown on B.B.C. television. The impact of the play 'Cathy Come Home', was tremendous. A national campaign for the homeless was launched under the name of Shelter. Shelter proved an extremely effective organization, one of several which in the late 1960s took up the cause of groups the welfare state had neglected. It eventually extended its concerns from straightforward homelessness to the virtual homelessness of the slum dweller. Under a photograph of unkempt children, one of whom is leaning against the last of a row of overflowing dustbins on waste ground behind stone-built tenements, a half-page Shelter appeal reads: 'You are looking at one of Britain's appalling slum areas. It wasn't much when it was built, exactly 100 years ago. Now its unbelievable. In Britain we've let our major cities fester. We've largely ignored the slums.'[5] The advertisement goes on: 'We're trying to change this. To mount a rescue operation. Rehousing families—4,000 already. Saving twilight areas from further deterioration. Educating young people to avoid being trapped into homelessness. But it takes money. Send a donation to Shelter. You'll help a family from breaking up. And you may save our cities from breaking down.' That is dramatic and effective. It is aimed to arouse public indignation against the conditions in twilight and slum areas—including areas such as Hendon in Sunderland. If it is successfully labelled 'slum' however, Millfield, a different sort of place altogether, is inevitably pictured as such an area, and its conflict with the planning department appears wrong-headed and almost incomprehensible to the outsider.

Better housing and particularly the eradication of slums had become by the end of the 1960s one of the few progressive causes which remained uncomplicated and, without question, desirable. Although it could have been a relevant factor for regionalism in comparatively few cases, exponents of strong regional government, however short their illustrative list, always included slum clearance as the one easily understood and universally approved enterprise. In defining 'the future of the left' in 1970 a former leader of the Liberal party gave the first among contemporary questions as the use of the potential of science for human purposes. The only *specific* thing he mentioned was slum clearance—'clearing the slums and providing services of various sorts'.[6]

Unlike, say, educational reform which meant the substitution of the comprehensive for the grammar school and even the end of superior privately-paid education, providing better housing involved no threat to privilege, except in the mild form of higher taxes or rates. Quite the opposite. Rehousing meant removal from one segregated residential location to another which was even more securely segregated, the municipal housing estate or flatted complex. It is not suggested that supporters of housing betterment were conscious of this, only that if rehousing had meant the invasion of private residential areas at public expense, slum clearance would have roused ambivalence among those who would conceive themselves as being to that extent adversely affected. For the mass of well-wishers, far removed geographically and experientially from working-class housing, slum clearance, lifing and so forth were self-evidently good things. Anyone who could label his activities with these names could automatically trigger a release mechanism of warm-hearted sympathy and support.

Historically, too, whatever enthusiasm an alert minority could generate and whatever public pressure could be brought to bear to accelerate the clearance of bad housing was justified by the severity of the problem and the lethargy of the responsible authorities. In terms of the end achieved, it did not matter what true or false reasons were presented; any clearance eventually accomplished was both necessary and still too little.[7]

It was therefore extraordinarily difficult to have it accepted that Millfield's problems in the late 1960s were less those of bad housing than those of bad administration, and that on the whole Millfielders suffered far more severely from the latter than from the former.

The ambience which does most to abate the influence of the public (and particularly that of the householder who is the institution's final consumer) is planning ideology, that is, the definition of the situation, the specification of the main kinds of problem that may be tackled, the major solutions, and the spirit of their application. British town planning is not monolithic.[8] But even those versions which are relatively modest make large claims which tend to raise sights above any target which would require familiarity with the needs and feelings of ordinary consumers in the here and now.[9] A principal tenet of planning faith is the priority of future over present needs. Short-term gains are to be willingly sacrificed in the interest of greater gains in the long run. The planner is freed from the present by his commitment to the future, and his scientificality can all be poured into anchorless data the validity of which cannot be checked.[10] He can strut on painted rainbows, betwixt false heaven and a false earth.[11]

The ideology of planning is built around self-evident truths and values which give complete authority to its main propositions and chains of reasoning. It bestows self confidence on its practitioners; which is another way of saying that it inoculates them against disturbing self-awareness and sceptical re-examination.[12] Behind their lack of interest in the proximate results of their proposals, planners have the solid weight of mutual admiration.

The local planning authority might have been capable of persuading Millfielders that lifing was to their ultimate benefit and that one or some of the various slum-clearance predictions were in their own or in the public interest. There is some reason to doubt that capability, but in any case the planning authority attempted to persuade no one. Instead, Millfielders were subject to the financial and emotional burdens of planning blight. They were punished not for any offence or even as suspects, but on the basis of a possible crime (which they were quite reluctant to commit), that is, allowing their homes to become unfit for human habitation.[13]

As the Millfield Residents' Association tried to convey to the planners, it is realistic to predicate policies on some future state of affairs which, without being able to bring it about, one is able to forecast. (One must be realistic, of course, about what is capable of being predicted with various degrees of reliability.) It is possible to predicate policies, too, on the basis of the power to bring about some future state of affairs.[14] Nothing is more striking in the history of Millfield's participation than the paradox of the planners' insistence on the soundness of their predictions on the one hand and on the other their determination to leave all options open. This will definitely happen; but if it doesn't, something else will. To all appearances both views were held simultaneously, with equal sincerity. The programme of redevelopment by 1972 remained unchanged as the statutory document. Behind this show of certainty, slum-clearance and lifing predictions, proposals, plans and operative policies came and went.[15] All, purportedly, were unavoidable expert deductions from hard technical evidence. All contradicted the statutory development plan, were mutually contradictory and flew in the face of the facts.

Generally, its proposals implied that what it had decided, it could realize. It treated intentions as if they were facts and ideals as if they were actualities. It planned as if the future were not uncertain and ignored the limits set by its inability either to predict influences which had not yet disclosed themselves or to control the conditions necessary for the fulfilment of their schemes.

Perhaps most damaging of all was its failure to pay sufficient attention to the existence of the democratic element in English local government, that is to say, the well-established institutions of councillor and political party, not simply what is acknowledged to be a newborn weakling, Skeffington-type participation. Parties and policies change and the desires of the professional planner are only one consideration in a complex play of influence. The planning department apparently took the line that if expertise and democracy were at variance, so much the worse for democracy. Some day that might be a reasonable view to take. The democratic element may be sufficiently weakened and the planning department's expertise may be sufficiently strengthened. As it was, one of the main reasons for the volatility of the plans was that when they were challenged, the planning department was able to produce no convincing data to support them. Planning is intended to increase the predictability of life and the scope for orderly control. Because they ignored the fact of uncertainty and the realities of power the planners decreased both.

The results for Millfielders were written large in distress and blight. The results for the planners, not as persons but as role-players caught in a trap they simply did not comprehend, were written large in their impotence once they were challenged to provide a convincing explanation of their own behaviour, and in the shifts and subterfuges to which in their discomfiture they found themselves driven.

If the institutional arrangements for raising housing standards by compulsion are to become more responsive to human needs, it is necessary for them to become more sensitive to the complaints of the clients.[16] The institutions of planning far from perfecting such arrangements for a heightened sensitivity, specialize in suppressing them. They emphasize their commitment to objective science, whether or not they are able to produce scientifically valid evidence to justify their assertions.[17] This fundamental defect is treated with extraordinary lightness by some writers. Dr. Suzanne Keller, for example, recognizes that the planner claims powers and indeed has statutory duties far in excess of those he can successfully redeem, yet passes this by with the remark: 'When planners start on a project they can scarcely afford the luxury of either doing surveys on local characteristics and attitudes or waiting for the results of such exhaustive surveys.'[18] The consequences of not affording the luxury and of not waiting are the fantastically large errors in all their forecasts. These scarcely lead to a saving in time. Imagine that sentence being written about any other set of technical experts. 'When civil engineers start on a dam . . .'

It is essential, of course, to build into any professional training a reasonably inflated conception of the contribution the profession makes to human welfare and the pure and powerful influence that the practitioner can exert. That the planning profession may go too far in this respect is hinted at in the title of two recent books, one German and one English. The title of the German book is *The Drawing-Board Preachers*.[19] The title of the English book is *The Evangelistic Bureaucrat*.[20] The details of the Millfield experience suggests, too, that the trainee planner could with advantage be prepared not only to face the scepticism of the lay mind and for the expanded role which he may one day be allowed to play (the basis of his present training) but also for the actual world through which for the time being he has to plot his course.

In due course the control of the town by the expert planner might reach the sophistication of medical practice. When that time comes householders may feel that the local planning authority provides treatment for their housing ills as reliable as that provided for their injuries and diseases at the local hospital. As it is, in Millfield at least, the situation is very similar to that in the early nineteenth century, when the patient stood a better chance of survival out of the surgeon's hands than in them.

It would be both attractive and easy to dismiss Sunderland as an exception. What prevents that is the fact that planning is a public function with extensive statutory powers. It is therefore necessary to ensure that throughout the whole range of authorities these public powers should be exercised by a sufficiently scrutinized apparatus. Even were Millfield to prove quite unique it could not be shrugged off. Either resources need to be increased to match its duties, or the duties need to be reduced to bring them into line with the capabilities of the agency undertaking them.

What planners think and want is a familiar subject. This research asks, however, not how things look from their point of view, but from the point of view of the recipients of their ideas and projects.[21] In the light of the Millfield participation experience, various contrivances for citizen protection and redress (actual and possible) need to be examined: the existing machinery of local democracy;[22] the improvement in the quality and reliability of information supplied to the public; tribunals, public inquiries and the projected local ombudsman; the press and pressure-group activity ('consumer syndicalism') and the development of a 'counter civil service' and advocacy planning (especially the role of the local university as the only institutional basis which matches that of the modern local authority). It is necessary, that is, to distinguish clearly between Millfield's housing problems (which were considerable in some parts of the area) and the more widespread and damaging defects of public administration. In Millfield the housing problem had changed from pressing a public authority to supply what the private market had failed to produce, to the problems of community action and personal liberty in the face of the same public authority. No matter how well-intentioned he may be, the advocate of housing policies which are based on yesterday's concerns rather than today's real difficulties may end up by creating more distress than he alleviates. He runs the risk of joining the company of all those who, as Burke said, in attending to the shell and husk of history think they are waging war with selfishness, intolerance and cruelty, 'whilst under the colour of abhoring the ill-principles of antiquated parties, they are authorising and feeding the same odious vices in different factions, and perhaps in worse'.[23]

## NOTES

1 Standing Orders No. 8 and No. 24.

2 The author became councillor for Millfield in the municipal election of May 1971. See above, footnote 1, p. 218.

3 A few reports are beginning to appear dealing with these processes. One of the first had, in fact, the title *The Forgotten People*. The author, N. S. Power, dedicated it to the people of Ladywood, Birmingham, and their 'years of endurance'. (Evesham: Arthur James, 1965.) In 1970 the Ministry of Housing and Local Government published two studies of St. Mary's, Oldham, *Living in a Slum* and *Moving from a Slum*. Under the scrutiny of M.H.L.G. researchers the 'Potts Street effect' did not show itself in its most virulent form. See also the article by Terence Bendixson in *New Society* (July 11th 1970) on a conference organized by the South-wark Council of Social Serivce, 'From Rumour to Removal'. A Peckham doctor is reported as saying that slum clearance is unnoticed only because of its gradualness. 'If you saw the process speeded up you would see it as a human disaster, a man-made catastrophe.' One can imagine official reaction to that. But which exaggerated response is most creditable, the anger of someone who has seen suffering at first hand, or the equanimity which springs from lack of knowledge?

4 On the policy of Newcastle upon Tyne local planning authority in Rye Hill, see Jon Gower Davies, 'Pollution by Planning', *Official Architecture and Planning*, 32, 2, June 1969, as well as his *The Evangelistic Bureaucrat*, cited elsewhere.

5 *Sunday Times*, September 20th 1970.

6 *The Times*, September 22nd 1970.

7 Norman Dennis, 'Mass Housing and the Reformer's Myth', *Planning Outlook*, New Series, VI, Spring 1969.

8 William Ashworth, *The Genesis of Modern British Town Planning*, London: Routledge and Kegan Paul, 1954; Donald L. Foley, 'British Town Planning: One Ideology or Three?', *British Journal of Sociology*, 11, 3, September 1960.

9 The reduction of costs is an example of a relatively limited aim in land-use planning. The planners' task is to reduce costs, both public and private, in a way which '*is in accord with current social conscience*'. Nathaniel Litchfield, *The Economics of Land Use Planning*, London: Estates Gazette 1956, p. 277. (Emphasis added.)

10 See Hannah Arendt, *The Origins of Totalitarianism*, Second Edition, New York: Meridan Books, 1958, p. 346, for a more generalized discussion of this. The point about the hallucinatory safe-haven for reformers in a too-far future where they can cogitate without the need for the anchors of information is also made in C. Wright Mills, 'The Social Role of Intellectuals', *Politics*, 1, 3, 1944.

11 The phrase is Nietzsche's. *Thus Spake Zarathustra* (1883–91), London: Everyman, 1933, p. 263.

12 Foley, *op. cit.* See also H. W. Volmer and D. L. Mills (eds.), *Professionalization*, Englewood Cliffs, New Jersey: Prentice Hall, 1966.

13 For a discussion of the concept of the 'possible crime', see Arendt, *op. cit.*, pp. 426–7.

14 For a study which concentrates on the problems of mustering the resources of energy, time, skills, money and political muscle for urban redevelopment, see Robert A. Dahl, *Who Governs? Democracy and Power in an American City*, New Haven: Yale University Press, 1961, pp. 115–40.

15 For a discussion of the implications for the power, responsibility and competence of decision-takers of the combination of an ostensible legal framework and an actual cats' cradle of policies, see Arendt, *op. cit.*, pp. 393ff.

16 For experimental evidence on the connection between client feedback and the responsibility felt by the practitioner, see H. A. Tilkes' study of forty-five experimental subjects who were told they were taking part in an investigation of learning techniques. The experimental subject acted as a teacher who gave a 'pupil' an electric shock when he answered wrongly, and stepped up the voltage with continued wrong answers. The experimental subject was given the responsibility of terminating the experiment when he thought it appropriate. Of the fifteen subjects who could neither hear nor see the 'pupil', only three made any protest as the level of voltage was raised. Both the level of voltage at which protests were made and the time taken to stop the experiment were highly correlated with the level of feedback allowed the experimental subjects, some of whom could both see and hear the pupil, some of whom could only see but not hear him and some of whom could neither see nor hear him. *Journal of Personality and Social Psychology*, 14, 2, 1970.

17 See the report of the Standing Joint Committee of the R.I.B.A., the

R.I.C.S., the T.P.I. and the Institute of Civil and Municipal Engineers (the Buchanan Committee) of April 1970, which stated that research in planning was 'far too small in relation to present needs'.

18 *The Urban Neighbourhood*, New York: Random House, 1968, p. 149.

19 Eberhard Schulze, *Die Prediger mit dem Reissbrett*, Stuttgart: Verlags-Anstalt, 1964.

20 *Op. cit.*

21 In this regard it is an attempt which resembles that of H. S. Becker's *Boys in White: Student Culture in a Medical School*, Chicago: University of Chicago Press, 1961, which was one of the first books in medical sociology to look at things from the perspective of the patient. Portions of a later book in the same genre find eerie echoes in Millfield's participation; see, 'The Problem of False Hope', in Jules Henry, *Culture Against Man*, London: Tavistock Publications, 1966, pp. 396–400.

22 Especially the extent to which the councillor is 'captured' by the official and the concomitants of this and other styles of enacting the role of ward representative.

23 Edmund Burke, *Reflections on the Revolution in France* (1790), in *The Works of Edmund Burke*, Volume IV, Oxford: The World's Classics, 1907, p. 156.

# CHAPTER 19

# TYPES OF PARTICIPATION

---

The business of this book has been simply to say, 'This is what happened.' The story is not about some communal disaster, flood, earthquake, famine, epidemic disease, crippling physical and mental disorder, or personal tragedy. It is about discordance in decisions affecting dwellings and neighbourhoods—the effects of urban renewal.

It is important to keep a proper perspective. Suffering from planning blight is not the same as suffering from totalitarian terror or civil strife. If at all, life and death were at stake in very few instances, and then only in the case of the old and the emotionally weak. The worst results, in the main, were that people felt more or less severely upset for a fairly large number of years. Outsiders could easily ignore complaints, or, if they momentarily registered they could soon forget them. Most of the time distress was contained within the walls of private homes and notoriously this is not news. As Camus says of the fictional Oran plague, so long as the victims were rats the news coverage was lavish. When human beings began to succumb, the press had nothing to say. 'For rats die in public; men in their homes. And newspapers are concerned only with the street.'[1] The planning department was naturally anxious that the personal and social problems raised by their activities should remain the business of separate families and that they should never become a subject of public disclosure and comprehension.

A case could easily be made out that to concentrate on problems so trivial on a world scale is a disgraceful waste of time— that, in fact, the insouciance of the planning department was an attitude to be cultivated, not condemned. The indifference of the public generally, including sociological and other researchers, could perhaps be praised because they ought to worry about more important things. But the ignorance and indifference of planners cannot be excused on the same grounds. They have made Millfield and places like it their full-time job. Whether benefits and losses on an absolute scale of suffering are great or small, concern with participation and planning blight is their career commitment.

It is important to see also that this case is not a description of all planning practice (although, as the concluding chapter will suggest, there may be something very general about bureaucracies of the town-planning type which raise for them particular problems of rationality). This chapter, therefore, will attempt to make clear that Millfield's experience was only one of a large number of variants. In principle this task turns the book away from a straightforward chronicle of events and trivial-sounding details towards comparative government, findings and theories in the field of political sociology and the enormous literature of political and social doctrines. Once the researcher leaves the haven of his case study, participation and opposition to participation are unavoiably revealed as part of the great ocean of political fact and speculation with its boundless horizons.

*Interested Parties*

Participation experiences vary with the size and nature of the stake various interested parties hold in any particular outcome. Davies's study of urban renewal projects in New York (Seaside-Hammels, Rockaways, West Village and West Side) demonstrated the influence on patterns of participation of the economic, political, social and ideological interests of various individuals and groups.[2] Owner-occupiers participated with an intensity and in support of the neighbourhood *status quo* or in support of the planners partly in accordance with their economic calculations—would compensation and other arrangements be sufficient for them to obtain similar accommodation elsewhere? Owners of small businesses, dependent on the tastes, social ecology and financial standing of the population they serve have an economic stake in demolition and lifing proposals which puts their interest in particular outcomes at a different level of intensity to that of, say, the owners and managers of branch firms. Absentee landlords of dwellings are likely to base their attitudes to urban renewal proposals very largely upon the question of whether they are likely to gain or lose financially from compulsory purchase. The economic stakes of tenants in any outcome are likely to be less, and relate to a comparison of the rent of their existing and likely future dwellings, a calculation into which social security benefits, rent rebates etc. also enter. Institutions in the locality may also have important economic stakes in particular outcomes, especially if they are not part of a larger organization able to bear the costs of relocation. The levels of participation which emerge from the grass-roots are partly a consequence of economic stakes. Whether the intention of participation is to hurry or harass the planners depends on the existence of the particular pattern of economic interests in the specific locality.

The same applies when the nature and size of the political stakes in the *status quo* are analysed. The local councillor, for example, will tend to participate intensely (in support or opposition) if a high proportion of his constituents are affected, and less intensely if only a few are affected. If the basis of his office lies in a town-wide party caucus, his level of activity and his tendency to support the views of his grass-roots electorate will be different to what it would be if he holds his office on the basis of the agreement between his views and those of the local population. His attitude will be affected by the closeness or remoteness of the date of his re-election. Neighbourhood workers in positions of power and influence—clergymen, leaders of voluntary organizations, teachers etc.—will participate or not, and further or oppose planning proposals, according to the likelihood that they will gain or lose power as a result of them. Neighbourhoods differ in the composition of their politically interested workers, and differ therefore in the patterns of participation which emerge in the face of urban renewal schemes.

Neighbourhoods differ widely, also, in what Davies calls the size of the 'social' stakes of different groups of residents in the *status quo* or change. Mothers with young children are dependent on the existence of adequate schools and shops. If their neighbourhood is well-supplied, they will tend to oppose plans which would relocate them to areas less satisfactory in these respects. Relatively rich and well-educated families are more mobile and less dependent on strictly local services than are the relatively poor. The attachment of the very poor to any particular neighbourhood may also be weak for different reasons—the lack of interest of the parents in the character and location of their child's school; the unimportance of their family ties; and their anomie and isolation which mean that neighbourly contacts are minimal.

The vision of pure liberty, as Woodcock says, can be no more than a rather remote and admittedly unrealistic mental counterpoise to centralizing tendencies.[3] Practically speaking, the outstanding question is the character and direction of intervention and constraint—'the clear-cut choice between totalitarian and democratic planning'.[4]

1. *Participation as attention to consumer demands:* This form of participation emphasizes the responsibility and power of the decision-taking apparatus where, nevertheless, the participant is conceived of as a consumer to be satisfied. Under what conditions does it tend to emerge and predominate?

Centralized decision-making tends to be most appropriate where the decision concerns common rather than distributive goals (products and services benefiting the community as a whole, which cannot be split up for piecemeal consumption); where a greatest total benefit outcome is possible (illustrated at its simplest by two consumers X and Y and two outcomes, I and II, where X is indifferent but Y benefits from either I or II); and where there is inequality of influence, when the central decision-taker can redress the balance for the weaker party. When, however, there are no clear ultimate or common ends to be achieved; when there is low visibility with regard to the values involved; and where the demands of claimants are confused and complex, then the decision-taker is more likely to orient himself to the consumer and activate a market research style of participation.[5]

Participation as market research is seen by those responsible for planning (and for the delivery of social services) as a matter of securing reliable feedback from clients in the form of possibly useful advice and suggestions.[6] Lorraine Barie terms this indicative participation. The member of the public is an object of bureaucratic enquiry.[7] He is a member of a vast consumer panel whose opinions and preferences may be helpful in generating new or more effective service.[8] He is the consumer participant and citizen client.[9]

The praised pilot public participation schemes at Haringey, London (at Hornsey, Tottenham and Wood Green) were in large part, but not entirely (see below), of this type. In the pamphlet issued by the Council it was stated that every resident 'should have the opportunity of expressing his views . . . on what should or should not be done to make the borough a better and more pleasant place'.[10]

The pressure for consumer-client participation, which leaves the citizen as informant, not as decision-taker, comes not only from the bureaucracy. There is a strong strand in liberal philosophy, and (as conservative writers from de Tocqueville onwards have maintained) a tendency within mass democracy as such for the citizen himself to prefer this role of irresponsible demander and complainant. Thus, equality is fundamental to the liberalism of Bentham and James Mill; liberty and popular sovereignty are not, although they were regarded by Bentham and the elder Mill as on the whole useful. The favoured modern definition of democracy, popularized by Schumpeter and subsequently by Lipset emphasizes the passivity of the citizen. His power lies in his ability to change the decision-makers at regular intervals if they have failed to satisfy his demands.[11] This view is held not only by conservatives and liberals. Allen's view is that a trade union is not and need not be based on a concept of democracy, but on the end it serves. A trade union is there 'to protect and improve the general living standards of its members and not to provide workers with an exercise in self-government'.[12] Bullock makes a similar point in defending Bevin's behaviour as leader of the Transport and General Workers' Union.[13] It is sufficient that if the union fails a member, he can 'vote with his feet' (the great difference between voluntary organizations and state bureaucracies, as Allen stresses). The Millfield Residents' Association chose this style of participation as the one it preferred.[14]

2. *Participation as Partaking in Benefits:* Not only is there the question of willingness on the part of the citizen to go beyond market-research or consumer-client participation. There may also be some question of the citizen's capacity to do so. Rousseau continually pours scorn on the politically worthless strata of his own day:

> Of all the out-of-elbows rascals who today glitter in the armies of kings there is not one who would not, probably, have been driven with contempt from the ranks of a Roman cohort in the days when soldiers were defenders of liberty.[15]

Marx and Engels had a similar opinion of the lowest elements —the lumpenproletariat, the riff-raff:

> This scum of the depraved elements of all classes which establishes headquarters in the big cities, is the worst of all possible allies. This rabble is absolutely venal and absolutely brazen. If the French workers, in every

revolution inscribed on their houses: Death to the thieves! and even shot some, they did it not out of enthusiasm for property, but because they rightly considered it necessary above all to keep that gang at a distance.[16]

The people of Ship Street, Tally's Corner, or the Towpath—the sub-working class—are more likely to have passive market-research definitions of participation imposed on them by decision-takers than are citizens in other localities.[17] It is right that such people should receive humane treatment, perhaps, but it is out of the question that they should exercise control over what they receive, and scarcely reasonable that their own definitions of their needs should be taken seriously.

It came as a great surprise to many that the 'maximum feasible participation' clause (Section 202 (a)(3)) of the Economic Opportunities Act of 1964—the U.S. 'war on poverty' measure —had been thought of in terms of 'controlling' participation, at least so far as one drafter was concerned. It was inserted only to ensure that the poor should participate in the benefits of the Federal programmes.[18] 'Neither those who drafted it, those who sponsored it, nor those who enacted it ever in any way intended' that it should mean participation in any sense but this.[19]

But just who is incompetent, to what degree, in exactly which areas of public and private life is, of course, a crucial question. The pathology of participation takes the form of too large inclusions in this category. Participation deteriorates into a device for manipulation instead of discovery.[20] As people tend to take their self-image from the social situation in which they find themselves, planners generate another self-authenticating set of definitions, as citizens respond appropriately to the cues provided by forms of address and 'postures of attention'.[21] On reading the descriptions of idiots, imbeciles and the feeble-minded in Section 1 of the Mental Deficiency Act of 1927—idiots are those who cannot guard themselves against common physical dangers, imbeciles are those incapable of managing their affairs, and the feeble-minded are those requiring care, supervision and control—one cannot but be struck by their aptness as descriptions also of Millfielders as seen by planners.

3. *Participation in the decision-making process:* The style of participation in which the officials (elected or appointed) retain all formal powers and the citizen is a consenting or aggrieved spectator is only one of many. An alternative style is that in which the citizen as ardently involved in all community affairs. He is no longer a client who is either cossetted or duped, the beneficiary or victim of 'welfare colonialism'. He is cast in the role of policy-maker, a voting member of the governing board of directors. The ideas underlying the model citizen of classical liberal democracy enjoyed their greatest vitality before the advent of universal suffrage. The first amendment to the Constitution of the United States, for example, asserts the inviolability of the basic mechanisms of participation—the freedoms of speech, the press, religion, petition and assembly. It forbids, in Meiklejohn's phrase, 'the mutilation of the thinking process of the community'.[22] The belief in the worth and possibility of rational participation in policy-making by citizens is very much an Enlightenment view. Decisions can be influenced by bringing the message of social utility to those with power—the belief in the permeability to rational persuasion of even the most powerful, just as Voltaire and Diderot thought they could alter the course of history by educating Catherine the Great, Joseph, Louis, and the King of Prussia. Underlying this view are certain fundamental conceptions of 'Man and Society'—the reasonableness of men and the natural harmony of their interests (even though the 'natural harmony' may have to be discovered not in the 'will of all' or in 'apparent' or 'short-term' interest, but in the 'rational' will, the 'constant' will, the 'general' will, etc.).[23]

Direct and widespread citizen participation in decision-making is advocated in democratic theory not only for its desirable practical social consequences but also because of the intrinsic worth of such activity in the development of human personality. One of the final statements of liberal-democratic philosophy puts this point most clearly:

> No doubt many good things may be achieved for a people without responsive effort on their part. It can be endowed with good police, with an equitable system of private law, with education, with personal freedom, with a well organized industry. It may receive these blessings at the hands of a foreign ruler or from an enlightened bureaucracy or from a benevolent monarch. However obtained, they are all very good things.
>
> Within any peaceful order there is room for many good things to flourish. But the full fruit of social progress is only reaped by a society in which the generality of men and women are not only passive recipients but practical contributors.[24]

It may be wise to say once more that this was *not* the style Millfielders chose. They did not seek to persuade the planners on details of policy. What they said basically was, 'Let the planners only persuade *us*', i.e. they adopted the stance of 'consumers to be satisfied' not residents carrying out public duties or exercising civic virtues.

By the end of the 1960s enthusiasm for the 'active citizen' style of participation in the social services and planning was on the wane and attacks on its exponents began to appear.[25] But throughout the 1960s active-citizen participation enjoyed an immense vogue in social-service circles in the United States and helped determine not only that in the post-Franks period British planners turned to participation, but also that participation was frequently thought of in these terms.[26]

The 'active citizen' style is more likely to be adopted in preference to other styles in a particular locality at times when it is being widely and favourably discussed elsewhere. In the 1960s not only were American Poverty and Model Cities Programmes[27] ideas being disseminated, analogous ideas were being canvassed in the universities—'the infiltration of students into academic bureaucracies'[28] and in, for example, the Roman Catholic Church with discussions of collegiality and co-responsibility.

The likelihood that active-citizen participation will be sought by either officials or populace and succeed or be abandoned depends on factors which are extensively discussed in the literature of political sociology.[29] Both in America and in this country studies have been undertaken to explore the correlates of citizen activism in this sense. For example, two teams of planners in South End, Boston (Mass.), adopted different approaches under the general rubric of active-citizen type participation. One team aimed to involve 'the grass roots', the other adopted a quasi-elitest style of active participation, working with 'the community leaders'—headteachers, industrialists etc.[30] In a study of participation in government in this country one of the six projects which were undertaken concerned a comparison of planning participation in Newcastle upon Tyne, in the working-class area of Byker (not unlike Millfield) and the middle-class area of Jesmond.[31]

4. *Participation as the dissolution of organized opposition:* Generally, it can be presumed, the problem for those who are ideologically committed to the liberal ideals of self-direction and widespread acceptance within the population of responsibility for communal affairs is apathy.[32] According to Josephine Reynolds a well-advertised planning meeting in Liverpool, at Speke (population 40,000), attracted eight members of the general public. In Egremont, Lancs., more posters advertising a public planning meeting were displayed than there were inhabitants. Three people attended.[33] Margaret Harris and Monica Myers of the G.L.C. Research and Intelligence Unit calculated in the early part of 1970 the proportion of the total population of each London borough who attended a series of public meetings held by the G.L.C. to encourage public participation in planning. In Hackney the figure was as low as 0·0008 per cent.[34]

Sometimes, however, sections of the public are roused. Requests are made or agitation is undertaken for attention to be paid to specific consumer demands or for the closer involvement of excluded groups in decision-taking. One of the styles of participation which may then be operated by the decision-takers has been analysed by Philip Selznick in his influential study of the Tennessee Valley Authority. 'The forms of participation are emphasized by the administration, but action is channelled so as to fulfil administrative functions while preserving the locus of significant decision in the hands of the initiating group.'[35] Selznick pays particular attention to the technique of what he calls 'formal co-optation', by which the leaders of excluded groups are assimilated into the decision-making process in such a way that they lose the function of representing their constituents. They are formally or covertly 'co-opted into inactivity' as Silberman says when describing similar processes in Negro–white interaction in the United States and are reduced to the role of strengthening the 'rhetoric of justification' of the existing power-holders.[36]

The creation of the Citizens' Action Commission and its various committees by Richard Lee, mayor of New Haven, represents an exceptionally large-scale and skilful use of the co-optation of notables—in this case to forestall rather than combat opposition. Lee's success in radical redevelopment (including the Oak Street slum-clearance programme) depended on his conservatism with respect to the city's socio-economic structure and his care in securing the endorsement of his policies by a wide spread of influential interests.[37]

This device of urban-renewal agencies to prevent opposition by drafting community notables, 'such as local priests'[38] and securing their approval for the plans is precisely what was used in West Millfield. One of the chairmen of the residents' association eventually accepted the invitations of officials and the implicit suggestion that he alone might be spokesman for the residents' interests. 'The 31 Resolutions', he joked to the planners, 'are as dead as the 39 Articles.'[39] (The East Millfield chairman remarked, 'They may be for you. They aren't for me'.) In West Millfield the legitimacy of local approval and local communication afforded by the chairman's prior leadership of the residents' association and subsequent co-optation onto *ad hoc* planning officials' meetings (combined with the difficulty of publicly falling-out with virtually the single unambiguously high-status figure in West Millfield) meant that for the planners the problem of 'participation' was satisfactorily solved. In East Millfield, though the covert co-optation of the vicar was constantly attempted it was avoided out of principle and the principle was buttressed by episodes such as that afforded by the meeting of October 6th 1969.[40]

Other strategies of dissolutionary participation were activated, without success in Millfield, but (profiting from the Millfield experience) with more success elsewhere. The most important of these was to use the rhetoric of participation to inhibit the emergence of solidarity groups or justify the refusal to deal with them if they existed. 'Participation', to the administrator, may mean a convenient way of dealing with each resident *separately*, informing each *separately*, and not making public statements or unfairly favouring any special section of the population by dealing with particular structured groups. Especially after its participation experience in Millfield, the planning department aimed to deal only with individual queries. 'Which streets of houses will be sacrificed to make way for the Polytechnic? A spokesman for Sunderland Corporation planning department said that anyone wanting to know the details of the plans should get in touch with the planning department.'[41] 'Would the Housing Manager let the tenants know how long their houses have to stand? A spokesman for Sunderland planning department said . . . the planning department could answer such queries if tenants wrote to the Civic Centre. There was no need to write to the press, he said.'[42] Objectively, this standard advice did not make sense. It was in every way more satisfactory for householders to be informed publicly. It was cheaper, easier, quicker and gave wider coverage so far as the department was concerned to use the *Sunderland Echo*. It did make sense, however, in terms of 'perhaps the most fruitful distinction with which the sociological imagination works'—the 'personal troubles of the milieu' and the 'public issues of social structure', and preventing the former being turned into the latter.[43]

This, of course, is the classic pattern of political domination in a mass society. Totalitarianism succeeds when the population is amorphous and unorganized. Once in power totalitarian regimes attempt to complete the process of 'melting society down to a crowd', by disrupting all autonomous associations.[44]

As a way of paying lip-service to participation while using it to block genuine movements to affect the decisions of those in power, the official may also add to each statement about participation his own private qualification, *Immer langsam voran!* Forward!—at a snail's pace. You will get tired before I do.

5. *Participation as employment in programmes*: Participation as a matter of the citizen body being encouraged to swell the labour force available to carry out the work entailed in a public project is more characteristic of welfare programmes than of urban renewal. In the social services, the Seebohm report recommended maximum participation in, for example, a community-oriented family service. Individuals and groups should be involved not only in deciding what should be provided, but also in the provision of the service itself—foster-parents acting as agents to recruit others, children in hospital being cared for by their own mothers, and the day-by-day management of old people's clubs being partly the task of the members themselves.[45] Paid employment as aides and in other non-professional roles in programmes is described by Kramer as the least controversial way in which the poor in America could participate. A double benefit was supposed to flow from the employment of citizens affected by a project, changes in both the individual and the agency that employed him.[46]

The Skeffington report describes ways in which citizens can carry out unpaid tasks as their contribution to public participation in planning.[47] On the boundary of 'participation as decision-taking' and 'participation as employment on modest chores' are such schemes as that at Haringey, where the local authority offered the residents of each of the three pilot areas the chance to examine and itemize problems such as broken fences, overflowing dustbins and parked lorries, cost possible improvements and then choose between them for action up to the value of £10,000.

6. *Participation as grass-roots radicalism:* Participation as paid employment or volunteer work under the guidance and control of the planning agency represents the client at his most co-operative. The sixth type of participation represents the client at his most conflict-oriented. He participates by utilizing against the agency all available and tactically appropriate sanctions — rent strikes, demonstrations and other overt forms of protest.[47] Far from seeking to carry out tasks to alleviate the burden of the officials, such participation seeks to induce conflict, on the grounds that participation as employment reinforces the assumption of the clients' subordination in citizen-official interaction. According to the radical view of participation what is wanted is a challenge by the insurgent poor on behalf of their own interests to bureaucratic domination. This approach was, in fact, briefly commended by the U.S. Office of Economic Opportunity, which noted that a promising method of implementing maximum feasible participation was to assist citizens in developing autonomous organizations which would be competent to exert effective influence upon the decision-taking body by group forums, balloting, petitions, referendums and (specifically mentioned) protests.[49]

The Millfield Residents' Association's participation with the Sunderland planning authority was non-agitatory. Its use of reasoned arguments was a policy never departed from, except to the extent that the arguments gradually found themselves couched in sharp language, and eventually reliance was placed upon public debate through the local daily newspaper instead of letters to the planning authority. This was at a time, however, the late sixties, when the main media were reporting participation in many fields—race relations, university government, social welfare services—where the style was not that of Millfield, but of active dissent.[50] It seemed that in these fields modern society had succeeded in producing a race of what the Germans call *Umsturzmenschen*, men who want to tear up social institutions, even though they might have nothing better to put in their place.

### A Typology of Participation

The styles dealt with under the six headings of the previous section are little more than descriptions of empirically fairly common experiences in this particular field. They do not constitute a logically coherent range of models of participation. In other fields the headings dealing with types at a similarly low level of abstraction would be to varying degrees different. In industrial relations, for example, two such headings would be collective bargaining and joint consultation. Descriptions under these headings would resemble types of citizen participation in some respects. But there would also be considerable differences because of the simplicity of much industrial wage bargaining and 'the two sides of industry' when compared with urban renewal. There are differences in milieux, values at stake, established traditions and the particular aspects of participation which have proved important as discriminators in practice—in industry, for example, the question of the degree of freedom to exercise the sanction of a strike or lockout. A study of staff-student participation in universities would produce a list with similar analogues and contrasts.

The list itself could, of course, be extended endlessly by adding

new criteria, in the way that a student of comparative government and other political phenomena might wish to base his
distinctions upon structural questions of the degree or type of
leadership, mechanisms of voting, etc.; psychological questions
about the participants (authoritarianism, tough-mindedness/
tender-mindedness); or the participants' ideological (conservative, reformist, chiliastic) or non-ideological (e.g. wheeling-
dealing) outlook.

It might be useful in concluding this chapter to lay out a
simple typology of citizen participation. The following four
criteria will be used: (1) the locus of power, in the sense of the
right to participate at the point of authoritative consideration
of an issue; (2) the locus of influence, in the sense of the ability
to ensure that at the point of authoritative consideration the
outcome will be that which the wielder of influence intended;
(3) who benefits?—the key question of all politics; and (4) the
orientation of the participants to the rules of the game whatever
those rules may be. Again, for the sake of simplicity, these
variables will be considered within the framework of Western
democracy (say, the band which includes at least British and
American traditions and structures) and only polar types will be
considered.

Authoritative consideration may be in the hands of officials
(i.e. participation may be on the model of representative
democracy—as in the main structure of English local government). Alternatively it may be in the hands of the citizen body
generally—as when there are arrangements for elections or
referenda on certain issues. If urban-renewal decisions are
authoritatively considered only by officials there may be
demands that all or some of them should be authoritatively
decided by plebiscite or some other device for expressing 'the
will of the people', either those directly affected, or a wider
body. (Table 6.)

Secondly, officials may decide only on criteria they themselves
deem important (excluding 'the will of the people') i.e. only

they effectively influence their decisions at the point of authoritative consideration. At the other pole, officials may be guided exclusively by the demands placed upon them by the citizens. (Table 7.)

TABLE 6

LOCUS OF AUTHORITATIVE DECISION

| Officials | Citizens |
|---|---|
| AB<br>Representative<br>Democracy | CD<br>Direct<br>Democracy |

While the notion of the overwhelmingly influential citizen-body has principled exponents and there are therefore convenient terms available to describe its varieties,[51] in our society only derogatory terms are avilable to describe the notion of complete official influence; it will be simply referred to by convenient capital letters, AC.

TABLE 7

LOCUS OF INFLUENCE

| Officials | AC |
|---|---|
| Citizens | BD |

Thirdly, the criterion of 'who benefits?' In the case where officials exercise complete power and influence, the beneficiaries may be either the officials or the citizens. Again, in our society, usable names are lacking for cases where officials are 'feathering their own nests' either from bribes or quasi-bribes or else by idleness on the job which they are paid to do. They will be referred to simply as Aa and Ac (see Table 8) or as neglect, shielded incompetence and corruption. Where officials exercise power and control for the benefit of the citizens, there are barely acceptable, semi-derogatory terms such as 'paternalism' or 'do-goodism' (Ab, Ad).

TABLE 8

WHO BENEFITS?

| | | Locus of Authoritative Decision | | | |
|---|---|---|---|---|---|
| | | Officials | | Citizens | |
| | | Who Benefits? | | Who Benefits? | |
| | | Officials | Citizens | Officials | Citizens |
| Locus of Influence | Officials | Aa      Ac  Neglect of duties  Corruption | Ab      Ad  Paternalism | Ca      Cc | Cb      Cd |
| | Citizens | Ba      Bc | Bb      Bd  Consumer Sovereignty | Da      Dc | Db      Dd |

Cells Ba and Bc—i.e. where citizens are completely influential over the official decision-takers, but where that influence is exercised for the benefit of officials—will contain few if any cases. These can be regarded as purely notional types with no existence in any real situation. Cells Bb and Bd describe a situation of 'consumer sovereignty'.

Because of the rarity of plebiscitary arrangements all the C and D cells will contain relatively few cases, but clearly if and when such arrangements did exist, it would be expected that officials in some instances would influence the results for their own benefit. In other instances the officials would use their influence in the interests of the citizens, as the officials, not the citizens, saw them.

TABLE 9

I OFFICIALS' ARRAY

| | | | | Locus of Authoritative Decision | | | |
| --- | --- | --- | --- | --- | --- | --- | --- |
| | | | | Officials | | Citizens | |
| | | | | Who Benefits? | | Who Benefits? | |
| | | | | Officials | Citizens | Officials | Citizens |
| Locus of Influence | Officials | Orientation to Rules | Expedential | AaI | AbI | CaI | CbI |
| | | | Principled | AcI | AdI | CcI | CdI |
| | Citizens | Orientation to Rules | Expedential | BaI | BbI | DaI | DbI |
| | | | Principled | BcI | BdI | DcI | DdI |

268

Fourthly and finally the criterion of orientation to the rules of the game may be inserted. Cells Aa, Ab, Ca, Cb, Ba and Bb would include those cases where the rules of the game are used as and when it suits the officials' own purposes. This means, in practice, that the rhetoric of the rules should not be neglected, but the rules themselves should be violated when the occasion requires it:

> A prince ought to take care that he never lets anything slip from his lips that is not replete with fidelity, friendship, humanity and religion, that he may appear to him who sees and hears him altogether merciful, faithful, humane, upright and religious . . . because the vulgar are always taken in by what a thing seems to be . . . and in the world there is only the vulgar.[52]

Clearly, whether obtaining guidance directly from Machiavelli or not, instances of expediental adherence to the rules of participation (even as laid down by the officials themselves) would not be difficult to find.

Similarly, cells Ca, Cb, Ba, Bb, Da and Db would include those cases where the citizenry violated the rules of the game when it was expedient for them to do so. Cell Db, for instance, would contain examples of unprincipled, powerful mass-democratic situations, such as occasionally emerge at the height of revolutionary ardour (Jacobinism).

In any actual participatory exercise it is useful to consider which model the officials are attempting to adopt and have adopted, and which model the participating citizens would prefer. It is therefore useful to duplicate the final sixteen-fold table, showing one as the officials' array and the other as the citizens' array. (Table 9 and Table 10.)

In Millfield part of the difficulty arose from the fact that the officials were operating in the AI quarter. With evasive humility they occasionally dissembled that they were operating in the BI quarter or even (see p. 85 above) DI. Most of the time, however, they did not seem to have a very clear idea of what they ought to do, wanted to do or were doing, while the

# CONCLUSION

Millfield Residents' Association operated throughout on model BdII.

TABLE 10

II CITIZENS' ARRAY

| | | | | Locus of Authoritative Decision | | | |
|---|---|---|---|---|---|---|---|
| | | | | Officials | | Citizens | |
| | | | | Who Benefits? | | Who Benefits? | |
| | | | | Officials | Citizens | Officials | Citizens |
| Locus of Influence | Officials | Orientation to Rules | Expedential | AaII | AbII | CaII | CbII |
| | | | Principled | AcII | AdII | CcII | CdII |
| | Citizens | Orientation to Rules | Expedential | BaII | BbII | DaII | DbII |
| | | | Principled | BcII | BdII Millfield | DcII | DdII |

270

1 Albert Camus, *The Plague* (1947), *The Collected Fiction of Albert Camus*, London: Hamish Hamilton, 1960, p. 90.
2 J. Clarence Davies, *Neighbourhood Groups and Urban Renewal*. Metropolitan Politics Series No. 5, New York: Columbia University Press, 1966, pp. 154–67.
3 George Woodcock, *Anarchism*, Harmondsworth: Penguin Books, 1963, p. 450.
4 Philip Selznick, *T.V.A. and the Grass Roots* (1949), New York: Harper Torchbooks, 1966, p. 3.
5 See Edward C. Banfield's study of a set of public decisions in Chicago in the late fifties, *Political Influence: A New Theory of Urban Politics*, Glencoe: Free Press, 1961, and the results of his collaboration with James Q. Wilson, *City Politics*, Cambridge, Mass.: M.I.T. Press, 1963. See also James Q. Wilson, 'Planning and Politics', *Journal of the American Institute of Planners*, 29, November 1963; Harold Kaplan, *Urban Renewal Politics: Slum Clearance in Newark*, New York: Columbia University Press, 1963; and Edmund M. Burke, 'Citizen Participation Strategies', *Journal of the American Institute of Planners*, 34, September 1968.
6 Ralph H. Kramer, *Participation of the Poor*, New Jersey: Prentice-Hall, 1969, p. 11.
7 Lorraine F. Barie, 'The Meaning of Citizen Participation', *Urban Renewal*, Papers of Symposium held at University of Salford, 1968.
8 David R. Godschalk and William E. Mills, 'A Collaborative Approach to Planning through Urban Activities', *Journal of the American Institute of Planners*, 32, March 1966.
9 Frank Riessman, 'Anti-poverty Programmes and the Role of the Poor', in Margaret S. Gordon (Ed.), *Poverty in America*, San Francisco: Chandler Publishing Co., 1965.
10 Judy Hillman, 'Ratepayers Help in Planning of Borough', *The Observer*, September 21st 1969.
11 S. M. Lipset, *Political Man*, London: Heinemann, 1960, p. 45.
12 V. L. Allen, *Power in Trade Unions*, London: Longmans, Green, 1954, pp. 10–11, 15.
13 Alan Bullock, *The Life and Times of Ernest Bevin*, London: Heinemann, 1960, p. 206.
14 See above, p. 85.
15 J. J. Rousseau, *The Social Contract* (1762), London: Oxford University Press, World's Classics, 1947, p. 402.
16 Frederick Engels, Prefatory Note (1874) to *The Peasant War in Germany*

(1850) in Marx Engels Selected Works, Vol. I, Moscow: Foreign Languages Publishing House, 1958, p. 646.

17 Madeline Kerr, *The People of Ship Street*, London: Routledge & Kegan Paul, 1958; Elliott Liebow, *Tally's Corner, Washington D.C.: A Study of Negro Streetcorner Men*, Boston: Little, Brown, 1967; W. Lloyd Warner *et al.*, *Democracy in Jonesville*, New York: Harper 1949,; Herbert Gans, 'Urban Poverty and Social Planning', in Paul F. Lazarsfeld and others (Eds.), *The Uses of Sociology*, London: Weidenfeld and Nicolson, 1968, p. 443.

18 Daniel P. Moynihan, *Maximum Feasible Misunderstanding: Community Action in the War on Poverty*, New York: Free Press, p. 87.

19 *Ibid.*, p. 98.

20 R. A. B. Leaper, Foreword, *Participation and All That*, London: Report of Conference of Standing Conference of Council of Social Service, September 1969. (Mimeographed.)

21 Robert E. Lane, *Political Life* (1959), Glencoe: Free Press, 1964, p. 339.

22 Alexander Meiklejohn, *Political Freedom: The Constitutional Powers of the People*, London: Oxford University Press, 1966.

23 Rousseau, *op. cit.*, p. 390.

24 Leonard Trelawney Hobhouse, *Liberalism*, London: Home University Library, no date shown (about 1911), p. 228 and pp. 134–5.

25 Notably *Maximum Feasible Misunderstanding*, cited above. The book originated in a lecture delivered in the late Spring of 1967.

26 The best account of the development of such ideas during this period in the United States is Peter Marris and Martin Rein, *Dilemmas of Social Reform: Poverty and Community Action in the United States*, London: Routledge and Kegan Paul, 1967. The practical culmination was reached in the official *Community Action Programme Guide* issued by the Office of Economic Opportunity, October 1965, Volume I, pp. 27–8. A sample from the spate of diverse literature is given below. William C. Loring, Frank L. Sweetzer and Charles F. Ernest, *Community Organisation for Citizen Participation in Urban Renewal*, Boston, Mass.: Dept. of Commerce, 1957; Solomon Kobrin, 'The Chicago Area Project: A Twenty-five Year Assessment', *The Annals of the American Academy of Political and Social Science*, 322, March 1959; Charles E. Silberman, 'The Mixed-up War on Poverty', *Fortune*, 62, 2, August 1965; Richard A. Howard and Richard M. Elman, 'Poverty, Injustice and the Welfare State', *The Nation*, 202, 9, February 28th 1966; Richard W. Boone, 'What is Meaningful Participation?', *Community Development*, 1, 5, June 1966 (the journal was started in 1965); Lillian Rubin, 'Maximum Feasible Participation: The Origins, Implications and Present Status', *Poverty and Human Resources Abstracts*,

1, 1, 1967. An interesting set of essays is to be found in Fred M. Cox, John L. Erlich, Jack Rothman and John E. Tropman (Eds.), *Strategies of Community Organisation*, Itasca, Illinois: F. E. Peacock, 1970.

27 Model Cities Programmes were set up under the Demonstration Cities and Metropolitan Development Act of 1966. The Act laid down performance standards for participation as a condition of funding.

28 T. H. Marshall, 'Reflections on Power', *Sociology*, 3, 2, May 1969.

29 For an excellent discussion of these problems at the level of the local community, see Robert E. Agger, Daniel Goldrich and Bert E. Swanson, *The Rulers and the Ruled: Political Power and Impotence in American Communities*, New York: John Wiley, 1964.

30 Herbert H. Hyman, 'Planning and Citizens', *Journal of the American Institute of Planners*, March 1969.

31 Richard Batley, D. C. Galleymore and Henry Parris, Cambridge: Cambridge University Press (forthcoming).

32 For a vigorous general statement of this viewpoint, see C. Wright Mills, 'Liberal Values in the Modern World' (1952) in Irving Horowitz (Ed.), *Power, Politics and People*, New York: Oxford University Press, 1963.

33 Josephine P. Reynolds, 'Public Participation in Planning', *Town Planning Review*, July 1969.

34 Unpublished report.

35 *Op. cit.*, p. 14.

36 Charles Silberman, *Crisis in Black and White*, London: Cape, 1965, p. 204.

37 Dahl, *op. cit.*, pp. 130–9.

38 E. M. Burke, *op. cit.*

39 The planning department's minutes of the meeting read that the priest 'indicated that the 31 resolutions could now almost be disregarded'. Minutes of meeting held at planning office, April 27th 1970.

40 See above, pp. 209–12.

41 *Sunderland Echo*, April 3rd 1970.

42 *Ibid.*, January 6th 1971.

43 C. Wright Mills, *The Sociological Imagination*, New York: Oxford University Press, 1959, p. 8.

44 The phrase is that of Emile Lederer, *The State of the Masses*, New York: Norton, 1940. Hannah Arendt speaks of the atomisation of isolated individuals throughout the social structure as the basis for totalitarian rule. *Op. cit.*, p. 407.

45 *Report of the Committee on Local Authority and Allied Personal Services* (the Seebohm Report), Cmnd. 3703, London: H.M.S.O., 1968, Chapter 16.

46 Ralph H. Kramer, *op. cit.*, p. 18.

47 See above, pp. 225–7.

48 See William Hampton, *Democracy and Community: A Study of Politics in Sheffield*, London: Oxford University Press, 1970. This is a case study of the relationship between grass-roots agitation and local party politics.

49 *Community Action Programme Guide*, cited above, p. 16. The Guide was eventually withdrawn. It had stated that 'a vital feature' of every community action programme was the involvement of the poor in its planning, policy making and operation (p. 7).

50 See Norman F. Cantor, *The Age of Protest: Dissent and Rebellion in the Twentieth Century*, London: Allen and Unwin, 1970, Part IV.

51 A dominant concern of Samuel H. Beer's *Modern British Politics* (London: Faber and Faber, 2nd ed. 1969) is to discover, at each of the five stages he distinguishes, the degree of legitimacy accorded to the influence of the citizenry and the favoured mechanisms through which it might be expressed.

52 Nicolo Machiavelli, *The Prince* (1513), London: J. M. Dent, 1908, p. 140.

# CHAPTER 20

# CONCLUSION

---

The expression is generally written, 'Bureaucracy→ material efficiency + loss of human values'. Alternative forms of social organization represent possible gains in human values but inevitable losses in those other valued things, material goods and services. In productive enterprises, whether it is a matter of producing a motor car at Longbridge or producing a particular social worker on a doorstep at a pre-arranged time to cope with a problem for which her training has equipped her, this is almost certainly true. Anarcho-syndicalism, Guild Socialism and schemes for workers' control in industry generally, all must rest their case in part on human dignity, the intrinsic value of self-direction and questions of distributive justice. The technical efficiency of non-bureaucratic forms of industrial and commercial organization cannot be pressed, because (to say the least) their technical superiority has not been proved.

Bureaucracy offers, above all, the optimum possibility for carrying through specialization according to principles related solely to productivity. Individual performances are allocated to functionaries who have specialized training and who by constant practice learn more and more. The more complicated and specialized modern culture becomes, the more its external supporting apparatus demands the personally detached and strictly objective expert.

The second main advantage of bureaucratic organization is the calculability of its results. The peculiarity of modern culture and specifically its technical and economic basis demands complete predictability in the actions of all the many contributors to any final product. As Max Weber put it, this calculability is developed the more perfectly the more the organization is dehumanized and the more completely it succeeds in eliminating from its activities 'love, hatred, and all purely personal, irrational and emotional elements which escape calculation'. The watchword which governs the behaviour of the expert specialist is *sine ira et studio*, without passion and bias. More and more the material state of the masses depends upon the steady and correct functioning of the increasingly bureaucratic organizations, and the idea of eliminating them becomes more and more impractical.

It is a characteristic of modern society that the division of labour is carried to extreme lengths within organizations. But each organization is itself extremely specialized in its product. Given the very limited objective each organization sets for itself, the specialized functionaries, from labourer to managing director and from the newest clerk to the most senior official can turn their experience, skill and knowledge to the discovery and application of whichever resources and methods will prove the most effective and economical in achieving the pre-determined result. Research, therefore, becomes an integral function of such organizations. The use of researched facts and the emphasis on the necessity of allowing them to govern all activities is one sense in which the fully-developed bureaucracy is rational.

The notion of rationality does not seem to be exhausted, however, by the use of researched facts. What is a rational belief? Clearly, it is not 'a belief which is objectively correct'. One can reach a correct conclusion by a process which, on any normally accepted definition of the term is not rational. Although this sounds a little less likely, it would not ordinarily be felt that it was a contradiction to say that an incorrect version of the facts or an erroneous belief was nevertheless the result of a rational process of investigation and deduction. Rationality, then, appears to be something more than research and logic. The something more is this: openness to contradiction. A belief is rational in so far as it is open to inspection and modification in the light of new or contradictory data. In this broader sense, too, a fully-developed bureaucracy is fundamentally rational. Within the organization the appropriateness of a particular activity is constantly exposed to judgement. The effectiveness of the activity in obtaining the pre-defined ends is not itself a criterion of rationality, but the clarity of the organization's ends and the interlocking nature of the division of labour provides an incentive for mutual scrutiny. Each organization must then put its product to its consumers. The activities of modern organizations are essentially public and the public's scrutiny takes the highly disciplinary form of the acceptance or rejection of the organization's product by the process of the myriad individual decisions of value made by the consumers themselves. Bureaucratic organizations which are geared to the production of goods and services are, in the main, without the opportunity to evade the consequences of their mistakes, i.e. they do not have the right to make up by coercion for the failure of the appeal of their products or the effectiveness of their propaganda.

The bureaucracy of production has a single objective, or a set of objectives, to which the unified efforts of the whole organization can be bent. Tight, centralized direction is essential both to keep the organization moving towards its defined goals and in order to achieve the smooth articulation of the diversified efforts of the organization's personnel. If it is not to remain a more or less backward industry the production of dwellings is the task of such a centralized, hierarchical organization. This is so whether the organization is located within private industry, central government, or local government; whether it is a housing association; whether it works by tender or direct labour; and whatever the scheme of subsidies, if any.

This is an idealized picture of the modern organization. The public's values are themselves created, so far as it lies within their power to influence them, by the organizations themselves.

Empirical studies, not surprisingly, report error, idleness, over-staffing, incompetence. They show that all organizations suffer from lag, leak and friction.

There is, however, another and radically different type of bureaucracy, that which deals not with production but directly with standards of consumption. This study has thrown some light on the question of the validity of the claims of such a bureaucracy to the essential advantages of modern organizational procedure, namely, dependability, the possession of expertise, the use of research, and the rationality of decision-making, not in personal terms, but in terms of the fundamental structure, aims, and processes to which the organization is committed. The questions raised are: (1) to what degree are rationality and the objective utilization of researched data functional in this special field of planners' decisions about housing? and (2) in so far as the rational use of evidence can be shown to be functional, to what extent did it form part of the ideology and activity of the local planning authority?

In a bureaucracy of consumption, which local planning authorities are in their clearance and improvement schemes, everything depends upon the visibility and uniformity of the values at stake in what is being consumed. As was argued above (p. 254), if values are obvious and uncontroversial, the bureaucracy can supply its criteria and deliver accurate descriptions of cases falling below approved levels. But when the values are heterogeneous and opaque to the bureaucracy, it is essential that those whose values are being affected, in this case the consumers of housing, should find maximum scope for the expression of their preferences and that these preferences should be seriously considered as data: the wish to be rehoused by the Council, the wish to modernize, the wish to be left alone.

No one would deny that coercion will normally be resorted to in clearance and improvement schemes and that irreconcilable conflicts of interest between residents will be settled finally by administrative fiat. But the argument that there will inevitably be dissidents ought not to absolve the bureaucracy of consumption from discovering just who is agreeing with, and who is dissenting from its recommendations, and why. This argument about coercion at the margin only is, of course, meaningless to professionals whose conception of their role is that of arbiter of standards, and who set themselves as the best judges of what each separate family ought to value in housing and what their order of priorities should be, cost as against quality, size as against amenities, journey to work as against community attachment. Such professionals would define anything which differed from their own view of the right values for the consumer as irrelevant to the decision. They would take the view that the more the consumer's values differ from the bureaucrat's decision-of-value for him, the more urgent is the need to overcome his misguided opposition.

The extracts from *Millfield: Progress Report*—the planners' report to the planning committee of August 1969—and from other documents reveal in the treatment of the residents' association's correspondence and generally in the statements about Millfield a marked 'propensity to feign'. When the planning department said that all houses were inspected, and that they all were inspected internally, it did not feel consciously any ethical stress when the householders concerned denied this. It did not feel its case was weakened when the size of the survey and the time within which it was completed with the available manpower were shown to be incompatible. Given the task as defined for it by the office and profession, it enters the unconscious qualification: 'Sufficient have been inspected to justify the decision we have reached. We know enough about the state of these homes generally to reach the correct decision, whether they were literally and in the pedantic use of the word "inspected" or not.'

Decisively, this has not been an essay on integrity. Nothing is further removed from the argument and nothing less necessary to it than the postulate of ill-will. The issue is not that of moral turpitude, but of the institutional framework and constraints within which the relevance of particular facts to a particular decision, the importance of data to decision-making, and the very 'facticity' of fact are assessed. The status granted to information and its accuracy by the staff of an organization is not a function of their personal code or even their training so much as (1) the directness of the link between the quality of the decisions and the benefit or detriment to the decision-takers themselves; and (2) the permeability of their information structure to inspection. In the field of slum clearance, lifing and so forth, the planners' mistakes harm others but do not harm them. The people they harm are, furthermore, the Crustacea of the social and political world. Boiled alive, they utter no sound. Accurate and relevant facts, therefore, exercise no compelling force on the planners' decisions and the protection from scrutiny they enjoy or ensure means that they habitually get away, to use a homely phrase, with murder.

What are the lessons for participation and the wider framework of British-type democracy within which it was set? In Millfield, as a result of the very great advantages it enjoyed, specific issues connected with the planners' proposals were brought to a moderately successful conclusion (from the residents' point of view) only when the planners' rules were abandoned and the ordinary machinery of local councillor, M.P., publicity, public discussion and so forth was utilized.

The model of the active citizen, his receptive representative and their impartial servant, the official, still has amazing vitality, in spite of the fact that each component is stubbornly at variance with reality. This book is utopian neither about the political capacity of residents, nor the expertness of experts. The argument for democracy which draws it to its conclusion does not hold that all Millfields should have, or empirically are likely to have, anything reaching even the modest levels of activity of the Millfield Residents' Association. The argument for democracy, as thrown up by the Millfield experience, is that when by a flukish combination of circumstances a Millfield does happen, then the rhetoric of democracy and the homage paid to its symbols legitimizes scrutiny of the public authority as it affects ordinary people, while the rhetoric of alternative systems would condemn it.

When such grass-roots activity does infrequently emerge any healthy, confident bureaucracy can be expected to handle it with ease, especially by the management of data and communications generally. Alternatively, for the sake of a quiet life it can simply succumb in a piecemeal way to pressure from the normally inarticulate, just as it judiciously avoids the protests of the normally articulate.

Democracy also holds out the possibility, however, that very occasionally scrutiny from the grass-roots—from 'the toad beneath the harrow'—will lead the bureaucracy to pay more attention to the adequacy and relevance of its data and to the logic of its factual and social-philosophical arguments. Democracy does not mean that an active citizenry will always involve itself in community affairs. But put at its lowest, and this is democracy's fundamental and ineradicable justification, when it does so the public has a weapon, a frail and insubstantial weapon, but a weapon nevertheless, with which it can face the administration. And the importance of public scrutiny, including scrutiny by the general public by disclosure, as this book has argued, lies not only or even mainly in the opportunity it provides for the participants to press their own interests or for individuals to find personal fulfilment in civic activity. In the case of the bureaucracy of consumption it is a condition of its openness to contradiction, that is, it is an essential condition of the very rationality of the behaviour and beliefs of the bureaucracy itself.

# THE CORRESPONDENCE
# OF JULY–AUGUST 1969

Millfield Residents' Association                    July 21st 1969
to Town Clerk:

I am instructed to write to you in the following terms.

Millfield has suffered from planning blight since at least 1952, when the area was first officially shown as likely to be redeveloped before the end of 1971. In 1965 it was included definitely in the Council's clearance programme for 1965–70. In November 1967 it was publicly announced that the 1965 proposals were to be revised, and in March 1968 it was publicly announced that the plans would be prepared by the Autumn of 1968.

It was not until March 31st 1969 that the plans for West Millfield were at last revealed. These same plans were shown again at a public exhibition late in June of this year.

The Millfield Residents' Association, however, has been able to obtain no satisfactory answer on the status of these plans. Apparently they are not the concrete proposals of the Council nor of any of the departments concerned, but are to some unknown degree provisional.

In November 1967 the Corporation, through the chairman of the planning committee, announced that participation in planning would be sought from the residents of Millfield.

From November 14th 1968 until February 14th 1969 there was indeed participation of a sort over the plans for East Millfield. The association regrets that no official notification has been forthcoming since February 14th of the outcome of its hard work in the previous three months.

In connection with the plans for West Millfield, the association assisted the Council in every way it could in publicizing the public meeting of March 31st, and in publicizing and in other ways helping with the exhibition in June.

In spite of careful enquiries, the association has been unable to find satisfactory answers to the question of the status of these plans.

I am therefore instructed to write officially to you to enquire on this point.

In spite of equally diligent enquiries over many months the association has been unable to discover when participation in planning will commence. This is a matter of crucial importance to everyone in Millfield. As the association has always stressed, no one in the area itself benefits from delays. Blight has already bitten deeply into the area as a result of the plans to date, and bites in deeper with every additional day of uncertainty.

We therefore ask you, as a matter of great urgency, to expedite, in so far as it is within your power to do so, the Millfield plans and, as part of this, the consultation with the public which has been promised for so long, but which is still awaited.

As you know, the Minister of Housing has specifically required Sunderland to satisfy him that 'adequate participation' has been undertaken in its current plans. I have been asked to keep a careful record on these matters, because of its national importance in the light of the new Town and Country Planning Act. I regret that the record to date makes unhappy reading. I can only hope and suppose that things will improve as the Council and the association benefit from experience.

I look forward to your reply.

There are a number of particular points members of the association and of the public generally have asked me to write to you about. I shall make those the subject of separate letters.

Town Clerk to         July 24th 1969
Millfield Residents' Association:

MILLFIELD—CLEARANCE AND IMPROVEMENT

I thank you for your letter of the 21st instant and am arranging for the contents of the same to be considered by the planning
committee at their next meeting on August 27th.

Millfield Residents' Association    July 25th 1969
to Town Clerk:

MILLFIELD—CLEARANCE AND IMPROVEMENT

With reference to our letter of July 21st and to your reply of
July 24th, I am asked to thank you for arranging to have the
contents of our letter discussed by the planning committee at
their next meeting on August 27th.

The Millfield Residents' Association had been under the
impression, I think understandably, that the two questions
raised in our letter of July 21st could be answered immediately
—that there had simply been an administrative delay or an
oversight in letting us know things which had been long since
settled.

The secretary therefore addressed the letter to you and dealt
with the issues on the understanding that these were very well
known to the officials concerned in both your department and
in the town planning department.

As our original letter is to be put before the town planning
committee, however, I should like to take the opportunity to

clarify one or two points which were only implicitly dealt with in the letter of July 21st.

I believe that the following will be of assistance to the planning committee in considering our requests:

OUR REQUEST NUMBER ONE: The Millfield Residents' Association is asking first to be informed about the status of the present plans. *In particular* the association is interested in the present status of the plans for East Millfield (Central Ward). The most recent plans we possess are those shown on Plan PO 50/4/2, dated February 1969. These were presented to the Millfield Residents' Association on February 7th 1969. On February 14th the association met with Corporation representatives and discussed the association's views on Plan PO 50/4/2. These views were carefully expressed in resolutions of the association, and these resolutions were circulated to each member of the planning committee.

The association had heard nothing at all about the effect its resolutions might have had on plan PO 50/4/2. At the exhibition mainly devoted to the plans for *West* Millfield (Deptford ward), held in St. Mary Magdalene's Church Hall, Rutland Street, last month (June), there was one map showing the plans also for East Millfield. They appeared to reproduce almost exactly the details of Plan PO 50/4/2.

Our query, therefore, is: 'Is the map shown at the exhibition in June, which is almost identical with Plan PO 50/4/2, the final plan for East Millfield?'

Specifically, can the families in 'improvement areas', in the absence of further representations from the Millfield Residents' Association or other bodies or individuals, now organize their domestic affairs with the confidence that the Corporation has settled on the Plan PO 50/4/2 as its policy for the area? Can Building Societies, for example, now be informed that these proposals are firm proposals?

If not, could the association – or the public directly through the *Sunderland Echo* – be told what remains to be done in order to finalize these plans? In particular, are there any other steps the Millfield Residents' Association can take in order to assist the Corporation to reach an early decision?

As the association knows from the constant information reaching it from members and from the general public in the area, this 'ordeal by planning' is now building up resentment to explosive force.

OUR REQUEST NUMBER TWO: Our second request is simply to be informed of the date, or at least to be given some indication of the date, on which it is intended that public participation in planning—following on the June exhibition and the planning committee chairman's undertakings on his occasional visits to committee meetings of the Millfield Residents' Association —should take place.

In conclusion the association would like to take this opportunity to summarize its detailed resolutions. Briefly, the association's resolutions advocate (1) an end to uncertainty over what is planned for Millfield in both Central and Deptford wards; (2) representation to the Minister of dwellings and areas which the health department on the basis of survey define as 'unfit' or as clearance areas—if after public inquiry etc. the Minister approves the Corporation's case, the association advocates clearance and humane rehousing, together with adequate compensation, with all due speed; (3) a complete end to planning blight in all remaining areas.

This letter has been duplicated in order to ease the work of your department in having it circulated to the members of the planning committee in time for its August meeting.

Planning Department to                    July 28th 1969
Millfield Residents' Association:

MILLFIELD—PUBLIC PARTICIPATION

I refer to your letter of July 16th addressed to the chairman
of the planning committee which has been passed to me for
attention. I also have your letter of July 21st addressed to the
Town Clerk which I believe you have been informed will be
considered by the planning committee at their next meeting.

With regard to the points (1)–(3) raised in your letter, I am
sure you will recall that the the status of the proposals was
referred to by the chairman of the planning committee at the
first public meeting for West Millfield—they would be accepted,
changed or scrapped depending on (a) the views expressed by
the residents when the exhibition was held and (b) the outcome
of discussions with the Millfield Residents' Association. In other
words, the proposals for slum clearance, roads and lifing have
exactly the same status as the first proposals prepared in relation
to Millfield (the area east of the Durham railway).

So far I have received no communication from you regarding
the plans, only two letters regarding their status. I can hardly
believe that this is the only comment of the Millfield Residents'
Association? If it would assist, I would be willing to forward
copies of the two proposals maps showing (a) clearance/
improvement and (b) roads. I think you will agree that there
would be no point in presenting the present plans to Council
for their approval if they are going to be altered as a result of
discussions with the Millfield Residents' Association. This would
only cause further delay.

Residents' Association                                    July 29th 1969
to Town Clerk:

MILLFIELD

My instructions are to address future correspondence through
you, as well as to give maximum publicity to the problems of
Millfield, including publicity to correspondence dealing with
the public business of the area. This decision was taken after two
years of extraordinarily unsatisfactory communication with the
planning authority which, as the public record shows, was very
much a one-sided affair, namely, a one-way flow from the
association to the planning authority.

Of course I must follow out this instruction until it is amended
or reversed.

However, today I received *the very first communication in writing
through the post that has ever come to the association from the planning
authority* in the two years of the association's existence. The
association, over the same two years, has sent many, many
letters to the planning authority; it has sent hundreds of pages
of accounts of 'participation' between Corporation representatives and the association, accounts of public meetings, detailed
resolutions, none of which have been acknowledged; it has, on
extreme occasions, broken its rule of 'quiet consultation' by
writing letters to the local press.

The extent to which the association has been left in the dark
—I only give one example—is the fact that it was very well
known that the suggestion-box contents were to discussed at the
health and planning sub-committee at its meeting of July 23rd
1969. This box has been deliberately left to the unorganized
public by the association and as a matter of policy not used by
the association (although privately some members of the association did use it). The association took the view that suggestion
boxes are very poor instruments of public participation. This
was very well borne out by the fact that, for example, the road

proposals about which there is such strong feeling in the area, elicited only six comments, *three* of which came from committee members of the Millfield Residents' Association who could not forbear to comment. There was also a petition, again the work of committee members, privately. In the whole of the Booth Street clearance area (1972 clearance), where there is so much distress, only five comments were made. Two of these came from sisters, both who, as I know, spontaneously secured the help of the secretary's wife at the exhibition in filling out the comment slip. (We know all of this, of course, from *unofficial* sources closely connected with the planning department, not at all through formal channels.)

The association was not informed that the health and planning sub-committee would be dealing with Millfield on July 23rd 1969 (obviously, as the association has never been informed about anything officially and in writing). Yet it was against the background of these suggestion box comments only that the compulsory purchase order for the Washington Street area was discussed, and decisions reached on the fate of the south end of Washington Street itself.

Of course, a great deal remains to be said publicly about the quality of the surveys carried out in February and March of 1968, which ostensibly formed the basis of the planning department's recommendations—an absolutely crucial matter. The association has recorded from the exhibition plans the scores given on the evidence of amenities and there is a very large discrepancy between the facts of the situation and the scores. This is scarcely surprising, when it is borne in mind that the planning department/health department's survey, which was not commenced until some time after February 19th 1968, was claimed to have been completed for the whole of the south side of the river (*8,000* pre-1914 dwellings!) by March 18th 1968. Anyone with any knowledge of survey technique would know that such a claim was extravagant in the extreme with the resources in personnel devoted to the task by the planning and health departments (with the assistance of some workers from other departments). Objections at public meetings and among committee members of the Millfield Residents' Association themselves that they were not surveyed *at all* have always been denied by the planning department. But again, anyone with knowledge of door-to-door surveys can only look with amazement at the planning department's spokesman's claim that in a single month, when *8,000* households were miraculously surveyed, in only 'a few cases' were people not in when the surveyor called. This is contrary to all known experience of surveys. These comments refer only to press releases from the planning department. In participation meetings with the association, of which tape-transcripts are available, the story is, if anything, more sombre and less satisfactory still.

However, sir, when the association has at last 'broken' as far as its hitherto exemplary patience and forbearance is concerned, and has publicly stated that it is considering political action, when it has finally come to a decision that it is fruitless to pursue matters any further through the planning authority, when it has decided to make public the record, a letter is received for the first time from the planning authority. And—is it coincidence?—on the very day of the publication of the Skeffington report on public participation in planning which recommends disclosure and public debate going far beyond anything the Millfield Residents' Association itself has ever sought or even contemplated—on this very day the planning authority sends its first ever letter! (Dated July 28th 1969, received July 29th 1969.)

I enclose a copy of the letter, together with the association's reply. We should be grateful if you would channel the reply to the planning officer.

Millfield Residents' Association to Planning Department
(via the Town Clerk): July 30th 1969

MILLFIELD—CLEARANCE AND IMPROVEMENT

I received yesterday (July 29th 1969) the enclosed letter from the planning officer.

My instructions are that in future all correspondence must go through the Town Clerk, and I must abide by this instruction until it is modified or reversed. I should be glad, therefore, if you would convey this letter to the appropriate responsible officer.

*I. The Proposals Maps*

The planning officer refers in his paragraph No. 3 to the two maps dealing with the proposals: (a) clearance and improvement and (b) roads. The clearance and improvement map was asked for in our letter of April 11th 1969. On April 14th 1969 the association was verbally informed that this was contrary to planning committee policy and the sight of the maps was refused.

I assume that you will have no difficulty in finding the planning committee minute which lays down that policy, and the minute which now permits the planning officer to offer the Millfield Residents' Association a copy of the maps.

The Millfield Residents' Assocaition has now, under rather adverse circumstances, made careful notes of all these proposals.

However, it goes without saying that the association would find it useful to have copies of the maps showing the clearance/improvement proposals and the road proposals, as details are always cropping up which can only be answered with difficulty, or which cannot be answered at all, from our notes.

We should be extremely grateful, therefore, if you could arrange to have the two maps in question sent to the secretary as quickly as it can be arranged.

*II. The Status of the Present Proposals*

We are in some difficulty regarding the planning officer's 'clarification' of the position regarding the present status of the plans.

In particular, we are extremely puzzled by his reference to the East Millfield plans as the model of the status of the West Millfield plans. It is precisely because the association has been left so completely in the dark about the East Millfield plans that the question arose.

As I point out in the letter to you dated July 25th 1969, Plan PO 50/4/2 was shown to the association on February 7th 1969. On February 14th 1969 the association commented on that plan in the form of 9 resolutions. No further word reached the association about Plan PO 50/4/2 until it was seen *virtually unaltered* at the June exhibition. The association therefore has no idea whether Plan PO 50/4/2 is now the plan which the planning department intends to present to the Council (and that the recommendations of the association therefore had absolutely no effect whatsoever), or whether, after so long a delay the association's resolutions have not been considered yet.

It is essential for the people of Millfield to know soon whether their houses do have a life of thirty-plus years, and so on, and that these facts be publicly announced with great firmness so that families can start again to repair and improve their homes with some confidence in the future. Of course, definiteness of long life is a *sine qua non* for financial institutions which families need to approach for the necessary resources for major improvements. Because of the continued indefiniteness of the plans, Building Societies and so forth will 'not touch Millfield'.

The question of the status of the plans is therefore a tremendously important one, and it is clearly not answered by the planning officer in his letter of July 28th 1969.

In *West* Millfield the matter is, if anything, worse. The area is terribly blighted in parts by long-standing threats of slum-clearance (in some small parts resentful that long-standing *promises* of slum-clearance have been repeatedly unredeemed). The plans of March 31st 1969 has blighted nearly all the rest of the area with its maze of 'road proposals'. We notice that at the meeting of the health and planning sub-committee on July 23rd 1969 the members were told that the Shepherd Street 'road threat' was unreal, in that (I quote from the planning officer's document which has been passed to me unofficially from his department), 'This is a purely local road which is likely to be implemented when the houses are cleared'. If this means what it appears to mean, that the houses will not be cleared to make way for the road, but the road will only be built after the houses are demolished due to unfitness, then why cannot the minds of the families in Shepherd Street be put at rest in that knowledge?

(We know that it is not as clear as that, and we are obliged to wonder whether the sub-committee were fully appraised of the fact that *the other possibility* is that the road would be built when Shepherd Street was cleared *for industrial purposes*, as announced by the chairman of the planning committee at a meeting in Diamond Hall school on November 15th 1967.)

Shepherd Street is, of course, only one example. The same confusion on the status of the present proposals is present in a form very like this in every street in East and West Millfield.

Indeed, the degree of confusion is now so absolute that it is impossible to deal with it in the course of a single letter; the various strands would only be untangled at book length, even at this early stage.

The question of the status of the plans, however, is so important, that I should like to give one more specific example from many scores of examples, and perhaps an answer to this specific problem may be forthcoming. The association was aware that the south end of Washington Street, containing 39 dwellings, had been inspected by the health department. Twenty-two dwellings had been judged fit and 17 unfit. (The whole question of the objectivity of the 1957 Housing Act standard is an important but different matter which will not be pursued here.) On May 27th, however, the chairman of the planning committee appeared uninvited and unannounced (but none the less welcome) at a committee meeting of the Millfield Residents' Association purely in order to offer the Millfield Residents' Association a chance to express the opinion of the people in south Washington Street on whether or not they *wanted* to be cleared. The association's committee was assured in unambiguous terms that what the majority wanted would be implemented. The survey questionnaires from south Washington Street (the work of a Millfield Residents' Association street representative) were sent to the planning authority. Nothing more has been heard of them. (As usual, no acknowledgement of their receipt has been forthcoming.) Unofficially, one of the joint chairmen of the Millfield Residents' Association has been told that as a majority of the houses are fit, the popularity or otherwise of clearance is irrelevant. That is understandable. But what then was the status of the original proposal for the south end of Washington Street—i.e. what effect *could* the opinions, the work, the evidence, of the Millfield Residents' Association have in altering the proposals?

*III. Discussions with the Millfield Residents' Association*

The planning officer's letter of July 28th 1969 is, surprisingly, headed 'Millfield—Public Participation'.

It is important that the Millfield Residents' Association's view on this be recorded. The subject of our correspondence is not and never has been public participation. That is not the issue. The issue is the welfare of the residents of Millfield.

Public participation arises as an issue in so far as it results in furthering the welfare of the people of Millfield, and is of no relevance otherwise. I think it is fair to say that after its two years' experience of public participation many doubts have grown about its effectiveness as an instrument in furthering the interests of the people of Millfield, and it is obvious that new instrumentalities are now being very much canvassed.

I was, however, instructed to write to you on various topics, which I did, in my letter of July 21st 1969, to which the planning officer's letter of July 28th is a response. *One* of the points I raised was that of the long-awaited date of the commencement of 'participation'.

Quite simply, sir, the planning officer again neglects to answer that question, and presumably no answer can be forthcoming before the matter is discussed at the planning committee on August 27th 1969.

In the light of the documented history of the association's contact with the planning authority the rest of the planning officer's letter can only be regarded as extraordinary in its implication that the association has been inactive in pressing its views and, more importantly, the views of the public as expressed in public meetings etc.

As I have already pointed out, I am instructed to give the fullest publicity to these matters, this being a reversal of the association's policy of the previous two years of minimum publicity in order to assist the Corporation's proposals to be prepared under circumstances favourable to themselves. It is gratifying to see that the Skeffington committee report in fact recommends the course the association has recently adopted as its own.


Residents' Association                     August 1st 1969:
to Town Clerk:                             Reference No. 1

MILLFIELD RESIDENTS' ASSOCIATION

In my letter to you dated July 21st 1969 I said that there were a number of particular points I had been instructed to take up.

These have now been prepared in the form of a series of separate letters. I have shown today's date on all of them, and identified them with reference numbers.

In this letter, reference No. 1, I should like to make three points:

1. The accompanying letters, reference Nos. 2–6, are mainly requests for information or clarification.

In our contacts with the planning authority information and clarification have been exceedingly difficult to obtain. The grounds given for not providing information and clarification has been one or other variation on the argument that the plans and proposals are provisional, that this is not their definitive form, and that the *final* proposals at the end of the day (as they are submitted to the appropriate committee of the Council? as they are submitted by the appropriate committee of the Council to the Council for approval? as they are eventually approved after public inquiries etc.?) will be different.

I am instructed by the committee of the Millfield Residents' Association to say that this argument seems to the committee to have little value. It seems that *at each stage* it is necessary for everyone to be quite clear what the proposals are *at that stage*. It is, of course, impossible to discuss proposals if one does not know what the proposals are. If proposals are concrete and clear, then by discussion it is possible to move to a second set of concrete and clear proposals. That seems, to the committee of the Millfield Residents' Association, to be elementary. If the planning authority's view is different from this, then the Millfield Residents' Association would, I imagine, be glad to consider the basis of its contrary view.

2. If it is intended to submit these letters to the planning committee on August 27th 1969 or at some other time, we should be pleased if the association could be informed of the outcome.

The matters dealt with are inevitably complex—that is in the nature of the material. We recognize, however, that we have no control over the way in which these letters will be presented, if they are presented at all, and we confine our request to this: if they *are* précised we should be much obliged if the Millfield

Residents' Association could be forwarded a copy of each précis.

3. The Millfield Residents' Association appreciates the force of the argument of the report of the Skeffington committee in favour of maximum openness and of the full use of the media of communication. This is usually taken to apply only to the Corporation, in the sense that public business is the business of the public and ought to be made public, and the obligation appears only to lie with the Corporation to publicize its affairs. The Millfield Residents' Association, for its part, accepts the necessity of conducting its business in public, as expressed in a resolution presented to the Corporation representatives on February 14th 1969. At the appropriate time, therefore, we expect that this correspondence, together with relevant accounts of the transactions of the Millfield Residents' Association will be made public through one or more of the media.

August 1st 1969:
Reference No. 2

ROAD PROPOSALS—WEST MILLFIELD

I am instructed to draw your attention to the resolution proposed, seconded and passed *nem. con.* at the public meeting of July 8th 1969:

> That the people of Millfield do not think it necessary to have *road proposals* for through traffic in the area. This applies especially to the roads shown by broken lines on the Road Proposals Map displayed at the exhibition [in St. Mary Magdalene's Hall in June], but it also applies to other roads which would disrupt the community of Millfield.

The minutes of the public meeting note: 'It was generally felt that any road required to carry traffic "past" Millfield ought to be routed along the Penshaw branch railway and *not* along Shepherd Street and St. Luke's Road.'

When this minute was discussed at a subsequent meeting of the committee of the Millfield Residents' Association strong sentiments were expressed in support of this resolution.

The Millfield Residents' Association is keenly aware of the fact that road proposals concern the whole of the town, and an even wider area and population, and not solely Millfield. The association is sensitive to these possibilities, in so far as the case for (so to say) 'sacrificing' Millfield for the welfare of the town as a whole has ever been made by the planning authority.

We have been influenced, however, by the following considerations:

1. The road pattern seems to depend on the feasibility of utilizing the upper deck of Queen Alexandra Bridge for road traffic. (We say 'seems to' because it has been difficult to elicit any clear account of the factual basis of the road proposals. For example, these questions are relevant for a rational judgment on the part of the people of Millfield on the justifiability of demolition of homes to make way for roads: (i) Can the upper deck of Alexandra Bridge be so utilized? (ii) If the answer to that question is still unknown, what justification could be forthcoming for blighting wide areas of West Millfield before that crucial issue was settled?)

In so far as the use of Alexandra Bridge's upper deck remains dubious, it seems premature to present road proposals which depend upon its use, and most unfortunate and perhaps unnecessary in its effects on the security of Millfield families. If any information is available on this matter, we should, of course, be pleased to receive it.

In the meantime, it seems very understandable that families intensely resent the blighting effect of road proposals which appear to a great or lesser extent to depend upon another project of dubious feasibility, but one which will have to be decided sooner or later, and in the view of the M.R.A. should have been a decision *preceding* the road proposals for West Millfield. [*Author's note:* The Road Proposals Map showed four alternative roads. They all diverged from Queen Alexandra Bridge.]

2. Local knowledge of the deep dredging of the river in close proximity to the bridge in order to allow for the launching of the increasingly large ships from Doxford's yard, as well as the early discontinuance of the use of the top deck for rail traffic due to instability and the serious problems raised by mining subsidence in the late 1920s, makes local opinion sceptical of the possibilities of using the upper deck—I may record, sceptical in the extreme.

3. It appears that any through traffic could be accommodated on a road constructed along the old Durham–Sunderland and old Sunderland–Washington (i.e. trans-Alexandra Bridge) railway lines which lie to the south of the river, without affecting domestic property at all, thus benefiting the town, without harming Millfield, surely an ideal solution.

4. In so far as the roads shown are strictly local roads, for traffic with business within West Millfield, it would seem to be possible and desirable *either* (i) to utilize the existing road pattern with modifications to resolve conflicts of use, modifications which do not involve the demolition of property, such as are quite a familiar feature of the road engineer's trade; *or* (ii) to remove blight *resulting from road proposals* by making it clear that these local roads will only depart from the existing basic road pattern when clearance of domestic property *because of unfitness* makes the land available for such changes.

In the case of a 'long life' street such as Shepherd Street this would involve a clear public undertaking by the Corporation that *preservation* was *primary*, and the road proposals apparently affecting that street (of course it is badly blighted at this moment by the road proposals) are secondary considerations, and will only be implemented if and in so far as the 'preservation' policy of the Corporation has failed.

The committee of the Millfield Residents' Association was

shocked to discover that in the document discussed by the health and planning sub-committee on July 23rd 1969 the planning officer's observations on the Shepherd Street petition was to the effect that 'this is a purely local road which is likely to be implemented when the houses are cleared'.

*If* this means the same as the Millfield Residents' Association is advocating, namely the primacy of preservation and the complete removal of 'road proposals blight' (but, as usual, it is not clear what *is* meant by the observation, and we should be grateful for the same sort of clarification as the councillors present must have required), then why was not this stated in answer to the many queries along these lines which have been addressed to the planning authority in public meetings and elsewhere?

5. The fifth and final consideration studied by the Millfield Residents' Association was the evidence given by the planning authority at a recent public inquiry, where it was revealed that because of financial stringency the plans for the inner ring road had been severely curtailed. The M.R.A. considered that if the essential *central* traffic proposals were now in abeyance, it was unjust, iniquitous and scandalous to place dozens of Millfield families under the worry and distress of planning blight stemming from road proposals the time scale of which was so capricious.

We appreciate, sir, that much of the discussion at the public meeting and in committee might appear to someone thoroughly familiar with the details of the proposals as mistaken or irrelevant.

We wish to insist, however, that this is almost entirely due to the fact that the association has sought and been unable to obtain clear answers to the questions which would enable it to improve the quality and increase the constructiveness of its contribution. To the extent that the above five points are based upon correct information and understanding of the facts of the situation, they stand. In so far as they are based upon lack of knowledge of the facts, the association is immensely eager to be supplied with the facts in question.

August 1st 1969:
Reference No. 3

## MILLFIELD—CLEARANCE AND IMPROVEMENT: AREAS SHOWN WHITE

In discussing the maps displayed at the June exhibition, the association has had its attention drawn to certain apparent omissions, and I am instructed to enquire about them, through you.

1. Dwellings adjacent to the Villa bottling plant: A group of about half-a-dozen dwellings (roughly 14–22 Bell Street— even numbers) on the map entitled *Deptford—Clearance and Improvement* have been left 'white', i.e. they have not been coloured in any of the colours which indicate the nature of the proposals which will affect them.

If five or six dwellings can be left standing in an area of general clearance, this is an important consideration for the people of Millfield in arriving at a judgement about the proposals for other parts of the area.

I am therefore instructed to ask you for enlightenment on the proposals for this group of dwellings. As matters stand, it is only possible to speculate, and inevitably there are queries in Millfield about the possible basis for the exclusion of these particular dwellings from the proposals.

2. Another exclusion that the Millfield Residents' Association would like enlightenment on is the derelict building on the corner of John Candlish Road and Hylton Road.

There have *already* been adverse comments in the press about this property (formerly Dr. Mair's surgery), as well as strong words contained in minutes of the association which have been passed to the planning authority.

It is therefore exceedingly surprising to find that there are apparently no proposals for this property, which is perhaps the outstandingly ugly and dangerous structure in the whole district.

3. Other structures in the body of the area are also left 'white' without explanation, but these do not seem to raise the same problems as those shown in 1. and 2. above.

The association wishes to apologize for any vagueness in its identification of the problem areas. In spite of the most conscientious note-taking at the exhibition it proved impossible to record all details, and it is greatly regretted that the association's request for a copy of the proposals map was refused initially.

Future references will be greatly assisted when we do receive the relevant maps, which we expect to have shortly.

August 1st 1969:
Reference No. 4

GROUP OF DWELLINGS IN ST. LUKE'S ROAD

At the public meeting of July 8th 1969 a Mrs. Scorer asked the association to enquire on her behalf about the proposals for the group of houses which are roughly 87–95 St. Luke's Road.

As I understand it, Mrs. Scorer's is the dwelling that would appear to be scheduled to remain standing when all the others have been demolished.

Without the proposals' map to hand I regret that I cannot be more specific than this. No doubt, however, our request that the proposals for that particular small area be explained will enable us to be of assistance to the enquirer.

Although it might seem strange that Mrs. Scorer has not enquired herself directly to the planning authority, or if she has done so nevertheless has sought the assistance of the committee of the Millfield Residents' Association, the simple explanation is that the experience of enquirers in the past has not encouraged them to think that without the aid of a determined association a clear or helpful answer will be forthcoming.

I have been instructed to write to you about this matter, and I look forward to an early reply.


August 1st 1969:
Reference No. 5


ROAD PROPOSALS—EFFECTS ON PINE STREET

Residents of Pine Street have approached the committee of the Millfield Residents' Association seeking assistance over the matter of the road proposals.

Apparently a resident in the last few days had virtually completed the sale of his dwelling in Pine Street, when the buyer terminated negotiations on the grounds that her solicitor (the buyer's solicitor) had discovered that because of the road proposals 'Pine Street will be down in two or three years'.

The committee is not in a position to say whether this is an accurate account of what actually transpired on either side, but it agreed to take the matter up with the Town Clerk, at the enquirer's request.

On the Road Proposals map the road is indeed shown as affecting property in Pine Street.

We should be grateful for an answer that would be helpful to the enquirer.

August 1st 1969:
Reference No. 6

## OBJECTORS' COSTS OF REPRESENTATION AT PUBLIC INQUIRIES

I should like to thank you most sincerely for your prompt acknowledgement of our communications to you.[1] It is indeed most refreshing after the rather unsatisfactory state of affairs before the Millfield Residents' Association resolved to conduct its business through your department.

I am instructed to ask for clarification on the subject of objectors' costs at public inquiries connected with housing and planning proposals.

As I understand it the position at present is this: An objector to the Council's proposals at a public inquiry who has been wholly or partially successful may qualify for an award of costs within the terms of the Ministry of Housing and Local Government Circular 73/1965, but that, in the case of a claim for good maintenance in a public inquiry into a compulsory purchase order, this does not constitute 'an objection', and therefore even a successful claim in such a case does not attract an award of costs.

The association asks for an answer to the following questions:

1. Is this still, broadly, the legal position?

2. Are there any proposals which in the time period relevant to the planning and housing proposals for the area of East Millfield (Central ward) and West Millfield (Deptford ward) which would change (or have already changed) the provisions of Circular 73/1965, and which you think the association ought to consult?

3. Is the statement of our paragraph three of this letter correct? We should be glad of any written clarification of the position if our paragraph three is either incorrect in substance, or in one regard or another may be misleading.

304

Once again I should like to thank you for the promptness of your department in transacting the business which has been put to it, which is certainly appreciated by the secretary, and will be a great relief to the Millfield residents' committee, as well as to all the people in the area, who have been unable for so long to obtain anything but extremely vague, ambiguous and indefinite information or, more frequently, no information at all.

NOTE

1 The Town Clerk's department had sent a card acknowledging receipt of the letter of July 29th.

Town Clerk to                  August 5th 1969
Millfield Residents' Association:

I duly received your six separate letters dated the 1st instant and wish to confirm that these will be considered along with your other letters by the planning committee at their next meeting on the 27th instant. The chairman of the planning committee and the officials concerned have certainly during the past months got round a table to discuss matters with your association but I think it was apparent from the beginning that total agreement would not necessarily be reached and there was bound to be at some stage and on some points a clash of interests. It is for the Council to decide policy and I hope to let you know what their plans are for Millfield as soon as possible. However, I cannot do so until after the 27th instant. Every attempt seems to have been made to involve the residents in town planning the chairman of the planning committee and the chairman (*sic*) have done their best to explain what they are doing.

Residents' Association                 August 8th 1969
to Town Clerk:

MAPS OF HOUSING AND ROAD PROPOSALS:
WEST MILLFIELD

I refer to our letter of July 30th 1969.

You will remember that certain maps were exhibited by the planning authority at a public meeting it organized in West Millfield on March 31st 1969. Because of the inappropriate scale, members of the audience were unable to see how the proposals affected their particular property, and on April 11th 1969, therefore, the M.R.A. wrote to the planning authority offering to display them again at its own public meeting on April 14th 1969.

The use of the maps was refused.

After your intervention the planning authority wrote on July 28th 1969 offering the maps to the association. The offer was accepted, through you, by return of post.

I regret to say that I am as yet still without the maps in question.

The committee had expected that at its meeting on August 7th several outstanding details could have been cleared up— more than four months after the original display— by consulting these maps. This is, of course, much more than four months after the maps were originally promised by the 'Autumn' of 1968.

I am asked to write to you once again, therefore, for your assistance in having the maps referred to in our letter of July 30th 1969 sent to the above address as soon as can be arranged.

Residents' Association                      August 9th 1969
to Town Clerk:


MILLFIELD: PLANNING PROPOSALS


In connection with your letter of August 5th 1969 which has
been considered by the committee of the Millfield Residents'
Association, I am instructed to reply in the following terms:

The committee expresses regret that the sense of several
remarks in your letter of August 5th 1969 is contrary to the
record. Summaries of the record have been transmitted to you.
The full version is in possession of the planning authority, having been conscientiously maintained by the association in the
interests of participation—accounts of the participation meetings for East Millfield November 14th 1968 to February 14th
1969; accounts of our own committee meetings; analyses of
public meetings with full public reactions to and preparation
for the Council's proposals; special interviews of householders;
etc.—and sent to the chairman of the planning committee.

The committee is therefore astonished at your statement that
'the chairman of the planning committee and the officials concerned have certainly during the past months got round a table
to discuss matters with your association'. There has never been
any meeting at all round a table or anywhere else between the
association and the planning committee chairman and the officials concerned to discuss West Millfield, the main area concerned in the original correspondence with you on July 21st
1969. Your statement as it applies to East Millfield depends up
'the past months', meaning, on August 5th, events which terminated on the previous February 14th.

Our original request in our letter of July 21st 1969 was to be
given the date of the commencement of the long promised
participation in West Millfield. It seems unhelpful, therefore,
for the people concerned to be told that 'certainly during the
past months' things have taken place that they know quite well

have not taken place, and which by no stretching of the English language could be said to have taken place.

Your assurance that 'every attempt has been made to involve the residents' depends upon the meaning given to the phrase 'every attempt'. On the Corporation's side the deliberations of the Skeffington committee have been held up as the pattern of what was to be hoped for. Now that the Skeffington committee has reported, and the M.R.A. committee has had the opportunity to study the report (*People and Planning*) the Skeffington version of every attempt and the attempts that have in fact been made in Millfield are clearly very much at variance.

Your statement that the chairman of the planning committee ('*and* the chairman' you write, much to our puzzlement) 'have done their best to explain what they are doing' may or may not be true. That it is 'the best they can do' is your judgement, not ours. But if it is you who are correct, and what has transpired is the best of which the people concerned are capable, then this puts the matter in a worse and not a better light.

The points you raise about the impossibility of 'total agreement' and about the 'clash of interests' which at some stage is 'bound to' arise are complex. What degree of agreement is possible, and the point at which any of the multitude of interests involved may clash are questions, however, which have not emerged. In East Millfield the plans of February 7th 1969 were not a response to the first twenty-two of the M.R.A.'s resolutions in any intelligible sense. The detailed resolutions 23–31 which were presented on February 14th 1969 have not been referred to again by the Corporation in any way that the Millfield Residents' Association knows of. In West Millfield no meetings between Corporation representatives and the Millfield Residents' Association have been arranged or held and therefore where agreement lies and where interests clash is necessarily not known.

I hope this response by the committee of the Millfield Residents' Association in reply to your letter of August 5th 1969 is of assistance in clarifying at any rate a few of the issues involved.

We were surprised to read that you intend to send all our letters of August 1st 1969 to the planning committee for consideration at its meeting on August 27th 1969, including, most surprising of all our reference No. 6, of August 1st 1969. The last seems to be pre-eminently a straightforward matter to be dealt with by the Town Clerk's department. It seems regrettable that a decision should have been made to postpone an answer until some time after August 27th, in view of the urgency of the suffering in Millfield due to delays to date.

There is some speculation in Millfield about the possibility that an explanation of the desperately prolonged agony of Millfield is the view in some quarters that the best way to deal with an active citizenry is to prevaricate until the active citizenry loses heart and lapses into apathy and passivity in the face of calculated obfuscation, ambiguity, dilatoriness and misrepresentation.

The Millfield Residents' Association is at pains to discount such rumours. It is too well aware that representatives and officials now know that the people of Millfield will pursue their rights and proclaim the truth against the greatest odds, and over whatever time period is necessary to see that justice is at last done.

P.S. This letter was withheld until today (August 13th) in order to amend it if necessary on receipt of the plans, which were 'offered' on July 28th 1969 and 'accepted' by letter delivered by hand by myself and the Reverend W. J. Taylor.

# MEETING BETWEEN MILLFIELD RESIDENTS' ASSOCIATION REPRESENTATIVES AND CORPORATION REPRESENTATIVES TOWN HALL, MONDAY, SEPTEMBER 15th 1969

Present: Representatives of the Millfield Residents' Association, the chairman, the Reverend W. J. Taylor and the joint chairman, Father C. Leslie Barron, Mrs. Brown, and Messrs. Darke, Dennis, Larcombe and Watson.

Six members of the planning (emergency) sub-committee, including the chairman of the planning committee.

Officers of the planning department, the Borough Engineer's department, the housing department, the health department, the Town Clerk's department, the Architect's department.

The representatives of the Millfield Residents' Association were admitted at 7.50 p.m.

*Chairman of the planning committee:* The meeting will be terminated at 8.30. I think the best way to begin is to ask the Millfield residents to say what they wish to say.

*Chairman of the association:* Well, as the secretary is the one who has been principally concerned with the correspondence which we are going to discuss, perhaps . . .

*Secretary:* I think that anyone who has looked at this correspondence will see that the contributions to it by the Millfield Residents' Association are considerably more bulky and voluminous than those from the Corporation. I am therefore somewhat surprised at the request.

What the Millfield Residents' Association has to say on the subject which we were asked here tonight to discuss has been said, after due consideration and careful thought, in those letters. One of the most shattering things I have ever heard was something a very senior councillor said to me a fortnight ago. He said, 'Nobody reads long letters'. Well, we are here at your request to discuss these 'long letters'. All the Millfield Residents' Association representatives, I assure you, have read them, and I assume you all have. I do not see I can add more at this stage. What we have to say has been said as clearly as we could say it in our letters, and it does not seem possible to make it any clearer with an impromptu summary now. What we have to say is in the correspondence, and I cannot say it again without simply reading it out aloud to the meeting.

I should, of course, be glad to clarify any particular points, at the request of any members of this committee, who have no doubt studied the letters, and may have questions to ask about them.

*Councillor:* There are two sets of proposals on the board. We have the history of the East Millfield proposals, and of the modifications as a result of the Millfield Residents' Association's counter-proposals.

We are not here to engage in recriminations about the past.

What we want to know is: Are the amended proposals broadly acceptable to the association?

*Chairman of the association:* We were given to understand at the last participation meeting in East Millfield—on February 14th—when we presented further resolutions, we were given to understand that these would be gone through, and that before the plan went to Council there would be a meeting. There would be at least two representatives of the Millfield Residents' Association who would meet the planning committee, or a group of representatives from various of the Corporation committees concerned.

We would be given the grounds for the changes in policy.

It therefore came as a great surprise to us to see that the Council had approved the clearance of Hedley Street area on April the 9th.

As amateurs we might think that on the whole it is the worst area.

But all we have ever said is that if the Corporation believes it can legally represent a particular area, then let it go ahead and represent it legally and put it to the test of a public hearing.

We felt let down over that.

*Councillor:* Let us take the point that the other councillor made.

What comments have you on these proposals?

Do you broadly agree or disagree?

*Chairman of planning committee:* The planning committee decided on February 26th 'that at the appropriate time' M.R.A. representatives would be invited to a special meeting of the planning committee. That has not been convened yet.

Building Societies have been contacted. We are looking into these things.

You will have this meeting.

*Chairman of the association:* I agree that all these things have to be seen to—Building Societies and so forth: lots of our proposals have nothing to do with the fabric of the area. There are all sorts of social implications.

But we wanted to be given an answer on any changes in policy which were based on our resolutions: *Why* should Hedley Street be cleared?

*Councillor:* There are two sets of proposals on the board there. The second set represents changes made after consultations with the M.R.A. The clearance of Alfred Street was put back because of what the M.R.A. said, together with the question of compensation under the Planning Acts when it was taken over for industry. The Hedley Street area is to be cleared as one operation, and not in bits and pieces. The area qualifying for discretionary grants has been extended.

What we want to know is, 'Is the M.R.A. broadly in agreement, or not?'

*Chairman of the planning committee:* Your proposals were put to the planning committee.

*Chairman of the association:* But these 'amended proposals'—so far as we are given to understand, they have no legal force, people cannot depend on them, they are still in the air.

*Councillor:* But let's face the question. Another councillor has put it twice, and I'll put it again.

The amended proposals are the bottom plan on the board.

Speaking generally, are the amended proposals acceptable to the association?

*Chairman of the association:* The association has not had an opportunity to discuss this.

*Councillor:* It *is* legal, because it is the subject of a planning committee minute.

You can take it back to the people. Those are the amended proposals, and they have been approved by the planning committee.

*Chairman of the association:* It is not just a matter of the proposals as such. What we need is the justification for the proposals. The people of Millfield need to be convinced that the proposals are well based. We need not just the proposals, but the basis for them, the reasons behind them, the statistical evidence on housing and so forth, to present to the people. The bare proposals are only a very small part of this.

*Councillor:* This does not seem sensible to me. The proposals were amended at the instance of the association!

'Put the clearance of Alfred Street back.'

'Treat the Hedley Street area as one.'

Yet you now say, 'Give us the statistical evidence for proposing to do that!'

*Chairman of the association:* We have done this as amateurs. We have suggested certain things that seemed to us to be sensible and necessary on the basis of our amateur's knowledge.

*We* obviously don't have the technical and legal expertise, or the time or the people to do the necessary studies.

All we can say, and all we have said, is, 'On the basis of our amateur's knowledge, this or this does not look right'.

We have told the departments concerned to go back and do their homework.

*But they must come back with their final plans because they make sense,* not because this or that body 'said so'.

*Councillor:* The residents know the area better than we do. They know it much better than we do. They had professional advice.

*Chairman of the association:* What we require is for the local authority to do its homework.

*Chairman of the planning committee:* This will be put to a subsequent meeting. We are having a meeting tomorrow morning. That is all information to be put to the meeting. We can't put information that we haven't yet got.

*Planning department:* We did our homework. These proposals come out of the homework we did.

*Councillor:* Surely these proposals must conform broadly to the general case the M.R.A. has been fighting for . . .? I am a new boy, so to speak, I am new to this, but surely . . .?

*Chairman of the association:* We've been fighting for Cirencester Street and St. Cuthbert's Terrace. That is not slum property. . . .

*Councillor:* That is conceded.

*Chairman of the association:* . . . We found tremendous conflict over the facts. A great amount of time at one of the four participation meetings was taken up, actually, with departmental wrangling—with departmental wrangling over whether surveys had been carried out, and who had or had not done the surveys!

*Planning department:* I'm sorry, but it was not 'departmental wrangling'. The question was, 'Who did the survey?', that is all.

Actually, this is the basis of a lot of . . . the distrust of the M.R.A. of the survey.

This survey has been carried out, make no mistake about that.

And it is an accurate survey. There have been some inaccuracies in minor cases, but in only six cases was an inaccuracy put to us after the West Millfield exhibition.

*Councillor:* I have taken a very slim, passive interest in Millfield until this evening. I am gaining the impression that the M.R.A. has an inclination to fight the battle after the battle is won.

There is no point in haggling over what went on in the past in these matters!

*Chairman of the association:* I accept that the homework did get done.

*Councillor:* Let us take this a stage further.

We have produced amended proposals.

Give the public an opportunity to give their views!

It is no good engaging in recriminations.

Then, if necessary, we will receive counter-proposals.

*Councillor:* The ball is in the M.R.A.'s court.

*Secretary:* If the councillor means by that, that here tonight you are now asking us to comment on those proposals, then the ball is not in our court.

The proposals are behind my back. They are out of range of vision across the table there.

They need to be studied.

We were not prepared for this request, and we are not ready to dispense instant wisdom.

We were invited here to discuss the correspondence of July 21st 1969, to date, not to give our reflections on proposals we have not had the opportunity to examine.

We were invited for 7.45, and told on entering this room that we had until 8.30. The ball is not in our court.

*Joint chairman of the association:* I am appalled that we have to finish this meeting in seventeen minutes' time.

The correspondence we came here tonight to discuss asks basically one simple question: 'When will participation begin?' That is the question we still want answering.

The ball is in your court.

There has been participation of some sort in East Millfield. There has not been participation in West Millfield.

*Chairman of the planning committee:* By 8.30 I don't mean on the dot. If it goes on . . .

*Councillor:* This does not help the issue at all.

We are here as new boys.

We want concrete proposals put as quickly as possible.

Take it back, find out what people think . . .

*Secretary:* Councillor, if I may address the councillor through the Chair, I do not believe that you are entitled to plead ignorance of the affairs of Millfield. Another councillor has just made a similar statement, that he is 'a new boy' and has come fresh to Millfield's problems.

We are here to discuss Millfield with members of the planning committee. The planning committee has undertaken to affect, and drastically affect, the lives of many hundreds of families. Millfield has been an issue since at least 1965, when the Council first approved definite plans for substantial slum clearance in the area. It has been a burning issue since 1967, when new plans were promised.

It is simply not good enough for members of the planning committee to turn round now and say, 'I am a new boy, the problem is new to me'. You are not entitled not to know about Millfield.

*Chairman of the planning committee:* These are the facts put to the planning committee. This is only Millfield. There is all the rest of the town to consider. Everybody can't be expected to know about every area. This is Millfield. Then it will be Southwick, and so on.

All the members can't have detailed or precise knowledge, but as a whole—have the whole town to consider.

*Councillor:* We are looking for agreement on East Millfield. We're not saying these are the final plans.

When all the information is in, then this will be made known, and further views collected.

This is not a *fait accompli.*

*Secretary:* You are saying that all the information will be forthcoming, and that the M.R.A. will see it?

*Councillor:* We are all saying one thing with one voice.

*Councillor:* We are prepared to supply it. Yes, we are.

*Secretary:* Is this an authoritative statement? Is this an authoritative statement, or is it only your own view?

*Councillor:* I am not in the habit of making statements that are not authoritative.

The association will be supplied with the reasons for the proposals, and we shall receive comments.

*Chairman of the planning committee:* We can give the outcome and the reasons, but we can't give the statistical information. That would be going against our officers. We cannot go against our officers. They have been appointed, and we cannot question the work that they do.

*Planning department:* We are not opposed to our work being queried.

*Chairman of the association:* This is the first time that we have had definite information that these plans are the 'amended proposals'. It was not until the middle of August that we received the February planning committee minutes where this was decided.

*Planning department:* We have erred. Yes.

*Chairman of the association:* We are prepared to 'present' these amended proposals, with the statistical evidence, stating the

housing conditions, and so forth, and put this to our people—
to our committee.

*Chairman of the planning committee:* We will have a meeting when
all the information we are now collecting is in, like the meeting tomorrow morning.

*Chairman of the association:* Since July we have become hot under
the collar, I think legitimately.

*Councillor:* We accept this.

*Councillor:* The vicar says that he can't talk for the people. But
these amended proposals are those which were decided by the
M.R.A.

*Secretary:* That is not so. The amended proposals shown on the
board behind me are the proposals that were put to the
M.R.A. on February 7th. On February 14th we met the Corporation again and put our counter-proposals in great detail.

We have heard nothing since, at least not until August 14th,
as described in the correspondence before you now.

In other words, these are not the proposals amended
according to the wishes of the M.R.A.

They are unaltered from the proposals of February 7th,
and the influence of the views of the M.R.A. was precisely . . .
nil.

*Planning department:* There is one difference from the proposals
of February 7th. In these streets here [*indicates*] the words
'by 1978' have been deleted.

*Councillor:* How can you say the impact is 'nil'?

*Secretary:* Would the planning department care to give the time-
tabling of the participation meetings over the East Millfield
plans? There were four meetings. The original plans were
presented at the first of them. At the second there was all this
wrangling between the planners and the health people over
whether surveys had been carried out, and if so, by whom:
but at that second meeting certain proposals of a general kind
mainly were put to the Corporation, and copies of the resolutions given to them. At the third meeting, of February 7th, the

amended proposals came back, purporting to be based on the views of the M.R.A. The M.R.A. was not satisfied at all with this contention. The plans were 'received'. At the fourth meeting further proposals were put, including the resolution stating that amendments purporting to be based on M.R.A. views should be based on what the M.R.A. said and wrote, and not what the Corporation chose to say that the M.R.A. said or wrote.

We were told that there would be further 'participation' in the light of the February 14th resolutions. We are now told that the Corporation proposals of February 7th are the definite proposals. That is what I mean when I say the impact has been 'nil'.

*Councillor:* I do not understand what the secretary is talking about. You are being asked to take these amended proposals away and consider them, and let us have your reactions.

So how can you say that the influence of the M.R.A. is nil?

*Secretary:* Now I do not understand what the councillor is talking about.

*Councillor:* Yes, the secretary and I are on entirely different wavelengths, I am afraid.

*Planning department:* The impact has been this—as the planning department has pointed out—that we have abandoned the 'short lives' policy. That was your strong recommendation.

*Chairman of the association:* I think we need to go no further.

We have these promises.

What we want is this—this map, or several maps, so that we can brief members of the committee on the statistical and factual basis of the proposals. The maps can be displayed at St. Mark's. Our committee members can then explain to small groups of people exactly what is being proposed by the Corporation, and the reasons for the proposals, the factual basis and what will be achieved by them.

We can then get the reactions street by street. That is necessary, I think, because there are differences between streets, as well as within streets.

*Chairman of the planning committee:* If you ask for anything in a normal, civil way, you will get it.

*Representative of M.R.A. (Mrs. Brown):* This '15-year life' for some of the streets ... Most of those houses could have a thirty-year life. There is no sense in giving houses 'fifteen years'. If you are wanting to improve, why go to all that trouble for only fifteen years?

And, say, middle-aged people: with 'fifteen years' they are being told that their house will be demolished at the very time when they want security, when they would want to feel that they are at peace and secure in their own home.

Nobody likes it, and nobody can see any sense in it.

*Chairman of the planning committee:* We are in the hands of legislation on this. We have to give these by law. We can't get out of that.

*Mrs. Brown:* You are breaking people's hearts, the way things are today. And you must work the roads and the houses together. It is no good telling people that their houses have fifteen or thirty years, and then make them frightened the whole time about the roads that might come through.

*Chairman of the planning committee:* We decided what was going to happen about the roads when we came to talk about the proposals for East Millfield.

*Councillor:* We have to make a decision.

*Chairman of the association:* We have always said that it is for the Council to make the decision: we are in no sense dictators of policy to the Council. The other side of that is that the Council takes the responsibility for what is decided.

And we have always realized that some people will be hurt, that you can't please everybody.

*Mrs. Brown:* I am not satisfied about the roads. People *are* worried and distressed about the roads.

*Chairman of the planning committee:* Well, now for West Millfield: Participation will take place. If anybody has read the Skeffington report . . .

*Joint Chairman of the association:* We have copies and several of us have studied the report.

*Chairman of the planning committee:* . . . There must be a public meeting giving lifings and alternative road proposals. Then there must be an exhibition, a display.

That is the procedure of Skeffington.

I am as frustrated as you are that the next stage has not taken place.

That has been due to holidays and analysing the results of the exhibition.

As soon as time is available and staff is available there will be participation, as in East Millfield.

*Representative of M.R.A. (Mr. Darke):* Oswald Street is affected by road Number . . . I cannot quite see the number there.

*Chairman of the planning committee:* We must give all information, that is why there are four alternative roads. One will be the road, the others won't.

*Mr. Darke:* The fact is that in Millfield there is tremendous psychological depression and unrest. There is the idea that the Corporation will do what they like, and when they like in Millfield.

*We've* asked for *no* roads in the full committee.

But in my sub-committee, in the meanwhile, we have asked if the Corporation, through the Borough Engineer, will choose one road—it is obviously a technical problem—and that way the anxiety in Millfield is immediately cut by three-quarters. Then the people in the area affected by the remaining road, and the m.r.a., can have their say about the road that remains.

You have asked for our opinions here.

What we have said time and time again is that there can be no concrete proposals from us until two things are known to us: What are the proposals for the roads, and what is going to happen to the houses in the top end of Washington Street?

*Chairman of the planning committee:* If we'd said, 'It will be road Number 3' it would have been dictation. So we've said, 'Here are four alternatives. Which in your opinion is the best?'

*Mr. Darke:* I am chairman of the environment sub-committee of the association. From that committee, and not from the full committee, and not even from all members of the sub-committee, I say, 'The road that interrupts the least'.

Even road Number 1 places Dene Street in blight.

*Councillor:* I think this matter can be cleared up if the Borough Engineer would describe now the bridges, if the Borough Engineer would now discuss the four roads—the bridges are the main thing there.

*Joint chairman of the association:* That is not the issue this evening.

There is one question only: *When does participation begin?*

People's minds must be put at rest.

A fortnight ago there was another survey at the top of Washington Street. One old lady at least was terribly upset. Who was doing the survey? I don't know.

*Planning department:* The Architect's department.

*Joint chairman of the association:* Well, this old lady said, 'Not another!' 'I'm afraid there are two more after me, the health department and the District Valuer. But you can rest assured that you will be here for fifteen years at least.'

*Architect's department:* She couldn't have been told that.

*Joint chairman of the association:* But she was!

*Architect's department:* She couldn't have been. Our people were told not to say anything.

*Joint chairman of the association:* Well, she was. And now it is referred back *again*! It is not clear from the *Sunderland Echo* whether only the top end of Washington Street is referred back or the whole of the area!

*Councillor:* The whole of the area.

*Joint chairman of the association:* People are in a ferment. We must put their minds at rest!

*Planning department:* We're doing that. The survey was requested by the planning committee in order to give lives. The survey results will be ready by next week.

*Architect's department:* The survey has been done for the top end of Washington Street, it is [being ?] typed, and will be ready next week.

*Planning department:* About the alternative roads: we are advised —in fact instructed—to do so. This is the first intimation we have had that you prefer route Number 4 [*sic*].

*Mr. Darke:* You have it wrong. I'm not saying we're in favour of route Number 4. I'm saying that you should decide on the best route, and then we can argue about the remaining route, but anxiety in the area would have been cut by three-quarters. It is the policy of the m.r.a. that *no* route should disrupt Millfield for the benefit of through traffic.

*Councillor:* When we know about south Washington Street, a decision about the roads will be facilitated. Obviously, if that whole area is cleared, that makes certain things possible with regard to roads.

*Chairman of the planning committee:* This is what participation is basically about.

All the relevant facts will be put on paper for you.

Then you can come back with a solution.

That is better than giving little bits of information now, out of context.

It is better to put it to the people when everything is known and we will be finding out more of these things tomorrow morning.

*Councillor:* The reference back, though it is the whole area, is only on account of the top of Washington Street, to await the survey. That survey has now been done.

*Now* we can say, 'This is the lifing'.

When the lifing is known, the residents might take a different view depending on whether it is a long or a short life. If it is a short life they may say, 'Well, take it all down'.

That would affect the roads—it may widen the choice available.

*Mr. Darke:* There is quite a lot of misery and upset in Millfield at the moment. There is a lot of unrest.

Let's be quite clear on what I was saying about the roads. I was only saying: 'Let's do something straight away to cut down the misery. Let's cut the misery caused by the road proposals by three-quarters straight away.' That's what I was saying. That [?] road will be built in the next seven years. Am I correct in saying this?

*Councillor:* No. [*Laughs*].

*Mr. Darke:* Well, that is what we were told at the public meeting you had in March!

*Engineer's department*: That may have been said then. But there have been changes in Council policy. My estimate now is 1980.

*Mr. Darke:* I want to correct the planning officer. When I said that about the roads, he said it was the first solid piece of information to come from the M.R.A.

On February 14th the M.R.A. put 31 resolutions. The general resolutions applied to West Millfield as well.

Incidentally, we are one association.

At our meeting on Wednesday, we will discuss those resolutions, and it is simply a matter of missing out specific references to East Millfield streets, etc.

Then we want a participation meeting.

*Chairman of the planning committee:* We have started on participation. We have had a public meeting and an exhibition.

*Joint chairman of the association:* This evening's meeting, this correspondence we were invited here to discuss, is to get an answer to that question: 'When does the next stage begin?' When do we move on to the next stage?

*Mr. Darke:* We want a date well in advance, so that we can prepare for the first meeting.

*Councillor:* Mr. Darke has made some very good points—the anxiety all this causes people.

But according to the Skeffington report we have to do it this way.

We want to get south Washington Street decided. We want a decision as soon as possible. As soon as it is known, it will be made public, including letting the M.R.A. know.

Speed is the essence.

*Secretary:* Speed, yes. But not speed at the expense of sense.

*Chairman of the planning committee:* The survey for south Washington Street should be ready next week. There is a meeting tomorrow morning with Building Societies etc.

As soon as the appropriate date is known, we will let you know.

We will not delay any longer than is possible.

We have shown you that participation is a thing to come.

You have had even more information than the planning committee has had: what you were told at the public meeting the planning committee didn't even know about.

So you have had the full text of what Skeffington is suggesting.

*Chairman of the association:* There is tremendous anxiety in the Washington Street area. They were given assurances that there would be no decision without participation—then we have the newspaper reports of April 10th. What can we say to those people?

All we can say is, 'I'm sorry, but we haven't had participation'.

*Chairman of the planning committee:* Health [the health department] is not bound by participation. Their statutory obligation is an inquiry. Those are the laws we are bound by—the health department by the inquiry, and the planning department by participation.

But the health department will help with participation.

*Planning department:* We'd like your observations before a participation meeting. Can we have your comments now?

*Mr. Darke:* We are having a meeting of the committee on Wednesday. There will be concrete proposals. They will be sent to your office.

Can someone come in and explain them to you?

*Planning department:* Yes. You are welcome to the planning office at any time, and we will be only too willing to give you any assistance we can.

*Mr. Darke:* We have sent several invitations to the chairman of the planning committee, but you haven't turned up. We are trying to work through our councillors, and I think we are succeeding in that.

But we still want participation.

We want something settled.

Some houses in Millfield are finished. But quite a number of them are little palaces—people want to get on with them, and live in them with some peace of mind.

I wouldn't swap my house for a Corporation bungalow, I can tell you that.

*Representative of M.R.A. (Mr. Larcombe):* We are under a moral obligation here. People in Washington Street and the area in which I live have no information whatsoever on what is to happen. We are under cross-fire of people who want to know, and we can only say that we have nothing we can tell them.

Speaking for my area within the M.R.A. I can only insist that we have this information as quickly as possible.

*Chairman of the planning committee:* If you ask simple questions in simple, straightforward language, you'll get all the answers. We are only too willing to do anything you ask for. Basically that is information, information from side to side.

*Councillor:* I hope this will mark a watershed, and from now on we will work in harmony. I think that there has simply been a failure in public relations, and now let's put that right.

*Chairman of the association:* I want to say this. Every word that has gone to the Corporation has been agreed: it has either been agreed in detail, or has been the clear expression of committee policy. No one individual has taken it upon himself to write anything that has not been fully discussed and agreed in committee.

We may at times appear aggressive. That is because we feel deeply about it.

We appreciate the position of the Corporation.

We will be satisfied if the Corporation can show that it has done its homework, if it can show that its policies for Millfield are well-based in fact and in principle.

No-one is hammering any particular individual, not the planning officer, not the chairman of the planning committee, nor the deputy.

We will be satisfied if what is proposed can be shown to be in the interests of the people of Millfield, and to that end we will continue to be forthright in what we have to say.

*Chairman of the planning committee:* You have been given according to Skeffington and you will get according to Skeffington in the future.

# THE PLANNING DEPARTMENT'S ANALYSIS OF THE JULY-AUGUST CORRESPONDENCE IN ITS REPORT TO THE PLANNING COMMITTEE MEETING HELD ON AUGUST 27th 1969

## MILLFIELD—PROGRESS REPORT

*East Millfield Proposals*

Following a meeting of chairmen and vice-chairmen of the health and planning committees on October 8th 1968, at which draft proposals for the Millfield area east of the Durham railway line were considered, a series of four meetings were held with the Millfield Residents' Association. These meetings resulted in certain modifications to the proposals which, it was explained to the association, would be considered by the planning committee on February 26th 1969, along with the resolutions of the Millfield Residents' Association. A comprehensive report was prepared for the planning committee which was approved in principle, along with certain other recommendations and decisions. [A copy of the decision of the planning committee of February 26th 1969 was enclosed with *Millfield: Progress Report*.]

These other matters are in course of being dealt with and it is expected that item (e) of the minute will be considered by the next meeting of the planning management working group (which now have before them the pre-1914 housing survey as a whole).

*West Millfield Proposals*

The draft proposals for the area west of the Durham railway line were put to a public meeting on March 31st 1969. The meeting was told that it was intended next to hold a public exhibition at which comments would be invited and that after this, meetings would be held with a residents' association formed to represent the interests of the area. In fact, the Millfield Residents' Association extended its scope to include representatives of each street in the area but under a different chairman.

The exhibition was held during the week June 23rd–27th and was staffed at all times by at least two members of the planning department.

Monday and Wednesday 6.00–9.00 p.m.
Tuesday, Thursday and Friday 3.00–5.00 p.m.

The exhibition seemed very well attended, especially on the first four days. Forty-one comments were received and two petitions. A schedule is attached which briefly describes them. Those comments which related to the Washington Street clearance area were considered by the planning and health (emergency) sub-committees held on July 23rd (see minutes). The number of comments received was disappointing and there was not a great deal of consistency in them—it would be difficult to use them as a basis for reconsidering the proposals. It is understood that the Millfield Residents' Association met to discuss the proposals during the week following the exhibition.

On July 21st, the secretary of the Millfield Residents' Association wrote to the Town Clerk asking about the 'status' of the plans shown at the exhibition and complaining that no official notification had been received regarding the plans for

East Millfield. (They had, of course, been told that the latest plans would be put to the planning committee on February 26th.) The point was also raised as to when 'public participation' for West Millfield would start. This latter was an odd question as public participation started with the first public meeting held on March 31st.

A further letter, dated July 25th, reiterated two of the points in the form of two requests:

(1) the position regarding the status of the plans, and
(2) when will public participation start in West Millfield?

The Town Clerk replied that the matter would be considered by the planning committee and the planning officer wrote the association clarifying the status of the East Millfield plans, and asking the association for their specific comments regarding the West Millfield plans. Up to this time (apart from periodic outbursts via the *Sunderland Echo*) relations with the Millfield Residents' Association had been reasonable considering the wide scope of the problems involved. The two letters received thus far were reasonable in tone, if critical. But between then and August 9th, nine further letters were received from the Millfield Residents' Association, six of them dated August 1st, containing four comments about the plans exhibited in June. [Subsequent to the drafting of the report two further letters have been received (as at August 22nd 1969), comprising a total of 10 pages (plus enclosures).] The four comments are summarized in this appendix and these together with the comments received at the exhibition will be the basis upon which amended proposals will be prepared for discussion with the Millfield Residents' Association. The comment regarding the road proposals has also been forwarded to the Borough Engineer.

The tenor of the letters dated July 29th (two-and-a-half pages long), July 30th (four pages long) and August 9th (three pages long) with all the innuendo and wilful misunderstanding inherent in this type of correspondence, is best gained by actually reading them (they are of course available). What seems to be the main points raised in the letters are noted below with comments:

## Millfield Residents' Association
## Letter of July 29th

| *Points Raised* | *P.O. Comments* |
|---|---|
| (1) Lack of communication. One-way communication. | In spite of this, two reports were circulated to the Millfield Residents' Association and four meetings held with them. The last letter addressed to an officer of the Corporation before the present series (commencing July 21st 1969) was in April 1968. |
| (2) Millfield Residents' Association not informed that contents of the exhibition 'suggestion box' were to be discussed on July 23rd 1969. | The comments as a whole were not then discussed (except insofar as they related to the Washington Street area). But in any case it is surely up to the committee to decide what it considers and when without the approval of the association. In this case they seem to have boycotted the suggestion-box, yet are concerned with what is in it. |
| (3) 'This (suggestion) box has been deliberately left to the "unorganized public" and as a matter of policy not used by the association.' | This is presumably why there were not as many comments as we had hoped for. |
| (4) 'The association took the view that suggestion boxes are very poor instruments of public participation.' | The Skeffington committee report states: 'The evidence received by the committee shows that exhibitions have contributed substantially to the understanding of planning proposals (para. 158). The exhibition should be used to |

| *Points Raised* | *P.O. Comments* |
|---|---|
| | sound out opinion, whether by inviting people to complete questionnaires or to make comments on panels specially provided for that purpose (para. 159 vi).' |
| (5) 'In the whole of Booth Street clearance area . . . only five comments were made. . . . (We know this from *unofficial* sources closely connected with the planning department.)' | There is an implication that someone has 'leaked' the comments. The committee can draw their own conclusions as to this implication and the way it is made. The document contains names and addresses of people making comments. It will be even more difficult in future to carry out public participation if people with views cannot be assured of anonymity when they desire it. If in these circumstances the document were to be released, it was certainly for the committee to decide. |
| (6) 'It was against the background of these suggestion box comments only that the c.p.o. for the Washington Street area was discussed.' | This is not true, both the health committee and the planning and health (emergency) sub-committees were made aware of the survey in south Washington Street carried out by the Millfield Residents' Association. |
| (7) Regarding the survey of pre-1914 houses, 'There is a very large discrepancy between the facts of the situation and the "scores" '. | Yet at the exhibition there were only six queries as to the accuracy of the survey. |
| (8) 'The planning/health departments' survey which was not commenced until some time after February 10th 1968, was claimed to have been completed for the whole of | As a matter of fact, it is quite within the capabilities of the planning department to survey 8,000 houses in a month, but it was never claimed that the whole |

| *Points Raised* | *P.O. Comments* |
|---|---|
| the south side of the river (8,000 dwellings) by March 18th 1968. Anyone with knowledge of door to door surveys can only look with amazement at the planning department's claim that in a single month, 8,000 houses were miraculously surveyed . . .' | of the south side of the river had been completed in that time. |
| (9) 'When it (the association) has finally come to a decision that it is pointless to pursue matters any further through the planning authority . . . a letter is received from the planning authority. And —is it coincidence?—on the very day of the publication of the Skeffington report . . .' | Of course, this letter is the first intimation received that the M.R.A. are now going to conduct their correspondence via the Town Clerk. As stated in (1) above, there were no previous letters to Council officers to reply to. The chairman of the planning committee specifically asked the M.R.A. to address their comments to the planning officer. |

## Millfield Residents' Association Letter of July 30th

| *Points Raised* | *P.O. Comments* |
|---|---|
| (10) The two maps dealing with proposals (a) clearance and improvement and (b) roads, were asked for in a letter dated April 11th 1969. On April 14th, there was a verbal refusal. | The planning officer received no letter asking for these plans, but in any case the exhibition material was still being prepared at this time and was not completed until mid-June. |
| (11) The status of the plans. 'In particular we are puzzled by his (the planning officer's) reference to the East Millfield plans as a model of the status of the West Millfield plans.' | This must be a deliberate misunderstanding as the letter to which this is a reply clearly stated 'the proposals . . . have exactly the same status as the *first* proposals prepared in relation to East Millfield'. |

| *Points Raised* | *P.O. Comments* |
|---|---|
| (12) The Millfield Residents' Association have not been informed of what happened to the East Millfield plans 'and the recommendations of the association had absolutely no effect whatsoever on them'. | The Millfield Residents' Association were told *what would be happening* to the plans but not what has happened—a copy of the planning committee minute of February 26th has now been sent. The point about the recommendations of the M.R.A. is blatantly not true. The changes made in the clearance/improvement programme had regard to the M.R.A. resolutions. The planning committee has recommended joint meetings of chairmen of affected committees regarding other resolutions. |
| (13) It is necessary to know definitely whether houses have a long life. | Agreed. |
| (14) West Millfield is terribly blighted. 'The plans of March 31st, blighted nearly all the area with its maze of road proposals.' | West Millfield is worse in this respect than the rest of the older parts of the town as it has unresolved road proposals in the area. The plan displayed at the public meeting on March 31st showed a road linking to the upper deck of the Queen Alexandra Bridge, as indicated in the consultant's report. For the exhibition, extended plans were displayed showing, in addition, three other alternatives. |
| (15) On July 23rd 1969, the planning and health sub-committee were told that the Shepherd Street road threat was 'unreal'. 'We wonder whether the sub-committee were fully appraised of the fact that the other possibility is that the road would be built when Shepherd | This was *not* discussed at this committee. Again the point about 'unofficial sources close to the planning department' is made (see (5) above). Shepherd Street is allocated for industry on the approved development plan and in November 1967 it is quite likely |

| *Points Raised* | *P.O. Comments* |
|---|---|
| Street was cleared for industrial purposes as announced by the chairman of the planning committee in November 1967.' | that no thought had been given to changing this. Detailed consideration of Millfield started at about this time. |

(16) 'I should like to give one more example from many scores of examples, and perhaps an answer to this may be forthcoming.' The point is then made again about the consideration of south Washington Street on July 23rd, the survey carried out there by the M.R.A. and what effect could the M.R.A. have in altering the proposals. 'Unofficially, one of the joint chairmen of the M.R.A. has been told that as a majority of the houses are "fit", the "popularity" or otherwise of clearance is irrelevant.'

The 'one more example' is a repetition of the point made in the previous letter (see (6) above). The last part of this statement is irrelevant, as the committee agreed with the majority's wishes.

(17) 'The planning officer's letter is surprisingly, headed "Millfield—Public Participation". The subject of our correspondence is not and never has been public participation.'

This is typical of the letters we receive. Apart from its irrelevancy, it is incorrect—there are two letters asking when it is going to start and it is mentioned again in the next paragraph.

(18) '*One* of the points I raised was that of the long awaited date of commencement of "participation".'

Public participation for West Millfield started with the public meeting held on March 31st and continued with the exhibition held in June. Now that comments have been received the proposals are being further considered. The comments arrived in August only as a result of the letter to which the M.R.A. seem to take exception.

(19) 'The planning officer's letter can    As stated in (1) above, the first

335

only be regarded as extraordinary in its implication that the association has been inactive in pressing its views.'

letter to a Council officer from the Millfield Residents' Association regarding West Millfield was received on July 21st 1969.

## Millfield Residents' Association Letter of August 9th

*Points Raised*        *P.O. Comments*

(20) 'Summaries of the record have been transmitted to you. The full version is in possession of the planning authority . . . and sent to the chairman of the planning committee.' (This refers to the M.R.A.'s transcript of their meetings with the Corporation.)

The 'summaries of the record' have been sent *only* to the chairman, not to the planning authority (in spite of his request). (See also (1), (9) and (19) above.)

(21) Regarding public participation in West Millfield 'it seems unhelpful therefore for the people concerned to be told that certainly during the past months, things have taken place that they know quite well have not taken place and which by no stretching of the English language could be said to have taken place'.

Again, the implication is that public participation has not started in West Millfield in spite of there having been a public meeting and an exhibition.

(22) 'Your assurance that every attempt has been made to involve the residents depends upon the meaning given to phrase every attempt.'

The attempts by the Corporation to involve the residents have resulted so far in four meetings with the Millfield Residents' Association, one public meeting and an exhibition.

(23) 'The East Millfield plans of February 7th, were not a response to the first twenty-two resolutions

The plans were not of course, a complete response and never could be, but the statement is

| *Points Raised* | *P.O. Comments* |
|---|---|
| of the M.R.A. in any intelligible sense.' | fatuous. The amended clearance/improvement proposals of February 7th, *were* a response to the resolutions referred to. |
| (24) 'Resolutions 23–31 have not been referred to again by the Corporation.' | *All* the resolutions (1–31 inclusive) were referred to in the report presented to the planning committee on February 26th, and the M.R.A. were told this. |
| (25) No meetings between the M.R.A. and the Corporation have yet been held regarding West Millfield. | Agreed, but the M.R.A.'s comments on the draft proposals were only received on August 4th. The exhibition was held as recently as June and the Corporation have been on vacation. |
| (26) 'There is some speculation in Millfield about the possibility that an explanation of the desperately prolonged agony of Millfield is the view in some quarters that the best way to deal with an active citizenry is to prevaricate until the active citizenry loses heart and lapses into apathy and passivity in the face of calculated obfuscation, ambiguity, dilatoriness and misrepresentation.' | There has been no prevarication and there would certainly have been no point in meeting the Millfield Residents' Association until some comments had been received from them. But these sort of comments are not only unhelpful, they are seemingly calculated to cause friction between the Corporation and the Millfield Residents' Association. *Planning Department, Burdon House. August 22nd 1969.* |

# NAME INDEX

# GENERAL INDEX